HOT!
INTERNATIONAL

GAY

MC...
EDIT...
DAVID...
PAUL...

V-XXI

babelcom
new york

à Luc,
ce «dictionnaire du cul»

THANKS TO ▼ WIR DANKEN ▼ GRACIAS A ▼ MERCI À
GRAZIE A ▼ AGRADECEMOS ▼ DĚKUJEME

Omar Beretta, Vincent Bontoux, Andreas Brücker, Václav Buriánek, Oscar Cid, Mark Coburn, Sabine Cousseau, Ignacio Darnaude, Claude Diotte, Carles Domènech, Josef Hruška, Jan Kábrt, Karel Kanda, Tomáš Kellner, Hartmut Kondoch, Martin Kryšpín, Luc Marmonier, Davide Maronati, Gabriel Martel, José Martínez, Fabrizio Mescoli, Corrado Orrù, Michael Paulus, Ricardo Paiva, Héctor Rey i Castells, PierPaolo Sabbatini, Jan Sebens, Michele Somaschini, Jaime Stankevicius, Jeff Taylor, Tim Temple, Thierry Torlai, Manuel Vidal, Roderick Young, Matthias Zerb

photos: John Healy / New York City

Copyright ©1996 by BabelCom, Inc.
Box 1209, Old Chelsea Station
New York City, New York 10113-1209 USA
212 627 2074 / 800 692 2235

ISBN 1-885948-18-2
Library of Congress Catalog Card Number: 95-78895

AT YOUR OWN RISK!

Hot! International / Gay is meant to be used responsibly and with common sense. The Editors and Publisher cannot be held liable in any way for any damages—physical or otherwise—that users of the book may cause or bring upon themselves by their own actions.

Manufactured in the United States of America

10   9   8   7   6   5   4   3   2

ENGLISH

DEUTSCH

ESPAÑOL

FRANÇAIS

ITALIANO

PORTUGUÊS

ČESKY

4 CONTENTS

The world today is smaller than it's ever been, and the number of people living and traveling outside their native countries goes up every year. With all this moving around, international romance is blooming like never before. But foreign-language phrasebooks that cover the real, "uncensored" vocabulary of love have been few, incomplete, and hard to find—until now.

Unlike traditional phrasebooks, *Hot! International / Gay* can help you with lots of different social situations—meeting, dating, relationships, steamy action in the bedroom, and more—whether you're an American in Paris, an Italian in Prague, or a Brazilian in Berlin.

Hot! International / Gay could even be good for your health. A few key words can prevent mixed signals and keep you away from unsafe or undesireable situations. Awareness of AIDS and other sexually-transmitted diseases can vary quite a bit from country to country and from person to person. Your new friend might be willing to jump into bed unprotected, but you shouldn't be—and now you can say so clearly, in his own language.

A few notes:

▼ Our unique "zebra-stripe" format makes it easy to chat up guys in any of six other languages. Just find the English phrase you want (always in the first black stripe, at the top of each page), then look below for its equivalents in German (DEUTSCH), Spanish (ESPAÑOL), French (FRANÇAIS), Italian (ITALIANO), Portuguese (PORTUGUÊS) or Czech (ČESKY). And your new boyfriend(s) can use the book just as easily to talk to you!

▼ Apart from English and the Brazilian-style Portuguese used in this book, all the languages here have two ways of saying "you"—one formal and one informal. To make things easier—and because these days younger people in many countries tend to use informal speech anyway—we stick with the familiar (like the French *tu* and the German *du*) instead of the formal (*vous* and *Sie*).

▼ Brackets [ ] offer a choice between two possibilities: *Let's go to [my / your] place.* Parentheses ( ), on the other hand, indicate an optional word or phrase: *Pull out (before you come).*

OK, have a good trip, and a great time!

The phonetic transcription under each phrase will help you sound out the words and make yourself better understood. Check the table below for the English equivalents of any sounds you're unsure of (just bear in mind that to keep things simple, our phonetic system is approximate—especially for vowels).

Stressed syllables are CAPITALIZED. Diphthongs (pairs of vowels, like in the word "chain," are shown as two separate vowels *(tsheîn)* with the second vowel marked with a circumflex (^) to remind you to pronounce both vowels together smoothly. Doubled vowels (such as *aa* or *EE*) are pronounced twice as long as a single vowel (remember, though, that doubling changes only the *length* of the vowel—*ee* is always a stretched-out version of the "e" in bed, *not* like "ee" in "meet," and *oo* is a stretched-out version of the "o" in "toes," rather than the "oo" in "moon").

SOUND	AS IN...	SOUND	AS IN...
a	father	ny	canyon
an	want, but nasal (as if holding your nose)	o	toe
		on	toe, but nasal
aîn	pint, but nasal	oîn	going, but nasal
aûn	amount, but nasal	œ	fur
b	boner	p	prick
d	dick	r	rear
dh	the	rr	"rápido" in Spanish; a rolled "r"
dzh	jack off	rzh	Dvořák the composer; a rolled
e	bed		"r" followed by a "zh"
en	bent, but nasal	s	sexy
ə	suck	sh	shy
f	fuck	t	sticky
g	guy	th	thick
h	hard	ts	tits
hh	Bach or loch, very aspirated	tsh	chat
i	penis	u	cool
in	lean, but nasal	un	cool, but nasal
k	condom	ü	"pute" in French; "e" as in
ks	sex		"penis," but with rounded lips
l	lesbian	v	love
ly	millionaire	w	wet
m	man	y	young
n	nude	z	zipper
ng	long	zh	massage

S ex can be romantic, fulfilling and fun, but you don't want to get sick—and you certainly don't want to die—for one night of passion. So when you do it, do it smart. It's not all that hard to avoid transmission of HIV and other nasty bugs if you and your partner follow a few simple guidelines:

▼ **ASSUME THAT EVERYONE** is potentially infected, no matter how cute or sexy, and act accordingly. You can't always tell someone's HIV status by his face or body.

▼ **SAFE & HOT:** Cuddling, nibbling, masturbating, and rubbing bodies together. Deep kissing is OK except when you have open sores or cuts in your mouth, or if you've just brushed or flossed (which can make your gums bleed).

▼ **FUCKING:** *Never* do it without a condom. It's also a good idea to pull out (or have him pull out) before coming.

▼ **SUCKING:** Less risky than fucking, but the experts say that if you want to be totally safe, lick your partner's shaft; don't take the head in your mouth. Or you can use a condom (unlubricated is fine, and usually tastes better than lubricated).

▼ **RIMMING:** Licking ass is generally considered not a high risk for AIDS, but is a higher risk for hepatitis and parasites.

▼ **TOYS:** Dildos and vibrators are fine, but don't share them (or if you do, clean them carefully with bleach or rubbing alcohol and put a condom on them).

▼ **RUBBER RULES!** Make sure your condoms are latex—not lamb or other animal skins. Also, never tear at condom packets with your teeth—you could rip the rubber!

▼ **GREASE IT UP:** Use plenty of lubricant, and make sure your brand is water-soluble (not oil or fat-based, like baby oil, lotions, Crisco, butter, or Vaseline; oil and fat will break down the rubber). The best lubes contain nonoxynol-9, a spermicide that may boost your protection (but *never* use a spermicidal lube alone without a condom).

▼ **DRINKING & DRUGS** don't mix well with safer sex. You need your wits about you to keep it safe, so don't overdo it!

▼ **POPPERS:** Apart from blurring your judgment in intimate situations, repeated use of poppers could screw up your immune system.

♂ refers to a man

♀ refers to a woman

adj adjective

adv adverb

Br British usage

LA Latin American Spanish

NE no exact equivalent

n noun

pl plural

Por Portuguese as spoken in Portugal

Qb French as spoken in Québec

s singular

v verb

INHALT

Die Welt von heute ist kleiner als je zuvor und die Zahl derer, die in fremden Ländern leben und reisen nimmt jedes Jahr zu. Bei all dieser Mobilität erlebt auch die Liebe eine internationale Blüte wie nie zuvor. Aber die Sprachführer, die ein echtes „Vokabular der Liebe" anbieten, sind selten oder schwer zu finden — bis jetzt.

Anders als traditionelle Sprachführer kann *Hot! International / Gay* in vielen Situationen helfen: Leute treffen, sich verabreden, Beziehungen aufbauen, miteinander schlafen, und vieles mehr — gleich, ob Du ein Deutscher auf Mallorca, ein Amerikaner in Berlin oder ein Brasilianer in Prag bist.

Hot! International / Gay könnte sogar hilfreich für Deine Gesundheit sein. Ein paar Schlüsselwörter können Mißverständnissen vorbeugen und Dich vor Situationen bewahren, die unsafe oder nicht wünschenswert sind. Das Bewußtsein von AIDS oder anderen Krankheiten, die sexuell übertragen werden, kann von Land zu Land und Person zu Person verschieden sein. Dein neuer Freund mag bereit sein, ungeschützt ins Bett zu hüpfen, aber Du solltest das nicht tun — und jetzt kannst Du ihm auch genau sagen, in seiner eigenen Sprache.

Einige Anmerkungen:

▼ Mit unserem „Zebrastreifen-System" verliert man nicht die Übersicht, wenn man mit ihm in einer von sechs Fremdsprachen spricht. Der deutsche Satz steht immer im ersten weißen Streifen auf jeder Seite. Oberhalb steht die englische Übersetzung (ENGLISH), unterhalb die Entsprechungen in Spanisch (ESPAÑOL), Französisch (FRANÇAIS), Italienisch (ITALIANO), Portugiesisch (PORTUGUÊS) und Tschechisch (ČESKY).

▼ Mit Ausnahme von Englisch und Portugiesisch haben alle Sprachen in diesem Buch, wie Deutsch, zwei Formen der Anrede, eine formelle wie „Sie" und eine informelle wie „Du". Der Einfachheit halber und da heutzutage die jüngeren Leute in vielen Ländern dazu tendieren, unabhängig von der Situation, das Äquivalent von „Du" zu gebrauchen, verwendet dieses Buch hauptsächlich die informelle Form der Anrede.

▼ Eckige Klammern [ ] werden verwendet, um Wahlmöglichkeiten aufzuzeigen: *Wir können zu [mir / dir] gehen.* Überdies handelt es sich bei allem in runden Klammern ( ) um Optionen: *Du bist (so) süß.*

Okay, wir wünschen eine gute Reise und viel Spaß!

Die Aussprachehinweise unter jedem Satz sollen Dir helfen, Dich verständlich zu machen. Du kannst sie phonetisch lesen, wie sie in der folgenden Tabelle aufgeführt werden; ziehe diese Tabelle bei speziellen Symbolen und schwierigen Klängen zu Rate. (Achte bitte darauf, alles so einfach wie möglich zu halten, bei unseren Richtlinien handelt es sich nur um eine Annäherung an die eigentlichen Klänge, besonders bei Vokalen.) Betonte Silben werden GROSSGESCHRIEBEN. Diphthonge (Vokalpaare, wie bei „klein") werden als zwei getrennte Vokale angegeben *(klaîn)*; der zweite Vokal wird mit einem Zirkumflex (^) angegeben, um Dich daran zu erinnern, beide Vokale zusammen schnell auszusprechen.

Klang	Wie bei...	Klang	Wie bei...
a	hart	o	Po
aⁿ	Chance; nasal, als ob man die Nase zuhält	oⁿ	Po, aber nasal
		oîⁿ	Feuer, aber nasal
aîⁿ	klein, aber nasal	œ	Körper
aûⁿ	Augen, aber nasal	p	Porno
b	Brust	r	Hure
d	Dildo	rr	„rápido" im Spanischen; stark gerollt
dh	„these" im Englischen; „s" in diese, aber gelispelt	rzh	der Komponist Dvořák; ein italienisches „r", schnell in Verbindung mit dem „g" aus Etage gesprochen
dzh	„Jeans" im Englischen		
e	kennenlernen		
eⁿ	Bett, aber nasal		
ə	bitte	s	süß; ein scharfes „s"
f	feucht	sh	Schatz
g	gut	t	Ständer
h	hart	th	„thin" im Englischen; „ß" in Kuß, aber gelispelt
hh	Nacht (im Rachen ausgesprochen)	ts	Zähne
i	spielen	tsh	Tschau
iⁿ	spielen, aber nasal	u	Muskeln
k	Kondome	uⁿ	Muskeln, aber nasal
ks	Sex	ü	küssen
l	lesbisch	v	wichsen
ly	Millionär	w	Whisky; englisches „w", mit gewölbten Lippen gesprochen
m	Mann		
n	Kondom	y	Junge
ng	Englisch	z	diese
ny	Champagner	zh	massage

Sex kann romantisch sein und Spaß machen, aber er sollte Dich nicht krank machen. Und um keinen Preis willst Du deswegen sterben. Wenn Du es also machst, mach' es clever. Es ist nicht so schwierig, eine HIV-Infektion oder andere unliebsame Krankheiten zu vermeiden, wenn Du Dich an die folgenden Richtlinien hältst:

▼ **NIMM AN, DASS JEDER** potentiell infiziert sein kann, egal wie süß oder sexy er aussieht. Also verhalte Dich entsprechend. Du kannst nicht festellen, ob jemand HIV-infiziert ist oder nicht, indem Du ihm ins Gesicht schaust oder ihn als Mensch beurteilst.

▼ **SAFE & HOT:** Knuddeln, Knabbern, Masturbation und die Körper aneinander reiben. Zungenküsse sind okay, außer wenn Du gerade offene Wunden oder Schnitte in Deinem Mund hast, Du Dir gerade die Zähne geputzt hast, oder Zahnseide verwendet hast (Dein Zahnfleisch könnte bluten).

▼ **BUMSEN:** *Nie* ohne Kondom. Es ist auch besser den Schwanz herauszuziehen bevor Du kommst (oder sag deinem Partner, er soll seinen Schwanz herausziehen).

▼ **BLASEN:** Weniger riskant als ficken, aber wenn Du vollkommen sicher sein willst, lecke nur den Schaft des Schwanzes und nimm nicht die Eichel in den Mund. Oder verwende ein Kondom (ohne Gleitmittel ist okay und schmeckt auch besser).

▼ **ARSCHLECKEN** gilt im allgemeinen nicht als großes Risiko in puncto AIDS, aber bedeutet ein großes Risiko für Hepatitis oder Parasiten.

▼ **HILFSMITTEL:** Dildos und Vibratoren sind in Ordnung, aber teile sie nicht mit anderen (oder wenn Du es tust, säubere sie sorgfältig mit Desinfektionsmittel oder hochwertigem Alkohol und zieh ein Kondom über sie).

▼ **REGELN FÜR KONDOME:** Achte darauf, daß die Kondome aus Latex sind — nicht aus Schafshaut oder anderen Tierhäuten. Außerdem öffne nie ein Kondompäckchen mit Deinen Zähnen — Du könntest das Kondom zerreißen!

▼ **EINFETTEN:** Wenn Du ein Gleitmittel verwendest, achte darauf, daß es wasserlöslich ist (nicht auf Öl oder Fett basiert, wie Babylotion und Hautcreme, Crisco, Butter oder Vaseline; Öl und Fett lösen das Kondom auf). Die besten Gleitmittel enthalten Nonoxynol-9, ein Spermizid — das Deinen Schutz erhöhen kann — jedoch Achtung: Verwende *nie* ein Spermizid ohne ein Kondom.

▼ **TRINKEN UND DROGEN** passen nicht zu Safer-Sex. Du brauchst Deinen Verstand, wenn es sicher bleiben soll!

▼ **POPPERS:** Wenn man beim Sex Poppers nimmt, kann man risikoreiche Situationen nicht mehr klar beurteilen. Poppers beeinträchtigt höchstwahrscheinlich das Immunsystem des Körpers, wenn es wiederholt gebraucht wird.

♂ wenn man einen
    Mann meint
♀ wenn man eine
    Frau meint
adj Adjektiv
adv Adverb

Br Britisches Englisch
LA Spanisch aus
     Lateinamerika
NE keine Entsprechung

n   Hauptwort
pl Plural
Por Portugiesisch
     aus Portugal

Qb Französisch
     aus Québec
s   Singular
v   Verb

14 CONTENIDO

El mundo es cada día más pequeño, y el número de personas que viajan o viven fuera de sus países aumenta cada año. Tanta movilidad ha llevado a una verdadera explosión de amoríos internacionales. Sin embargo, siempre ha sido difícil encontrar guías de conversación para viajeros que incluyan el vocabulario del amor. Pues ya no.

A diferencia de las tradicionales guías, *Hot! International / Gay* puede ayudarte en situaciones muy diversas: A ligar y salir con chicos, en tus relaciones y en tus revolcones — ya seas un español en Boston, un brasileño en París, o un alemán en Mallorca.

Hot! International / Gay podría resultar bueno hasta para la salud. Unas pocas palabras clave pueden desterrar malentendidos y mantenerte al margen de situaciones peligrosas o indeseables. La atención al SIDA y otras enfermedades de transmisión sexual varía mucho de un país a otro y de una persona a otra. Quizá tu nuevo amor estará dispuesto a saltar a la cama sin ninguna protección, pero tú no — y ahora se lo puedes decir en su propio idioma.

Unas cuantas notas:

▼ Con nuestro «formato cebra» es fácil charlar con chicos en seis idiomas. Sólo tienes que hallar la frase que deseas en español (siempre en la segunda raya negra de cada página). Encima encontrarás su equivalente en inglés (ENGLISH) y alemán (DEUTSCH). Abajo encontrarás el francés (FRANÇAIS), el italiano (ITALIANO), el portugués (PORTUGUÉS) y el checo (ČESKY).

▼ Excepto el inglés y el portugués, todas las lenguas de este libro tienen dos formas para la segunda persona, una formal (como «Usted») y una informal (como «tú»). Para simplificar, y porque la gente joven tiende a usar el equivalente de «tú», este libro usa sobre todo la versión informal.

▼ Los corchetes [ ] se usan para indicar dos o más opciones: *Vamos a [mi / tu] casa.* Por otro lado, lo contenido entre paréntesis ( ) es opcional: *Lo intentaremos otra vez (luego).*

Pues bien, ¡buen viaje, y que te diviertas!

Las guías de pronunciación debajo de cada frase te ayudarán a hacerte comprender mejor. Léelas fonéticamente, consultando la tabla siguiente para símbolos especiales y explicaciones de sonidos difíciles. (Ten en cuenta que, para simplificar, nuestras guías representan sólo una aproximación a los sonidos verdaderos, sobre todo en lo que concierne a las vocales.) Las sílabas acentuadas van en MAYÚSCULAS. Los diptongos (parejas de vocales, como en «coito») se indican como dos vocales distintas *(KOÎ-to)*; la segunda lleva un acento circunflejo (^), indicando que las dos vocales deben pronunciarse juntas y rápidamente. Cuando la vocal es doble (como *aa* o *EE*), se pronuncia más larga que una sencilla, como la «aa» de «Saavedra».

Sonido	Como en...	Sonido	Como en...
a	mano	oⁿ	con; «o» con la nariz tapada
aⁿ	ansias, «a» con la nariz tapada	oîⁿ	hoy, con la nariz tapada
aîⁿ	¡Ay! con la nariz tapada	œ	«feu» en francés; entre
aûⁿ	ciao, con la nariz tapada		«e» y «o»
b	beso	p	pelo
d	bien dura	r	cara
<u>dh</u>	Adonis	<u>rr</u>	guarro
dzh	«jeans» en inglés	<u>rzh</u>	Dvořák el compositor;
e	pecho		«r» y «<u>zh</u>» juntas
eⁿ	encular; «e» con la nariz tapada	s	sexo
ə	puta; una «a» débil	<u>sh</u>	«shit» en inglés; «ch» de
f	follar		«chupar» sin la «t» inicial
g	el golpe	t	tocar
h	joder, pero más suave	<u>th</u>	gracias, como en España
<u>hh</u>	joder	ts	mosca tse-tsé
i	lindo	<u>tsh</u>	chupar
iⁿ	insaciable; «i» con la	u	chúpame
	nariz tapada	uⁿ	un seductor; «u» con la nariz
k	culo		tapada
ks	éxtasis	ü	«pute» en francés; entre
l	lamer		«u» e «i»
lʸ	polla, o como «li» de «liado»	v	viejo verde, articulado con
m	macho		fuerza
n	nalgas	w	huevos
nᵍ	hincar	y	yo
nʸ	baño	z	«baise» en francés
o	orgasmo	<u>zh</u>	llorar, como en Argentina

El sexo puede ser romántico y divertido, pero no hay por qué ponerse enfermo — ni mucho menos morirse. Así que cuando hagas el amor, piensa con la cabeza. No es difícil evitar la transmisión del SIDA y otras enfermedades peligrosas si recuerdas que:

▼ **TODO EL MUNDO** puede estar infectado, incluso aquel chico tan guapo y musculoso. Ni la cara ni el cuerpo te dicen si una persona lleva el virus del SIDA. ¿Qué puedes hacer? Practica siempre el «sexo seguro».

▼ **SEGURO Y SEXY:** Acurrucarse, mordisquearse (¡suavemente!), masturbarse, frotarse. Un beso húmedo va bien mientras no tengas llagas o cortaduras en la boca, o si acabas de cepillarte los dientes o de usar hilo dental (las encías pueden sangrar).

▼ **FOLLAR:** *Nunca* folles sin condón. Y para mayor protección, ¡dile que la saque antes de correrse!

▼ **FELACIÓN:** Menos riesgo que follar, pero para evitar todo peligro, lámele la polla sin meterte el capullo en la boca. O puedes ponerle un condón (sin lubricante sabe mejor).

▼ **BESO NEGRO:** Lamer el culo no se considera peligroso para la transmisión del SIDA, pero sí para la hepatitis y varios parásitos.

▼ **JUGUETES:** Los consoladores y vibradores son muy seguros, mientras que no los compartas (si los compartes, lávalos bien con lejía o alcohol y ponles un condón antes de usarlos).

▼ **EL CONDÓN:** Asegúrate de que siempre sea de látex, no de tripa de cordero u otras pieles naturales. Y nunca abras un condón con los dientes — ¡si lo dañas, no te protege!

▼ **LUBRÍCALO:** Usa mucha crema, y asegúrate de que tu marca sea hidrosoluble (no hecha con aceite o grasa, porque éstos destruyen el látex). Tampoco uses aceite para bebés, loción para las manos, aceite vegetal, mantequilla, ni Vaselina. Los mejores lubricantes contienen nonoxynol-9, un espermicida que puede aumentar tu protección — pero *nunca* uses un espermicida sólo, sin condón.

▼ **DROGAS & ALCOHOL** en exceso no van con el sexo seguro. Para protegerte, ¡tienes que tener la cabeza clara!

▼ **POPPERS:** Aparte de afectar tu juicio en situaciones íntimas, los poppers pueden perjudicar tu sistema inmunológico si los usas con frecuencia.

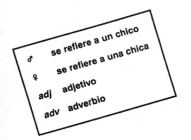

♂   se refiere a un chico
♀   se refiere a una chica
adj   adjetivo
adv   adverbio

Br   expresión británica
LA   español latino-
     americano
NE   sin equivalente
     preciso

n   sustantivo
pl   plural
Por portugués
     de Portugal

Qb   francés del
     Québec
s   singular
v   verbo

TABLE DES MATIÈRES 19

Aujourd'hui, le monde est plus petit que jamais, et le nombre de gens qui vivent et travaillent à l'étranger augmente chaque année. Tout ce mouvement fait naître les amours internationales comme jamais auparavant. Mais les manuels de conversation pour langues étrangères qui couvrent le vocabulaire de l'amour ont été jusqu'à présent soit très limités soit difficiles à trouver.

Contrairement aux recueils de phrases traditionnels, *Hot! International / Gay* peut vous aider à affronter les situations sociales les plus variées — rencontres, drague, jeux érotiques en chambre ou ailleurs — que vous soyez un Français à Miami Beach, un Américain à Paris, ou un Allemand à Majorque.

Hot! International / Gay peut même être bon pour votre santé. Quelques mots-clés permettent de clarifier les signaux un peu troubles et de rester à l'écart des situations dangereuses ou simplement indésirables. Quant au SIDA et aux autres maladies sexuellement transmissibles, leur perception varie énormément d'un pays ou d'une personne à l'autre. Votre nouvelle conquête peut vouloir se passer de protection, mais vous devriez l'éviter, et maintenant vous pouvez lui dire d'en faire autant, dans sa propre langue.

Quelques remarques:

▼ Notre unique format «zébré» facilite la conversation avec les garçons dans six langues. Trouvez simplement la phrase en français que vous voulez (toujours sur la deuxième bande blanche, juste au milieu de chaque page), et regardez au dessus pour ses équivalents en anglais (ENGLISH), allemand (DEUTSCH) et espagnol (ESPAÑOL), ou au dessous pour les traductions en italien (ITALIANO), portugais (PORTUGUÉS), et tchèque (ČESKY).

▼ Toutes les langues dans ce livre, sauf l'anglais et le portugais, ont deux formes pour la deuxième personne, comme «tu» (informelle) et «vous» (formelle) en français. Pour simplifier les choses, et étant donné que dans de nombreux pays aujourd'hui les jeunes ont tendance à utiliser l'équivalent de «tu» les uns avec les autres quelle que soit la situation, ce livre utilise surtout les façons de parler informelles.

▼ Les crochets [ ] indiquent un choix entre deux possibilités: *Allons chez [moi / toi].* De plus, tout ce qui est entre parenthèses ( ) est à prendre comme une option: *Retire-toi (avant de jouir).*

Et bien, bon voyage, et amusez-vous bien!

En dessous de chaque phrase, des conseils pour la prononciation vous aideront à vous faire comprendre. Vous pouvez les lire phonétiquement selon la table de correspondances suivante (mais n'oubliez pas que, par souci de simplicité, nos conseils ne donnent qu'une approximation des sons réels, surtout pour les voyelles). Les syllabes accentuées sont en CAPITALES. Les diphtongues (comme dans le mot «coït») sont notées comme deux voyelles séparées (koît); la seconde porte le signe d'un accent circonflexe (^) pour que vous vous souveniez de prononcer rapidement les deux voyelles ensemble. Enfin, quand une voyelle est doublée (aa, EE), il faut doubler la durée de la prononciation.

Son	Comme dans...	Son	Comme dans...
a	**a**ctif	nʸ	oign**on**
aⁿ	b**an**der	o	vibr**o**
aîⁿ	m**aï**s, nasalisé et sans aspiration finale	oⁿ	bât**on**
		oîⁿ	c**oï**t, nasalisé
aûⁿ	ch**ao**s, nasalisé	œ	c**œu**r
b	**b**ite	p	**p**orno
d	**d**raguer	r	**r**ouge
dh	«**th**e» en anglais; comme «s» dans «cho**s**e», mais zézayé	rr	«**r**ápido» en espagnol; fort «**r**» roulé
dzh	«**j**eans» en anglais	rzh	D**v**ořák le compositeur;
e	f**e**sses		«**r**» et «**zh**» dits rapidement
eⁿ	m**ain**		ensemble
ə	**je**	s	**s**ucer
f	**f**ellation	sh	**ch**armant
g	**g**odemiché	t	**t**oucher
h	«**h**ello» en anglais; aspiré	th	«gra**c**ias» en espagnol; comme
hh	«Ba**ch**» en allemand; fortement aspiré		«**s**» dans «**s**ucer», mais zézayé
i	l**i**t	ts	la mouche **ts**é-**ts**é
iⁿ	p**in**e, nasalisé	tsh	caou**tch**ouc
k	**c**aresse	u	ch**ou**quette
ks	se**x**e	uⁿ	ch**ou**quette, nasalisé
l	**l**esbienne	ü	c**u**l
lʸ	mi**ll**ion	v	**v**iril
m	**m**asturbation	w	**ou**i
n	**n**iquer	y	h**i**er
nᵍ	lo**ng**ueur	z	cho**s**e
		zh	**g**entil

Le sexe peut être romantique et agréable — à condition cependant de ne pas tomber malade. Et vous n'avez sûrement pas envie de mourir non plus. Alors quand vous faites l'amour, faites-le intelligemment. Il n'est pas difficile d'éviter la transmission du SIDA et d'autres maladies; suivez simplement ces quelques indications.

▼ **FAITES** comme si chacun était susceptible d'être infecté, aussi beau ou sexy qu'il soit, et agissez en conséquence. Vous ne pouvez pas savoir si quelqu'un est effectivement séropositif en regardant son visage ou son corps.

▼ **SAIN ET SENSUEL:** Les caresses, les chatouilles, la masturbation et les câlins. Les baisers «profonds» ne posent pas de problème sauf si vous avez des plaies ou des coupures dans la bouche, ou si vous venez de vous brosser les dents ou d'utiliser un fil dentaire (vos gencives pourraient saigner).

▼ **PÉNÉTRATION:** *Jamais* sans préservatif. Et dites-lui de se retirer avant de jouir!

▼ **FELLATION:** Moins dangereuse que la pénétration; cependant, si vous voulez être entièrement en sécurité, contentez-vous de lécher la verge de votre partenaire; ne la prenez pas dans la bouche. Ou sinon, utilisez un préservatif (sans lubrifiant, c'est parfait, et cela aura meilleur goût).

▼ **LÉCHER LE CUL** est généralement considéré comme peu dangereux dans le cas du SIDA, en revanche risque élevé d'hépatite et de parasites.

▼ **ACCESSOIRES:** Les godemichés et les vibromasseurs sont acceptables à condition de ne pas les partager (sinon, il faut les nettoyer minutieusement avec de l'eau de Javel ou de l'alcool et les recouvrir d'un préservatif).

▼ **PRÉSERVATIFS:** Ils doivent être en latex. De plus, il ne faut jamais ouvrir l'étui avec les dents — on pourrait déchirer le préservatif!

▼ **GRAISSEZ LA MACHINE!** Utilisez beaucoup de lubrifiant, et assurez-vous que le produit utilisé est soluble dans l'eau (pas d'huile ou de matières grasses, comme le lait de toilette, les lotions, le beurre ou la vaseline; l'huile et la graisse attaquent le latex). Les meilleurs lubrifiants contiennent du nonoxynol-9, un spermicide (ce qui améliore la protection). Attention: ne *jamais* utiliser un spermicide sans préservatif.

▼ **ALCOOL ET DROGUES:** Souvent incompatibles avec le safe sex. Gardez votre présence d'esprit pour vous protéger!

▼ **POPPERS:** Outre le fait qu'ils brouillent votre perception des choses en situation intime, les poppers risquent fort de mettre à mal votre système immunitaire, à usage répété.

♂ un homme
♀ une femme
adj adjectif
adv adverbe

Br anglais britannique
LA espagnol de l'Amérique Latine
NE aucun équivalent exact

n nom
pl pluriel
Por Portugais du Portugal

Qb français du Québec
s singulier
v verbe

24   ELENCO VOCI

Oggi il mondo è più piccolo che mai, e la quantità di persone che viaggiano e vivono fuori dal loro paese nativo, cresce ogni anno. Con tutta questa mobilità, gli idilli internazionali sbocciano come non mai. Ma trovare frasari che coprano il vocabolario esplicito dell'amore è sempre stato difficile se non impossibile — almeno fino ad ora.

Hot! International / Gay, differentemente dai tradizionali frasari, può aiutarti in molte situazioni sociali di diversa natura: nell'incontrare amici, negli appuntamenti galanti, in una relazione, nel pieno della passione in camera da letto, ed altro ancora. E ti aiuterà sia se sei un italiano a Los Angeles, un americano a Firenze, o un tedesco a Praga.

Hot! International / Gay può essere utile anche alla tua salute. Poche parole adeguate possono prevenire segnali sbagliati e tenerti alla larga da situazioni pericolose o indesiderate. La conoscenza dell'AIDS e di altre malattie a diffusione sessuale può variare notevolmente da paese a paese e da persona a persona. Il tuo nuovo amico potrebbe forse volere entrare «in azione» senza alcuna protezione, ma tu no — e adesso glielo potrai dire nella sua lingua.

Alcune note:

▼ Con la nostra unica impaginazione «zebrata» potrai facilmente parlare con ragazzi in sei lingue diverse. Basta trovare la frase in italiano che ti interessa (sempre nella terza riga nera) e guardare sopra per l'equivalente in inglese (ENGLISH), tedesco (DEUTSCH), spagnolo (ESPAÑOL), o francese (FRANÇAIS), e sotto per il portoghese (PORTUGUÊS) o per il ceco (ČESKY).

▼ Ad eccezione dell'inglese e del portoghese, tutte le lingue in questo libro utilizzano, come l'italiano, due forme per il «tu»: una formale come «Lei», e una informale come «tu». Per ragioni di semplicità ed anche perché oggigiorno i giovani di molti paesi tendono ad usare il «tu» tra di loro, questo libro usa la forma informale.

▼ Le parentesi quadre [ ] sono usate per indicare una possibilità di scelta: *Andiamo da [me / te].* In oltre, tutto quello contenuto tra due parentesi tonde ( ) è facoltativo: *Tiralo fuori (prima di venire).*

Bene, ti auguriamo buon viaggio, e divertiti!

Le guide di pronuncia sotto ogni frase ti aiuteranno a farti capire. Per di più, puoi leggerle foneticamente, seguendo la tavola qui sotto. (Ricorda che per semplicità, le nostre guide sono solo una approssimazione del suono effettivo, in particolare con le vocali.) Le sillabe da accentare sono MAIUSCOLE. I dittonghi (come nella parola «chiappe») sono indicati come due vocali separate *(KIÂP-pe)*; la seconda vocale è marcata con un accento cinconflesso (^) per ricordarti di pronunciare insieme entrambi le vocali. La vocale doppia *(aa, EE)* si pronuncia rafforzata, cioè, più lunga di quella semplice.

Suono	Come...	Suono	Come...
a	cazzo	oⁿ	bacio, detto in modo nasale
aⁿ	cazzo, detto in modo nasale	oîⁿ	vuoi, detto in modo nasale
aîⁿ	dai, detto in modo nasale	œ	«Sant'Ambrœus» in
aûⁿ	ciao, detto in modo nasale		Milanese; «e» detto a
b	bacio		labbra tonde
d	duro	p	peloso
dh	«the» in inglese; come «d»	r	caro
	ma con la lingua tra i denti	rr	arrapato
dzh	orgia	rzh	Dvořák il compositore;
e	sesso		«r» e «zh» dette veloce-
eⁿ	sesso, detto in modo nasale		mente insieme
ə	«je» in francese	s	succhiare
f	frocio	sh	pisciare
g	gola	t	toccare
h	«hello» in inglese; aspirato	th	«gracias» in spagnolo;
hh	«Bach» in tedesco; molto		come «s» ma pronunciato
	aspirato		con la lingua tra i denti
i	lingua	ts	cazzo
iⁿ	lingua, detto in modo nasale	tsh	ciao
k	chiappe	u	succhiotto
ks	ex	uⁿ	culo, detto in modo nasale
l	lesbica	ü	«pute» in francese; «i»
lʸ	coglioni		detto a labbra tonde
m	mordere	v	venire
n	natiche	w	uomo
nᵍ	lingua	y	iena
nʸ	bagno	z	cosa
o	bacio	zh	«je» in francese

Il sesso può essere romantico e divertente, ma non vuoi certo ammalarti — e sicuramente non vuoi morire. Quindi quando fai sesso, usa il cervello. Non è così difficile evitare la trasmissione dell'AIDS e di altre spiacevoli malattie; basta seguire le seguenti semplici indicazioni:

▼ **PENSA CHE CHIUNQUE** è potenzialmente infetto, non importa quanto sia dolce o sexy e comportati di conseguenza. Non è possibile capire lo stato clinico di una persona rispetto all'AIDS guardandolo in viso o osservando il suo corpo.

▼ **SICURO & ECCITANTE:** Abbracciarsi, coccolarsi, masturbarsi e strofinare il proprio corpo contro quello del partner. Baciarsi con la lingua è consentito, tranne quando si hanno ferite o tagli all'interno della bocca, oppure se lavandosi i denti poco prima, le gengive hanno sanguinato.

▼ **SCOPARE:** Non farlo *mai* senza il preservativo. E non dimenticare: tiralo (o digli di tirarlo) fuori prima di venire.

▼ **SUCCHIARE:** Meno rischioso che scopare, ma se vuoi essere totalmente sicuro, limitati alla base del pene; non prendere in bocca la cappella. Oppure usa un preservativo (va bene non lubrificato, il sapore è più gradevole).

▼ **LECCARE IL CULO** è considerato generalmente non rischioso per l'AIDS, ma molto rischioso per epatiti e parassiti vari.

▼ **GIOCATTOLI:** L'uso di dildi e di vibratori è consentito, ma non farli usare ad altre persone (oppure se lo fai, lavali accuratamente con della candeggina o alcool denaturato e infilaci sopra un preservativo).

▼ **PRESERVATIVI:** Usa sempre preservativi in lattice e non quelli fatti in materiali organici animali. Inoltre non aprire la confezione con i denti — potresti rompere il preservativo.

▼ **LUBRIFICANTI:** Usa molto lubrificante con i preservativi e fai in modo di usarne sempre uno idrosolubile (non a base di olio o grasso, come il baby-oil, il Crisco, il burro o la vaselina — l'olio e il grasso rompono il lattice). I migliori lubrificanti contengono lo spermicida nonoxynol-9; questo può aumentare la tua protezione. Ma non usare *mai* uno spermicida da solo senza un preservativo.

▼ **ALCOOL & DROGHE:** Non abusarne se vuoi che il tuo sesso sia sicuro. Hai bisogno di lucidità per non fare cazzate!

▼ **POPPERS:** Oltre ad alterare le tue capacità di giudizio in situazioni intime, i poppers possono danneggiare il tuo sistema immunitario se ripetutamente usati.

♂ un uomo

♀ una donna

adj aggettivo

adv avverbio

Br inglese britannico

LA spagnolo dell'America Latina

NE non esattamente equivalente

n sostantivo

pl plurale

Por Portoghese del Portogallo

Qb francese del Québec

s singolare

v verbo

ÍNDICE

O mundo hoje em dia está menor do que nunca, e o número de pessoas vivendo e viajando fora do seu país de origem aumenta a cada ano. Com toda essa mobilidade, o romance internacional vem se expandindo como nunca. Entretanto, livros de expressões que cobrem o vocabulário explícito do amor têm sido sempre poucos ou difíceis de se encontrar — até agora.

Ao contrário dos tradicionais livros de expressões, *Hot! International / Gay* pode ajudar você em muitas situações sociais diferentes — como conhecer pessoas, iniciar namoros, relacionamentos, ações eróticas no quarto e muito mais — seja você um brasileiro em Miami, um alemão na Argentina, ou um americano em Lisboa.

Hot! International / Gay pode até ser bom para a sua saúde. Algumas palavras-chave podem prevenir confusão de sinais e evitar situações inseguras ou indesejáveis. A concientização no que diz respeito a AIDS e outras doenças sexualmente transmissíveis pode variar um bocado de país para país e de pessoa a pessoa. Seu novo amigo pode ir se entregando sem proteção, mas você não deve fazer o mesmo. E mais, você agora pode dizer a ele o que você quiser, na língua dele.

Algumas notas:

▼ O nosso formato de "listras em zebra" permite o diálogo fácil com homens em qualquer uma das seis línguas. Basta encontrar a frase que você quer em português (sempre na terceira listra branca), e ver o correspondente em inglês (ENGLISH), alemão (DEUTSCH), espanhol (ESPAÑOL), francês (FRANÇAIS) e italiano (ITALIANO), acima, e tcheco (ČESKY) abaixo.

▼ Exceto em inglês, todas as línguas neste livro têm duas formas para "você", uma formal e outra informal (como "tu" em Portugal). Hoje em dia, pessoas mais jovens em muitos países têm a tendência de usar espressões informais ao se dirigir a outra pessoa em muitas situações, se não em quase todas. Portanto, para tornar mais simples o uso desse pronome e da língua em geral, esse livro usa expressões de linguagem informal.

▼ Colchetes [ ] são usados para indicar mais de uma possibilidade: *Vamos à [minha / sua] casa.* Além disso, tudo em parênteses ( ) é opcional: *Tira (antes de gozar).*

Bem, tenha uma boa viagem — e bom proveito!

Os guias de pronúncia abaixo de cada frase ajudarão você a ser melhor compreendido. Para símbolos especiais e sons difíceis, confira a tabela abaixo. Lembre-se de que, para manter as coisas simples, nossos guias são somente sons aproximados dos reais, principalmente com as vogais. Sílabas tônicas são marcadas com letras MAIÚSCULAS. Ditongos (pares de vogais, como na palavra "eu") são indicados como duas vogais separadas *(eû)*; a segunda vogal é marcada com um circunflexo (^) para lembrar você de pronunciar ambas as vogais juntas rapidamente. As vogais duplas *(aa, EE)* são pronunciadas duas vezes mais longas do que uma vogal só.

Som	Como em...	Som	Como em...
a	n**a**morado	oîⁿ	aç**ões**
aⁿ	irm**ã**	œ	"c**œu**r" em francês; "e"
aîⁿ	m**ãe**		pronunciado com os labios
aûⁿ	masturbaç**ão**		arredondados
b	**b**issexual	p	**p**ornô
d	**d**uro	r	t**r**epar
dh	"**th**e" em inglês; "z" com a	rr	"**r**ico" em espanhol
	língua entre os dentes	rzh	Dvo**řá**k o compositor; "r" de
dzh	**d**inheiro		t**r**epar e em seguida "g" de
e	s**e**xo		**g**ilete, pronunciados juntos
eⁿ	b**em**		e depressa
ə	b**u**nda	s	**s**exi
f	**f**oder	sh	**ch**upetinha
g	**g**ozar	t	**t**repar
h	**r**apidinha, como em **R**io	th	"gra**c**ias" no espanhol de
hh	**r**apidinha, mas mais gutural		Espanha; "s" com a língua
i	f**i**na		entre os dentes
iⁿ	s**im**	ts	mosca **ts**e-tse
k	**c**unete	tsh	**tch**eco
ks	se**x**o	u	tes**u**do
l	**l**ascivo	uⁿ	b**un**da
ly	co**lh**ões	ü	"k**ü**ssen" em alemão; fale "i"
m	**m**achão		fazendo a boca de "u"
n	**n**oitada	v	**j**ovem
ng	ci**nc**o	w	líng**u**a
ny	camisi**nh**a	y	**i**ate
o	**o**rgia	z	te**s**ão
oⁿ	c**om**	zh	**g**ilete

O sexo pode ser romântico e divertido, mas não compensa quando causa doença — e você certamente não quer morrer. Então, quando tiver uma relação sexual, faça-o com inteligência. Não é tão difícil evitar a transmissão da AIDS e outros indesejáveis organismos se você seguir algumas normas simples.

▼ **PARTA** do principio de que todo mundo está potencialmente infetado, não importa quão gostoso ou sexy seu parceiro seja — e aja de acordo. Você não pode dizer se alguém tem o vírus somente pela cara ou físico.

▼ **SEGURO E "QUENTE":** Carícias, mordiscadas, masturbação, e roçar corpo com corpo. Beijo de língua tudo bem, exceto se você tiver feridas abertas ou cortes na sua boca, ou se você acabou de escovar os dentes ou usar o fio dental (sua gengiva pode estar sangrando).

▼ **TREPAR:** *Nunca* o faça sem camisinha. E lembre-se que é melhor tirar antes de ejacular.

▼ **FELAÇÃO:** Menos arriscado que trepar, mas se você quiser estar totalmente seguro, somente lamba a base do pênis do seu parceiro; não ponha a cabeça na sua boca. Ou você pode usar uma camisinha (a não lubrificada está bem, e tem gosto melhor).

▼ **CUNETE:** Lamber o cu é geralmente considerado de baixo risco para AIDS mas de alto risco para contrair hepatite e parasitas.

▼ **BRINQUEDOS:** Consolos e vibradores tudo bem, mas não os compartilhe com ninguém (ou se o fizer limpe-os cuidadosamente com desinfetante, água sanitária ou álcool e ponha uma camisinha neles).

▼ **REGRAS DA CAMISINHA:** Tenha certeza de que suas camisinhas sejam de latex — não de pele de carneiro ou outro animal qualquer. Outra coisa: Nunca abra a embalagem da camisinha com os dentes — você pode rasgar o conteúdo.

▼ **LUBRIFIQUE:** Use bastante lubrificante; é importante que ele seja solúvel em água (não à base de óleo ou gordura, tipo óleo para bebê, loção cremosa, gordura vegetal, manteiga, ou vaselina; o óleo e a gordura destroem o latex). Os melhores lubrificantes contém nonoxynol-9, um espermicida — o que pode pode aumentar sua proteção — mas *nunca* use só o espermicida sem a camisinha.

▼ **BEBIDAS & DROGAS** em geral não se misturam muito bem com sexo seguro. Você precisa de astúcia para manter-se seguro!

▼ **POPPERS:** Além de confundir seu julgamento em situações de intimidade, poppers podem afetar seu sistema de imunidade se usados com frequência.

♂ um homem
♀ uma mulher
adj adjetivo
adv advérbio

Br expressão britânica
LA espanhol da América Latina
NE não existe equivalente exato

n substantivo
Por português de Portugal
pl plural

Qb francês de Québec
s singular
v verbo

OBSAH

Dnešní svět se zdá menším než kdykoli v minulosti, množství lidí cestujících do zahraničí nebo žijících v cizině každým rokem roste. Tento pohyb přináší proti dřívějším letům i mnohem větší pravděpodobnost milostných setkání a vztahů mezi příslušníky různých národů. Avšak najít konverzační příručku cizího jazyka, která by se necensurovaně zabývala i oblastí lásky a sexu bylo velmi těžké — až do této chvíle.

Na rozdíl od tradičních slovníků je *Hot! International / Gay* připraven pomoci v mnoha rozličných společenských situacích — při setkáních s lidmi, schůzkách, vztazích, žhavých ložnicových scénách a navíc — stejně dobře poslouží Čechovi v New Yorku, Američanovi v Praze nebo Italovi na Kanárských Ostrovech.

Hot! International / Gay Vám může dokonce pomoci uchovat si zdraví. Několik základních výrazů může pomoci zabránit vzájemnému nedorozumění a nepochopení situace a tím Vás ochránit od nebezpečných nebo nechtěných zážitků. Vědomí rizika AIDS a dalších pohlavních nemocí se v jednotlivých zemích značně liší a stejně tak rozdílný je i přístup konkrétních jedinců. Váš nový přítel bude například chtít „jít na věc" bez ochrany, ale Vy se chránit chcete — teď máte možnost vše uvést na pravou míru, díky *Hot! International / Gay*.

Několik poznámek:

▼ Naše jedinečná „zebra" úprava zjednodušuje komunikaci s klukama v kterémkoli ze šesti jazyků. Pouze si najděte českou frázi, která Vás zajímá (vždy v černém poli na spodním okraji stránky), a v horní části stránky naleznete její jazykový ekvivalent v angličtině (ENGLISH), němčině (DEUTSCH), španělštině (ESPAÑOL), francouzštině (FRANÇAIS), italštině (ITALIANO), nebo portugalštině (PORTUGUÊS).

▼ Všechny jazyky v této knize (kromě angličtiny a portugalštiny) mají tak jako čeština dva způsoby oslovení druhé osoby; jeden formální (jako „vy") a jeden neformální (jako „ty"). Pro zjednodušení i proto, že dnes mladí lidé častěji používají ekvivalent českého „ty", většinou tato kniha uvádí neformální oslovení.

▼ Hranaté závorky [ ] upozorňují na více eventuálních možností: *Pojď'me [ke mně / k tobě]*. Kromě toho, všechny výrazy v kulatých závorkách ( ) znamenají též možnost volby: *(Moc) tě miluji*.

Takže, šťastnou cestu a dobře se bavte!

Přepis výslovnosti pod každou frází Vám pomůže lépe porozumět. Speciální symboly najdete v následujících tabulkách. (Mějte prosím na paměti, že pro jednoduchost uvádíme pouze přibližný přepis zvuku, hlavně pokud se jedná o samohlásky). Místa s přízvukem jsou psána VELKÝMI písmeny. Dvouhlásky (jako „souložit") jsou popisovány jako dvě samostatné samohlásky *(SOÛ-lo-zhit)* druhá z nichž je přízvuk (^) abychom Vám připomněli nutnost vyslovit obě hlásky rychle dohromady.

Zvuk	Vysloví se jako...	Zvuk	Vysloví se jako...
a	aférka	nʸ	ňadra
aⁿ	aférka, vyslovte se	o	lovit
	zacpaným nosem	oⁿ	lovit, vyslovte se
aîⁿ	čaj, vyslovte se		zacpaným nosem
	zacpaným nosem	oîⁿ	trojka, vyslovte se
aûⁿ	čau, vyslovte se		zacpaným nosem
	zacpaným nosem	œ	„hören" v němčině; „e" se
b	bisexuál		rty do kroužku
d	dvoření	p	půlky
<u>dh</u>	„the" v angličtině; „z" se	r	robertek
	„šlapáním si" na jazyk	<u>rr</u>	striptýz, nebo „rápido" ve
<u>dzh</u>	džínsy		španělštině
e	sex	<u>rzh</u>	kouřit
eⁿ	sex, vyslovte se	s	sperma
	zacpaným nosem	<u>sh</u>	šukat
ə	„bitte" v němčině	t	travestie
f	felace	<u>th</u>	„gracias" ve španělštině;
g	genitalie		„s" se „šlapáním si" na jazyk
h	homosexuál	ts	cucflek
<u>hh</u>	chlípný	<u>tsh</u>	čurák
i	milovat	u	guma
iⁿ	milý, vyslovte se	uⁿ	guma, vyslovte se
	zacpaným nosem		zacpaným nosem
k	kurva	û	„küssen" v němčině; „i" se
ks	sex		rty do kroužku
l	láska	v	vylízat
lʸ	klient	w	oáza
m	mrdat	y	ujetý
n	nudipláž	z	zádek
nᵍ	mango	<u>zh</u>	souložit

Sex je zábavný a romantický, ale určitě nechcete onemocnět — a už rozhodně ne zemřít. Takže když to děláte, dělejte to s rozumem. Není tak těžké vyhnout se riziku přenosu AIDS a dalších nepříjemných pohlavních chorob, dodržíte-li několik jednoduchých zásad.

▼ **MĚJTE NA PAMĚTI**, že každý je potenciální přenašeč, nezáleží na tom, jak krásně nebo sexy vypadá, a podle toho se chovejte. Není možné odhadnout, jak na tom kdokoli pokud jde o AIDS je podle tváře nebo postavy.

▼ **BEZPEČNÉ A VZRUŠUJÍCÍ:** Objímání, štípání, masturbace, vzájemné tření těl. Líbání je OK s výjimkou situace, kdy máte otevřenou ránu v ústech, nebo těsně po čištění zubů kartáčkem nebo nití (Vaše dásně mohou krvácet).

▼ **ŠOUSTÁNÍ:** *Nikdy* nesouložte bez kondomu, a je lepší ho vytáhnout dříve než se uděláš.

▼ **KOUŘENÍ PTÁKŮ** je méně riskantní než šoustání, ale chcete-li si být skutečně jisti, olizujte jenom strany údu, neberte do úst žalud. Nebo použijte kondom (nelubrikovaný má lepší chuť).

▼ **LÍZÁNÍ ZADKU** všeobecně není pokládáno za hodně riskantní pokud jde o AIDS, ale nebezpečné pro přenos žloutenky a parazitů.

▼ **„HRAČKY":** Robertky a vibrátory jsou v pořádku, ale nepůjčujte je (pokud ano, pak pořádně umyté dezinfekcí či alkoholem a pokryté kondomem).

▼ **„GUMOVÁ" PRAVIDLA:** Přesvědčte se, že Váš kondom je z latexu a ne z nějakých zvířecích materiálů. Nikdy také neotevírejte balíček kondomů za pomoci zubů — guma by se mohla protrhnout.

▼ **JAK TO NAVLHČIT:** Používejte hodně lubrikantu, a dbejte na to, aby byl rozpustný ve vodě (ne na mastném nebo tukovém základě, jako dětský olej, emulze, máslo, stolní tuk, krém, vazelína; oleje a tuky ničí gumu). Nejlepší lubrikanty obsahují nonoxynol-9, spermicid, což může zvýšit Vaši ochranu — ale *nikdy* nepoužívejte pouze spermicid bez kondomu.

▼ **ALKOHOL A DROGY** nejdou s bezpečným sexem moc dohromady. Potřebujete mít čistou hlavu a sebekontrolu, chcete-li mít „safe" jistotu.

▼ **POPPERS:** Nejen že Vám otupí Vaši soudnost při intimních situacích, ale „poppers" také mohout poničit Váš imunitní systém, pokud se požívají opakovaně.

♂   o mužovi
♀   o ženě
adj   přídavné jméno
adv   příslovce

Br   britský výraz
LA   španělština Latinské Ameriky
NE   neexistuje rovnocenný výraz

n   podstatné jméno
pl   plurál, množné číslo
Por   portugalská portugalština

Qb   francouzština Québeca
s   singulár, jednoté číslo
v   sloveso

[Yes / No / Maybe]. *[yes / noû / MEÎ-bi].*	**Please.** *pliiz.*	**ENGLISH** the basics
[Ja / Nein / Vielleicht]. *[yaa / naîn / fii-LAÎSHT].*	**Bitte.** *BI-tə.*	**DEUTSCH** wichtiges
[Sí / No / Quizá]. *[si / no / ki-THA].*	**Por favor.** *por fa-BOR.*	**ESPAÑOL** lo básico
[Oui / Non / Peut-être]. *[wi / noⁿ / pœ-TE-trə].*	**S'il te plaît.** *sil tə ple.*	**FRANÇAIS** b a ba
[Sì / No / Forse]. *[si / no / FOR-se].*	**Per favore.** *per fa-VO-re.*	**ITALIANO** le basi
[Sim / Não / Talvez]. *[siⁿ / naûⁿ / təl-VES].*	**Por favor.** *puhh fə-VOHH.*	**PORTUGUÊS** o básico
[Ano / Ne / Možná]. *[A-no / ne / MOZH-naa].*	**Prosím.** *PRO-siim.*	**ČESKY** základy

ENGLISH *the basics*	**Thank you (very much).** *thenk yu (VE-ri mətsh).*	**[You're welcome / Not at all (Br)].** *[yœr WEL-kəm / not et ool].*	
DEUTSCH *wichtiges*	**Danke (schön).** *DAN-kə (shœn).*	**Bitte.** *BI-tə.*	
ESPAÑOL *lo básico*	**(Muchas) gracias.** *(MU-tshas) GRA-thiás.*	**De nada.** *de NA-dha.*	
FRANÇAIS *b a ba*	**Merci (beaucoup).** *mer-SI (bo-KU).*	**Pas de quoi.** *pad kuâ.*	
ITALIANO *le basi*	**(Molte) grazie.** *(MOL-te) GRA-tsiê.*	**Prego.** *PRE-go.*	
PORTUGUÊS *o básico*	**(Muito) obrigado.** *(MUÎᴺ-tu) o-bri-GA-du.*	**De nada.** *dzhi NA-də.*	
ČESKY *základy*	**Díky (moc).** *DII-ki (mots).*	**Není zač.** *NE-nii zatsh.*	

Excuse me. *eks-KIÚZ mi.*	**I'm sorry.** *aîm SA-ri.*

ENGLISH the basics

Entschuldigung. *en-TSHUL-di-gung.*	**Es tut mir leid.** *es tut MI-ər laît.*

DEUTSCH wichtiges

Perdón. *per-DON.*	**Lo siento.** *lo SIÉN-to.*

ESPAÑOL lo básico

Pardon. *par-DON.*	**Désolé.** *de-zə-LE.*

FRANÇAIS b a ba

Scusa. *SKU-za.*	**Mi dispiace.** *mi dis-PIÂ-tshe.*

ITALIANO le basi

Com licença. *kon li-SEN-sə.*	**Sinto muito.** *SIN-tu MUÎN-tu.*

PORTUGUÊS o básico

Promiň. *PRO-miny.*	**Je mi líto.** *ye mi LII-to.*

ČESKY základy

ENGLISH — the basics

[Hello / Hi].
[hə-LOÛ / haî].

Good [morning / afternoon / evening].
gud [MOR-ninᵍ / af-tœr-NUN / IIV-ninᵍ].

DEUTSCH — wichtiges

Hallo.
HA-lo.

Guten [Morgen / Tag / Abend].
GUU-tən [MOR-gən / taak / AA-bənt].

ESPAÑOL — lo básico

Hola.
O-la.

[Buenos días / Buenas tardes *(12:00→)* / Buenas tardes *(18:00→)*].
[BUÊ-nos DI-as / BUÊ-nas TAR-des / BUÊ-nas TAR-des].

FRANÇAIS — b a ba

Salut.
sa-LÜ.

Bon [jour *(06:00→)* / jour *(12:00→)* / soir].
boⁿ [zhur / zhur / suâr].

ITALIANO — le basi

Ciao.
TSHA-o.

[Buon giorno *(06:00→)* / Buon giorno *(12:00→)* / Buona sera].
[buôn DZHOR-no / buôn DZHOR-no / BUÔ-na SE-ra].

PORTUGUÊS — o básico

Oi.
oî.

[Bom dia / Boa tarde / Boa noite].
[boⁿ DZHI-ə / boâ TAHH-dzhi / boâ NOΊ-tshi].

ČESKY — základy

[Ahoj / Nazdar].
[A-hoî / NAZ-dar].

[Dobré ráno / Dobrý den / Dobrý večer].
[DO-bree RAA-no / DO-brii den / DO-brii VE-tsher].

How's it going? *haúz it GOÛ-inᵍ?*	**Fine, thanks.** *faîn, <u>thenks</u>.*	**ENGLISH** the basics
Wie geht's? *vii geîts?*	**Gut, danke.** *guut, DAN-kə.*	**DEUTSCH** wichtiges
¿Qué tal? *ke tal?*	**Bien, gracias.** *biên, GRA-<u>thi</u>âs.*	**ESPAÑOL** lo básico
Ça va? *sa va?*	**Très bien, merci.** *tre biêⁿ, mer-SI.*	**FRANÇAIS** b a ba
Come va? *KO-me va?*	**Bene, grazie.** *BE-ne, GRA-tsiê.*	**ITALIANO** le basi
Como vai? *KO-mu vaî?*	**Bem, obrigado.** *beⁿ, o-bri-GA-du.*	**PORTUGUÊS** o básico
Jak se máš? *yak se maa<u>sh</u>?*	**Dobře, díky.** *DOB-<u>zhe</u>, DII-ki.*	**ČESKY** základy

ENGLISH · the basics

Not bad. And you?
nat bed. end yu?

[Goodbye / Bye]!
[gud-BAI / baî]!

DEUTSCH · wichtiges

Nicht schlecht. Und du?
nisht shlesht. unt du?

[Auf Wiedersehen / Tschüß]!
[aûf VII-dər-zeîn / tshüs]!

ESPAÑOL · lo básico

Tirando. ¿Y tú?
ti-RAN-do. i tu?

¡[Adiós / Ciao]!
[a-DHIÓS / TSHA-o]!

FRANÇAIS · b a ba

Ça peut aller. Et toi?
sa pœ a-LE. e tuâ?

Au revoir!
or-VUÂR!

ITALIANO · le basi

Non c'è male. E tu?
non tshe MA-le. e tu?

[Arrivederci / Ciao]!
[a-rri-ve-DER-tshi / TSHA-o]!

PORTUGUÊS · o básico

Nada mal. E você?
NA-də maû. i vo-SE?

[Até logo / Tchau]!
[ə-TE LO-gu / tshaû]!

ČESKY · základy

Jde to. A ty?
i-DE to. a ti?

[Na shledanou / Čau]!
[nas HLE-da-noû / tshaû]!

See you soon. *sii yu sun.*	**Good night.** *gud naît.*	**ENGLISH** the basics
Bis bald. *bis balt.*	**Gute Nacht.** *GUU-tə na<u>hh</u>t.*	**DEUTSCH** wichtiges
Hasta luego. *AS-ta LUÊ-go.*	**Buenas noches.** *BUÊ-nas NO-<u>tsh</u>es.*	**ESPAÑOL** lo básico
À bientôt. *a biêⁿ-TO.*	**Bonne nuit.** *bən-NÜÎ.*	**FRANÇAIS** b a ba
A presto. *a PRES-to.*	**Buona notte.** *BUÔ-na NOT-te.*	**ITALIANO** le basi
Até mais. *ə-TE maîs.*	**Boa noite.** *boâ NOÎ-<u>tsh</u>i.*	**PORTUGUÊS** o básico
Uvidíme se brzy. *u-VI-dii-me se BƏR-zi.*	**Dobrou noc.** *DO-broû nots.*	**ČESKY** základy

ENGLISH understand?	(Sorry,) I don't understand. *(SA-ri,) aî doûnt ən-dœrs-TEND.*	Slower, (please). *SLOÛ-œr, (pliiz).*
DEUTSCH verstehen	(Entschuldigung,) ich verstehe nicht. *(en-TSHUL-di-gung,) ish fersh-TEÎ-ə nisht.*	Langsamer, (bitte). *LANG-za-mər, (BI-tə).*
ESPAÑOL ¿entiendes?	(Lo siento,) no entiendo. *(lo SIÉN-to,) no en-TIÊN-do.*	Más despacio, (por favor). *mas des-PA-thiô, (por fa-BOR).*
FRANÇAIS comment?	(Pardon,) j'ai pas compris. *(par-DON,) zhe pa kon-PRI.*	Plus lentement, (s'il te plaît). *plü lant-MAN, (sil tə ple).*
ITALIANO capito?	(Mi dispiace,) non ho capito. *(mi dis-PIÂ-tshe,) non o ka-PI-to.*	Più lentamente, (per favore). *più len-ta-MEN-te, (per fa-VO-re).*
PORTUGUÊS compreende?	(Desculpe,) eu não compreendo. *(dis-KUL-pi,) eû naûn kon-pri-EN-du.*	Mais devagar, (por favor). *maîs di-və-GAHH, (puhh fə-VOHH).*
ČESKY rozumíš?	(Promiň,) nerozumím. *(PRO-miny,) NE-ro-zu-miim.*	Pomaleji, (prosím). *PO-ma-le-yi, (PRO-siim).*

Do you speak [English / German / Spanish / French]? *du yu spiik [ING-lish / DZHŒR-mən / SPE-nish / frentsh]?*	**I (don't) speak [Italian / Portuguese / Czech].** *aî (doûnt) spiik [i-TA-liën / POR-tshə-giiz / tshek].*	**ENGLISH** understand?
Sprichst du [Englisch / Deutsch / Spanisch / Französisch]? *shprishst du [ENG-lish / doîtsh / SHPA-nish / fran-TSŒ-zish]?*	**Ich spreche (kein) [Italienisch / Portugiesisch / Tschechisch].** *ish SHPRE-shə (kaîn) [i-ta-LIÊ-nish / por-tu-GII-zish / TSHE-shish].*	**DEUTSCH** verstehen
¿Hablas [inglés / alemán / español / francés? *A-blas [in-GLES / a-le-MAN / es-pa-NYOL / fran-THES?*	**(No) hablo [italiano / portugués / checo].** *(no) A-blo [i-ta-LIÁ-no / por-tu-GES / TSHE-ko].*	**ESPAÑOL** ¿entiendes?
Tu parles [anglais / allemand / espagnol / français]? *tü parl [aⁿ-GLE / al-MAⁿ / es-pa-NYOL / fraⁿ-SE]?*	**Je parle (pas) [italien / portugais / tchèque].** *zhə parl (pa) [i-ta-LIÊⁿ / por-tu-GE / tshek].*	**FRANÇAIS** comment?
Parli [inglese / tedesco / spagnolo / francese]? *PAR-li [in-GLE-ze / te-DES-co / spa-NYO-lo / fran-TSHE-ze]?*	**(Non) parlo [italiano / portoghese / ceco].** *(non) PAR-lo [i-ta-LIÁ-no / por-to-GE-ze / TSHE-ko].*	**ITALIANO** capito?
Você fala [inglês / alemão / espanhol / francês]? *vo-SE FA-lə [in-GLES / a-le-MAÛN / es-pa-NYOL / fraⁿ-SES]?*	**Eu (não) falo [italiano / português / tcheco].** *eû (naûⁿ) FA-lu [i-tə-LIÁ-nu / por-tu-GES / TSHE-ku].*	**PORTUGUÊS** compreende?
Mluvíš [anglicky / německy / španělsky / francouzsky]? *MLU-viish [AN-glit-ski / NIÊ-met-ski / SHPA-niêl-ski / FRAN-tsoûz-ski]?*	**(Ne) mluvím [italsky / portugalsky / česky].** *(ne) MLU-viim [I-tal-ski / POR-tu-gal-ski / TSHE-ski].*	**ČESKY** rozumíš?

ENGLISH pickups	**Do you have the time?** *du yu hev <u>dhə</u> taîm?*	**Do you have a [cigarette / light]?** *du yu hev ə [SI-ga-ret / laît]?*
DEUTSCH abschleppen	**Wie spät ist es?** *vii <u>shpeît</u> ist es?*	**Hast du [eine Zigarette / Feuer]?** *hast du [AÎ-nə tsi-ga-RE-tə / FOÎ-ər]?*
ESPAÑOL ligues	**¿Tienes hora?** *TIÉ-nes O-ra?*	**¿Tienes [un cigarrillo / fuego]?** *TIÉ-nes [un <u>thi</u>-ga-<u>RRI</u>-lʸo / FUÈ-go]?*
FRANÇAIS draguer	**Tu as l'heure?** *tü a lœr?*	**Tu as [une cigarette / du feu]?** *tü a [ün si-ga-RET / dü fœ]?*
ITALIANO l'approccio	**Sai l'ora?** *saî LO-ra?*	**Hai [una sigaretta / da accendere]?** *aî [U-na si-ga-RET-ta / da at-<u>TSHEN</u>-de-re]?*
PORTUGUÊS cantadas	**Que horas são?** *ki O-rəs saûⁿ?*	**Você tem [um cigarro / fogo]?** *vo-SE teⁿ [uⁿ si-GA-<u>hh</u>u / FO-gu]?*
ČESKY balení	**Máš čas?** *maa<u>sh</u> <u>tsh</u>as?*	**Máš [cigaretu / oheň]?** *maa<u>sh</u> [TSI-ga-re-tu / O-henʸ]?*

Do you come here a lot? *du yu kəm HI-œr ə lat?*	**What cologne are you wearing?** *wət kə-LOÛN ar yu WE-ə-ring?*	**ENGLISH** pickups
Kommst du oft hierher? *komst du oft HI-ər-he-ər?*	**Welches Eau de Toilette nimmst du?** *VEL-shəs o də tuâ-LE-tə nimst du?*	**DEUTSCH** abschleppen
¿Vienes mucho por aquí? *BIÊ-nes MU-tsho por a-KI?*	**¿Qué colonia llevas?** *ke ko-LO-niâ LYE-bas?*	**ESPAÑOL** ligues
Tu viens souvent ici? *tü viêⁿ su-VAⁿ i-SI?*	**Qu'est-ce que tu portes comme parfum?** *kes kə tü pərt kəm par-FEⁿ?*	**FRANÇAIS** draguer
Vieni spesso qua? *VIÊ-ni SPES-so kuâ?*	**Che colonia porti?** *ke ko-LO-niâ POR-ti?*	**ITALIANO** l'approccio
Você vem muito aqui? *vo-SE veⁿ MUÎN-tu ə-KI?*	**Que colônia você está usando?** *ki ku-LO-niâ vo-SE is-TA u-ZAN-du?*	**PORTUGUÊS** cantadas
Chodíš sem často? *HHO-diish sem TSHAS-to?*	**Co to máš za kolínskou?** *tso to maash za KO-liin-skoû?*	**ČESKY** balení

ENGLISH / pickups

Want to dance?
want tu dens?

You're a great dancer.
yœr ə greít DEN-sœr.
☞ COMPLIMENTS, P. 192

DEUTSCH / abschleppen

Willst du tanzen?
vilst du TAN-tsen?

Du bist ein guter Tänzer.
du bist aîn GUUT-ər TEN-tsər.
☞ KOMPLIMENTE, S. 192

ESPAÑOL / ligues

¿Quieres bailar?
KIÊ-res baî-LAR?

Bailas muy bien.
BAÎ-las muî biên.
☞ CUMPLIDOS, PÁG. 192

FRANÇAIS / draguer

Tu veux danser?
tü vœ dan-SE?

Tu danses très bien.
tü dans tre biên.
☞ COMPLIMENTS, P. 192

ITALIANO / l'approccio

Vuoi ballare?
VUÔ-i bal-LA-re?

Balli molto bene.
BAL-li MOL-to BE-ne.
☞ COMPLIMENTI, P. 192

PORTUGUÊS / cantadas

Quer dançar?
kehh dan-sahh?

Você dança bem.
vo-SE DAN-sə ben.
☞ ELOGIOS, PÁG. 192

ČESKY / baleni

Zatancujeme si?
za-TAN-tsu-ye-me si?

Dobře tancuješ.
DOB-zhe TAN-tsu-yesh.
☞ LICHOTKY, STR. 192

Let me buy you a drink. *let mi baî yu ə drink.*	**What'll you have?** *WƏT-əl yu hev?*	**ENGLISH** drinks
Ich möchte dich zu einem Drink einladen. *ish MŒSH-tə dish tsu AÎ-nəm drink AÎN-laa-dən.*	**Was nimmst du?** *vas nimst du?*	**DEUTSCH** trinken
Te invito a una copa. *te in-BI-to a U-na KO-pa.*	**¿Qué tomas?** *ke TO-mas?*	**ESPAÑOL** copas
Je veux t'offrir un verre. *zhə vœ to-FRIR eⁿ ver.*	**Qu'est-ce que tu prends?** *KES-kə tü praⁿ?*	**FRANÇAIS** boire
Ti posso offrire qualcosa da bere? *ti POS-so of-FRI-re kuâl-KO-za da BE-re?*	**Cosa vuoi da bere?** *KO-za VUÔ-i da BE-re?*	**ITALIANO** drinks
Deixa eu te oferecer um drinque. *DEÎ-sha eû tshi o-fe-re-SER uⁿ drink.*	**O que é que você quer?** *u ki e ki vo-SE kehh?*	**PORTUGUÊS** drinques
Chci tě pozvat na panáka. *hhə-TSI tiê POZ-vat na PA-naa-ka.*	**Co si dáš?** *tso si daash?*	**ČESKY** skleničky

ENGLISH drinks	Do you want a [beer / red wine / white wine]? *du yu want ə [BI-ər / red waîn / waît waîn]?*	I'll take a [mineral water / coffee / juice]. *aîl teîk ə [MI-ne-rəl WA-tœr / KA-fi / <u>dzh</u>us].*
DEUTSCH trinken	Willst du [ein Bier / einen Rotwein / einen Weißwein]? *vilst du [aîn BI-ər / AÎ-nən ROT-vaîn / AÎ-nən VAÎS-vaîn]?*	Ich nehme [ein Mineralwasser / einen Kaffee / einen Saft]. *ish NEÎ-mə [aîn mi-nə-RAAL- va-sər / AÎ-nən ka-FEÎ / AÎ-nən zaft].*
ESPAÑOL copas	¿Quieres [una cerveza / un vino tinto / un vino blanco]? *KIÊ-res [U-na <u>ther</u>-BE-<u>tha</u> / un BI-no TIN-to / un BI-no BLAN-ko]?*	Tomo un [agua mineral / café / zumo]. *TO-mo un [A-guâ mi-ne-RAL / ka-FE / <u>THU</u>-mo].*
FRANÇAIS boire	Tu veux [une bière / du vin rouge / du vin blanc]? *tü vœ [ün bièr / dü veⁿ ru<u>zh</u> / dü veⁿ blaⁿ]?*	Je prends [une eau minérale / un café / du jus]. *<u>zh</u>ə praⁿ [ün o mi-ne-RAL / eⁿ ka-FE / dü <u>zh</u>ü].*
ITALIANO drinks	Vuoi [una birra / del vino rosso / del vino bianco]? *VUÔ-i [U-na BI-<u>rra</u> / del VI-no ROS-so / del VI-no BIÂN-ko]?*	Prendo un [acqua minerale / caffè / succo]. *PREN-do un [AK-kuâ mi-ne- RA-le / kaf-FE / SUK-ko].*
PORTUGUÊS drinques	Você quer [uma cerveja / vinho tinto / vinho branco]? *vo-SE ker [U-mə se<u>hh</u>-VE- <u>zh</u>ə / VI-nʸu TSHIⁿ-tu / VI-nʸu BRAⁿ-ku]?*	Eu aceito [uma água mineral / um cafezinho / um suco]. *eû ə-SEÎ-tu [U-mə A-guə mi-ne-RAÚ / uⁿ kə-fe-ZI-nʸu / uⁿ SU-ku].*
ČESKY skleničky	Chceš [pivo / červené víno / bílé víno]? *<u>hh</u>ə-TSESH [PI-vo / TSHER- ve-nee VII-no / BII-lee VII-no]?*	Dám si [minerálku / kávu / džus]. *daam si [MI-ne-raal-ku / KAA-vu / <u>dzh</u>us].*

Do you smoke? *du yu smoûk?*	**I (don't) smoke.** *aî (doûnt) smoûk.*	**ENGLISH** smoking
Rauchst du? *raûhhst du?*	**Ich rauche (nicht).** *ish RAÛ-hhə (nisht).*	**DEUTSCH** rauchen
¿Fumas? *FU-mas?*	**Yo (no) fumo.** *yo (no) FU-mo.*	**ESPAÑOL** tabaco
Tu fumes? *tü füm?*	**Je fume (pas).** *zhə füm (pa).*	**FRANÇAIS** fumer
Fumi? *FU-mi?*	**(Non) fumo.** *(non) FU-mo.*	**ITALIANO** sigarette
Você fuma? *vo-SE FU-mə?*	**Eu (não) fumo.** *eû (naûⁿ) FU-mu.*	**PORTUGUÊS** cigarros
Kouříš? *KOÛR-zhiish?*	**Já (ne) kouřím.** *yaa (ne) KOÛR-zhiim.*	**ČESKY** cigarety

ENGLISH smoking	**Do you mind not smoking?** *du yu maînd nat SMOÛ-king?*	**Do you mind if I smoke?** *du yu maînd if aî smoûk?*
DEUTSCH rauchen	**Macht es dir was aus, nicht zu rauchen?** *mahht es DI-ər vas aûs, nisht tsu RAÛ-hhən?*	**Macht es dir was aus, wenn ich rauche?** *mahht es DI-ər vas aûs, ven ish RAÛ-hhə?*
ESPAÑOL tabaco	**¿Te importaría no fumar?** *te im-por-ta-RI-a no fu-MAR?*	**¿Te molesta si fumo?** *te mo-LES-ta si FU-mo?*
FRANÇAIS fumer	**Ça te dérangerait de ne pas fumer?** *sa tə de-ran-zhə-RE də nə pa fü-ME?*	**Ça te gêne, si je fume?** *sa tə zhen, si zhə füm?*
ITALIANO sigarette	**Ti dispiace non fumare?** *ti dis-PIÂ-tshe non fu-MA-re?*	**Ti dispiace se fumo?** *ti dis-PIÂ-tshe se FU-mo?*
PORTUGUÊS cigarros	**Você se incomodaria de não fumar?** *vo-SE si in-ku-mu-də-RI-ə dzhi naûⁿ fu-MAHH?*	**Você se incomodaria se eu fumasse?** *vo-SE si in-ku-mu-də-RI-ə si eû fu-MA-si?*
ČESKY cigarety	**Mohl bys nekouřit?** *MO-həl bis NE-koûr-zhit?*	**Vadilo by ti kdybych si zapálil?** *VA-di-lo bi tig-DI-bihh si ZA-paa-lil?*

What's your name? *wɐts yœr neîm?*	**My name is _____.** *maî neîm iz _____.*	**ENGLISH** names
Wie heißt du? *vii haîst du?*	**Ich heiße _____.** *ish HAÎ-sə _____.*	**DEUTSCH** namen
¿Cómo te llamas? *KO-mo te LᵞA-mas?*	**Me llamo _____.** *me LᵞA-mo _____.*	**ESPAÑOL** nombres
Comment tu t'appelles? *kə-MAᴺ tü ta-PEL?*	**Je m'appelle _____.** *zhə ma-PEL _____.*	**FRANÇAIS** noms
Come ti chiami? *KO-me ti KIÂ-mi?*	**Mi chiamo _____.** *mi KIÂ-mo _____.*	**ITALIANO** nomi
Qual é o seu nome? *kuâl e u seû NO-mi?*	**Meu nome é _____.** *meû NO-mi e _____.*	**PORTUGUÊS** nomes
Jak se jmenuješ? *yak seî-ME-nu-yesh?*	**Jmenuji se _____.** *i-ME-nu-yi se _____.*	**ČESKY** jména

ENGLISH — names

Nice to meet you.
naîs tu miit yu.

Are you here alone?
ar yu HI-œr ə-LOÛN?

DEUTSCH — namen

Nett dich kennenzulernen.
net dish KE-nən-tsu-ler-nən.

Bist du alleine hier?
bist du a-LAÎ-nə HI-ər?

ESPAÑOL — nombres

Mucho gusto.
MU-tsho GUS-to.

¿Estás aquí solo?
es-TAS a-KI SO-lo?

FRANÇAIS — noms

Heureux de te rencontrer.
œ-RŒD tə ran-kon-TRE.

Tu es seul?
tü e sœl?

ITALIANO — nomi

Piacere.
piâ-TSHE-re.

Sei qui da solo?
seî kuî da SO-lo?

PORTUGUÊS — nomes

Prazer em conhecê-lo.
prə-ZER en ku-nʸe-SE-lu.

Você está aqui sozinho?
vo-SE is-TA ə-KI su-ZI-nʸu?

ČESKY — Jména

Těší mě.
TIÊ-shii miê.

Jsi tady sám?
si TA-di saam?

Are you together? *ar yu tu-GE-<u>dh</u>œr?*	**We're (not) together.** *WI-œr (nat) tu-GE-<u>dh</u>œr.*	**ENGLISH** together?
Seid ihr zusammen? *zaît I-ər tsu-ZA-mən?*	**Wir sind (nicht) zusammen.** *VI-ər zint (ni<u>sh</u>t) tsu-ZA-mən.*	**DEUTSCH** zusammen?
¿Estáis juntos? *es-TAÎS <u>HH</u>UN-tos?*	**(No) estamos juntos.** *(no) es-TA-mos <u>HH</u>UN-tos.*	**ESPAÑOL** ¿juntos?
Vous êtes ensemble? *vuz et aⁿ-SAⁿ-blə?*	**Nous sommes (pas) ensemble.** *nu səm (pa) aⁿ-SAⁿ-blə.*	**FRANÇAIS** ensemble?
State insieme? *STA-te in-SIÊ-me?*	**(Non) stiamo insieme.** *(non) STIÂ-mo in-SIÊ-me.*	**ITALIANO** insieme?
Vocês estão juntos? *vo-SES is-TAÛⁿ <u>ZH</u>UⁿΝ-tus?*	**Nós (não) estamos juntos.** *nos (naûⁿ) is-TA-mus <u>ZH</u>Uⁿ-tus.*	**PORTUGUÊS** juntos?
Chodíte spolu? *<u>HH</u>O-dii-te SPO-lu?*	**(Ne) chodíme spolu.** *(ne) <u>HH</u>O-dii-me SPO-lu.*	**ČESKY** spolu?

ENGLISH together?	**Is this your boyfriend?** *iz dhis yœr BOÎ-frend?*	**We're just friends.** *WI-œr dzhəst frendz.*
DEUTSCH zusammen?	**Ist das dein Freund?** *ist das daîn froînt?*	**Wir sind nur Freunde.** *VI-ər zint nuur FROÎN-də.*
ESPAÑOL ¿juntos?	**¿Es tu novio?** *es tu NO-biô?*	**Somos sólo amigos.** *SO-mos SO-lo a-MI-gos.*
FRANÇAIS ensemble?	**C'est ton copain?** *se toⁿ kə-PEᴺ?*	**Nous sommes juste amis.** *nu səm zhüst a-MI.*
ITALIANO insieme?	**Questo è il tuo fidanzato?** *KUÊS-to e il TU-o fi-dan-DZA-to?*	**Siamo solo amici.** *SIÂ-mo SO-lo a-MI-tshi.*
PORTUGUÊS juntos?	**Este é seu namorado?** *ES-ti e seû nə-mu-RA-du?*	**Nós somos só amigos.** *nos SO-mus so ə-MI-gus.*
ČESKY spolu?	**To je tvůj kluk?** *to ye TVUU-i kluk?*	**Jsme jen přátelé.** *sme yen PSHAA-te-lee.*

Where are [you / you guys] from?	**[I'm / We're] from _____.**	**ENGLISH** where from?
WE-œr ar [yu / yu gaîz] frəm?	*[aîm / WI-œr] frəm _____.* ☞ COUNTRIES, P. 258	
Woher [kommst du / kommt ihr]?	**[Ich bin / Wir sind] aus _____.**	**DEUTSCH** woher?
vo-HE-ər [komst du / komt I-ər]?	*[ish bin / VI-ər zint] aûs _____.* ☞ LÄNDER, S. 258	
¿De dónde [eres / sois]?	**[Soy / Somos] de _____.**	**ESPAÑOL** orígenes
de DHON-de [E-res / soîs]?	*[soî / SO-mos] de _____.* ☞ PAÍSES, PÁG. 258	
[Tu es / Vous êtes] d'où?	**[Je viens / Nous venons] de _____.**	**FRANÇAIS** d'où tu es?
[tü e / vu-ZET] du?	*[zhə viên / nuv-NON] də _____.* ☞ PAYS, P. 258	
Di dove [sei / siete]?	**[Vengo / Veniamo] da _____.**	**ITALIANO** di dove sei?
di DO-ve [seî / SIÊ-te]?	*[VEN-go / ve-NIÂ-mo] da _____.* ☞ PAESI, P. 258	
De onde [você é / vocês são]?	**[Eu sou / Nós somos] _____.**	**PORTUGUÊS** de onde?
dzhi ON-dzhi [vo-SE e / vo-SES saûn]?	*[eû soû / nos SO-mus] _____.* ☞ PAÍSES, PÁG. 258	
Odkud [jsi / jste]?	**[Já jsem / My jsme] _____.**	**ČESKY** odkud jsi?
OT-kut [si / ste]?	*[yaa sem / mi sme] _____.* ☞ ZEMĚ, STR. 258	

ENGLISH *where from?*	I live [there / here]. *aî liv [DHE-œr / HI-œr].*	Have you been there? *hev yu bin DHE-œr?*
DEUTSCH *woher?*	Ich wohne [dort / hier]. *ish VOO-nə [dort / HI-ər].*	Bist du dort gewesen? *bist du dort gə-VEÎ-zən?*
ESPAÑOL *orígenes*	Vivo [allí / aquí]. *BI-bo [a-LYI / a-KI].*	¿Has estado? *as es-TA-dho?*
FRANÇAIS *d'où tu es?*	J'habite [là-bas / ici]. *zha-BIT [la-BA / i-SI].*	Tu connais? *tü kə-NE?*
ITALIANO *di dove sei?*	Abito [lì / qui]. *A-bi-to [li / kuî].*	Ci sei stato? *tshi sei STA-to?*
PORTUGUÊS *de onde?*	Eu vivo [lá / aqui]. *eû VI-vu [la / ə-KI].*	Você já esteve lá? *vo-SE zha is-TE-vi la?*
ČESKY *odkud jsi?*	Žiji [tam / tady]. *ZHI-yi [tam / TA-di].*	Byl jsi tam? *bil si tam?*

How long are you staying? *haû lon⁹ ar yu STE-yin⁹?*	**I'm leaving [tomorrow / in (three) days / in a month].** *aîm LII-vin⁹ [tu-MA-roû / in (thrii) deîz / in ə mənth].*

ENGLISH where from?

Wie lange bleibst du hier? *vii LAN⁹-ə blaîpst du HI-ər?*	**Ich fahre [morgen / in (drei) Tagen / in einem Monat].** *ish FAA-rə [MOR-gən / in (draî) TAA-gən / in AÎ-nəm MOO-nat].*

DEUTSCH woher?

¿Cuánto tiempo te vas a quedar? *KUÂN-to TIÊM-po te bas a ke-DHAR?*	**Me voy [mañana / dentro de (tres) días / dentro de un mes].** *me boî [ma-NYA-na / DHEN-tro dhe (tres) DHI-as / DHEN-tro dhe un mes].*

ESPAÑOL orígenes

Tu restes combien de temps? *tü rest koⁿ-BIÊⁿ də taⁿ?*	**Je pars [demain / dans (trois) jours / dans un mois].** *zhə par [də-MEⁿ / daⁿ truâ zhur / daⁿz eⁿ muâ].*

FRANÇAIS d'où tu es?

Quanto tempo resti? *KUÂN-to TEM-po RES-ti?*	**Parto [domani / fra (tre) giorni / fra un mese].** *PAR-to [do-MA-ni / fra (tre) DZHOR-ni / fra un ME-ze].*

ITALIANO di dove sei?

Quanto tempo você vai ficar aqui? *KUÂⁿ-tu TEⁿ-pu vo-SE vaî fi-KAR ə-KÎ?*	**Eu vou partir [amanhã / em (três) dias / em um mês].** *eû voû pəhh-TIR [ə-mə-NYAⁿ / eⁿ (tres) DZHI-əs / eⁿ uⁿ mes].*

PORTUGUÊS de onde?

Jak dlouho se zdržíš? *yak DLOÛ-ho sez-DƏR-zhiish?*	**Odjíždím [zítra / za (tři) dny / za jeden měsíc].** *od-YIIZH-diim [ZII-tra / za (trzhi) dni / za YE-den MIÊ-siits].*

ČESKY odkud jsi?

ENGLISH — age

How old are you?
haù oûld ar yu?

How old do you think I am?
haù oûld du yu <u>think</u> aî em?

DEUTSCH — alter

Wie alt bist du?
vii alt bist du?

Wie alt denkst du, bin ich?
vii alt denkst du, bin i<u>sh</u>?

ESPAÑOL — edad

¿Cuántos años tienes?
KUÂN-tos A-nʸos TIÊ-nes?

¿Cuántos años me echas?
KUÂN-tos A-nʸos me E-<u>tsh</u>as?

FRANÇAIS — âge

Quel âge tu as?
kel a<u>zh</u> tü a?

Quel âge tu me donnes?
kel a<u>zh</u> tüm dən?

ITALIANO — età

Quanti anni hai?
KUÂN-ti AN-ni aî?

Quanti anni mi dai?
KUÂN-ti AN-ni mi daî?

PORTUGUÊS — idade

Quantos anos você tem?
KUÂⁿ-tus A-nus vo-SE teⁿ?

Quantos anos você me dá?
KUÂⁿ-tus A-nus vo-SE mi da?

ČESKY — věk

Kolik je ti let?
KO-lik ye ti let?

Kolik si myslíš, že mi je?
KO-lik si MIS-lii<u>sh</u>, <u>zh</u>e mi ye?

ENGLISH — age

I'm [twenty / thirty-two] years old.
aîm [TUÊN-ti / THŒR-ti-tu] yiirz oûld.
☞ NUMBERS, P. 260

You look younger.
yu luk YƏN-gœr.

DEUTSCH — alter

Ich bin [zwanzig / zweiunddreißig] Jahre alt.
ish bin [TSVAN-tsish / TSVAÎ-unt-DRAÎ-sish] YAA-rə alt.
☞ ZAHLEN, S. 260

Du siehst jünger aus.
du ziist YÜNG-ər aûs.

ESPAÑOL — edad

Tengo [veinte / treinta y dos] años.
TEN-go [beîn-te / TREÎN-ta i dhos] A-nyos.
☞ NÚMEROS, PÁG. 260

Pareces más joven.
pa-RE-thes mas HHO-ben.

FRANÇAIS — âge

J'ai [vingt / trente-deux] ans.
zhe [vent / trant-DŒZ] an.
☞ NUMÉROS, P. 260

Tu fais plus jeune.
tü fe plü zhœn.

ITALIANO — età

Ho [venti / trentadue] anni.
o [VEN-ti / tren-ta-DU-e] AN-ni.
☞ NUMERI, P. 260

Sembri più giovane.
SEM-bri più DZHO-va-ne.

PORTUGUÊS — idade

Eu tenho [vinte / trinta e dois] anos.
eû TE-nyu [VIN-tshi / TRIN-ta i dois] A-nus.
☞ NÚMEROS, PÁG. 260

Você parece mais jovem.
vo-SE pə-RE-si maîs ZHO-ven.

ČESKY — věk

Je mi [dvacet / třicet dva] let.
ye mi [DVA-tset / TRZHI-tset dva] let.
☞ ČÍSLA, STR. 260

Vypadáš mladší.
vi-PA-daash MLAT-shii.

ENGLISH / zodiac	**What's your sign?** *wəts yœr saîn?*	**I'm [an Aries / a Taurus / a Gemini / a Cancer].** *aîm [ən EE-riz / ə TO-rəs / ə <u>DZHE</u>-mə-naî / ə KEN-sœr].*
DEUTSCH / tierkreis	**Was ist dein Sternzeichen?** *vas ist daîn <u>SH</u>TERN-tsaî-<u>sh</u>ən?*	**Ich bin [Widder / Stier / Zwilling / Krebs].** *i<u>sh</u> bin [VI-dər / <u>SH</u>TI-ər / TSVI-lin^g / kreps].*
ESPAÑOL / zodiaco	**¿De qué signo eres?** *de ke SIG-no E-res?*	**Soy [aries / tauro / géminis / cáncer].** *soî [A-riês / TAÛ-ro / <u>HH</u>E-mi-nis / KAN-<u>ther</u>].*
FRANÇAIS / zodiaque	**Tu es de quel signe?** *tü ed kel sin^y?*	**Je suis [Bélier / Taureau / Gémeaux / Cancer].** *zhə süî [be-LIÊ / to-RO / <u>zh</u>e-MO / kaⁿ-SER].*
ITALIANO / zodiaco	**Di che segno sei?** *di ke SE-n^yo seî?*	**Sono [Ariete / Toro / Gemelli / Cancro].** *SO-no [a-RIÊ-te / TO-ro / <u>dzh</u>e-MEL-li / KAN-kro].*
PORTUGUÊS / zodiaco	**Qual é o seu signo?** *kuâl e u seû SIG-nu?*	**Eu sou de [Áries / Touro / Gêmeos / Câncer].** *eû soû <u>dzh</u>i [A-riês / TOÛ-ru / <u>ZH</u>E-meûs / KA^N-sehh].*
ČESKY / zvěrokruh	**V jakém jsi znamení?** *V-YA-keem si ZNA-me-nii?*	**Jsem [Beran / Býk / Blíženec / Rak].** *sem [BE-ran / biik / BLII-<u>zhe</u>-nets / rak].*

Are you a [Leo / Virgo / Libra / Scorpio]? *ar yu ə [LI-où / VŒR-goù / LI-brə / SKOR-pi-où]?*	**... [a Sagittarius / a Capricorn / an Aquarius / a Pisces]?** *... [ə se-dzhi-TE-riəs / ə KE-pri-korn / ən ə-KUÊ-riəs / ə PAÎ-siiz]?*	**ENGLISH** zodiac
Bist du [Löwe / Jungfrau / Waage / Scorpion]? *bist du [LŒ-və / YUNᴳ-fraû / VAA-gə / SHKOR-piôn]?*	**... [Schütze / Steinbock / Wassermann / Fisch]?** *... [SHÜ-tsə / SHTAÎN-bok / VA-sər-man / fish]?*	**DEUTSCH** tierkreis
¿Eres [leo / virgo / libra / escorpión]? *E-res [LE-o / BIR-go / LI-bra / es-kor-PIÔN]?*	**... [sagitario / capricornio / acuario / piscis]?** *...[sa-hhi-TA-riô / ka-pri-KOR-niô / a-KUÂ-riô / PIS-this]?*	**ESPAÑOL** zodiaco
Tu es [Lion / Vierge / Balance / Scorpion]? *tü e [liôⁿ / viêrzh / ba-LAⁿS / skər-PIÔⁿ]?*	**... [Sagittaire / Capricorne / Verseau / Poissons]?** *... [sa-zhi-TER / ka-pri-KƏRN / ver-SO / puâ-SOⁿ]?*	**FRANÇAIS** zodiaque
Sei [Leone / Vergine / Bilancia / Scorpione]? *seî [le-O-ne / VER-dzhi-ne / bi-LAN-tsha / skor-PIÔ-ne]?*	**... [Sagittario / Capricorno / Acquario / Pesci]?** *... [sa-dzhit-TA-riô / ka-pri-KOR-no / ak-KUÂ-riô / PE-shi]?*	**ITALIANO** zodiaco
Você é de [Leão / Virgem / Libra / Escorpião]? *vo-SE e dzhi [li-AÛⁿ / VIHH-zheⁿ / LI-brə / is-kuhh-pi-AÛⁿ]?*	**... [Sagitário / Capricórnio / Aquário / Peixes]?** *... [sə-zhi-TA-riû / kə-pri-KOHH-niû / ə-KUÂ-riô / PEÎ-shis]?*	**PORTUGUÊS** zodiaco
Jsi [Lev / Panna / Váha / Štír]? *si [lef / PA-na / VAA-ha / shtiir]?*	**... [Střelec / Kozoroh / Vodnář / Ryba]?** *... [stər-ZHE-lets / KO-zo-roh / VOD-naarzh / RI-ba]?*	**ČESKY** zvěrokruh

ENGLISH	yes or no?	**Do you like guys?** *du yu laîk gaîz?*	**Are you gay?** *ar yu geî?*
DEUTSCH	ja oder nein?	**Stehst du auf Männer?** *<u>sh</u>teîst du aûf ME-nər?*	**Bist du schwul?** *bist du <u>sh</u>vul?*
ESPAÑOL	¿sí o no?	**¿Te gustan los chicos?** *te GUS-tan los <u>TSH</u>I-kos?*	**¿Eres gay?** *E-res geî?*
FRANÇAIS	oui ou non?	**Tu aimes les garçons?** *tü em le gar-SON?*	**Tu es homo?** *tü e o-MO?*
ITALIANO	sì o no?	**Ti piacciono i ragazzi?** *ti PIÂT-<u>tsh</u>o-no i ra-GAT-tsi?*	**Sei gay?** *seî geî?*
PORTUGUÊS	sim ou não?	**Você curte rapazes?** *vo-SE KU<u>HH</u>-<u>tsh</u>i <u>hh</u>ə-PA-zis?*	**Você é gay?** *vo-SE e geî?*
ČESKY	ano / ne?	**Jsi na kluky?** *si na KLU-ki?*	**Jsi homosexuál?** *si HO-mo-sek-su-aal?*

I'm [gay / bisexual / straight]. *aîm [geî / baî-SEK-shuâl / streît].*	**Do you have a boyfriend?** *du yu hev ə BOÎ-frend?*

ENGLISH yes or no?

Ich bin [schwul / bisexuell / hetero]. *ish bin [shvul / bi-sek-SUÊL / HE-te-ro].*	**Hast du einen Freund?** *hast du AÎ-nən froînt?*

DEUTSCH ja oder nein?

Soy [gay / bisexual / hétero]. *soî [geî / bi-sek-SUÂL / E-te-ro].*	**¿Tienes novio?** *TIÊ-nes NO-biô?*

ESPAÑOL ¿sí o no?

Je suis [homo / bi / hétéro]. *zhə süî [o-MO / bi / e-te-RO].*	**Tu as un copain?** *tü a eⁿ kə-PEᴺ?*

FRANÇAIS oui ou non?

Sono [gay / bisessuale / etero]. *SO-no [geî / bi-ses-SUÂ-le / e-TE-ro].*	**Hai un fidanzato?** *aî un fi-dan-DZA-to?*

ITALIANO sì o no?

Eu sou [gay / bissexual / heterossexual]. *eû soû [geî / bi-sek-su-AÛ / e-te-ro-sek-su-AÛ].*	**Você tem namorado?** *vo-SE teⁿ nə-mu-RA-du?*

PORTUGUÊS sim ou não?

Jsem [homosexuál / bisexuál / normál]. *sem [HO-mo-sek-su-aal / BI-sek-su-aal / NOR-maal].*	**Máš kluka?** *maash KLU-ka?*

ČESKY ano / ne?

yes or no?	**ENGLISH**	I don't have a boyfriend. *aî doûnt hev ə BOÎ-frend.*	I have a [boyfriend / girlfriend]. *aî hev ə [BOÎ-frend / GƏR-əl-frend].*
ja oder nein?	**DEUTSCH**	Ich habe keinen Freund. *ish HAA-bə KAÎ-nən froînt.*	Ich habe [einen Freund / eine Freundin]. *ish HAA-bə [AÎ-nən froînt / AÎ-nə FROÎN-din].*
¿sí o no?	**ESPAÑOL**	No tengo novio. *no TEN-go NO-biô.*	Tengo [novio / novia]. *TEN-go [NO-biô / NO-biâ].*
oui ou non?	**FRANÇAIS**	J'ai pas de copain. *zhe pad kə-PE^N.*	J'ai [un copain / une copine]. *zhe [e^n kə-PE^N / ün kə-PIN].*
sí o no?	**ITALIANO**	Non ho un fidanzato. *non o un fi-dan-DZA-to.*	Ho [un fidanzato / una fidanzata]. *o [un fi-dan-DZA-to / U-na fi-dan-DZA-ta].*
sim ou não?	**PORTUGUÊS**	Eu não tenho namorado. *eû naû^n TE-nʸu nə-mu-RA-du.*	Eu tenho [namorado / namorada]. *eû TE-nʸu [nə-mu-RA-du / nə-mu-RA-də].*
ano / ne?	**ČESKY**	Nemám kluka. *NE-maam KLU-ka.*	Mám [kluka / holku]. *maam [KLU-ka / HOL-ku].*

I'm divorced. *aîm di-VORST.*	**I'm married.** *aîm MEE-rid.*

ENGLISH — yes or no?

Ich bin geschieden. *ish bin gə-SHII-dən.*	**Ich bin verheiratet.** *ish bin fer-HAÎ-ra-tet.*

DEUTSCH — ja oder nein?

Estoy divorciado. *es-TOÎ dhi-bor-THIÂ-dho.*	**Estoy casado.** *es-TOÎ ka-SA-dho.*

ESPAÑOL — ¿sí o no?

Je suis divorcé. *zhə süî di-vər-SE.*	**Je suis marié.** *zhə süî ma-RIÊ.*

FRANÇAIS — oui ou non?

Sono divorziato. *SO-no di-vor-TSIÂ-to.*	**Sono sposato.** *SO-no spo-ZA-to.*

ITALIANO — si o no?

Eu sou divorciado. *eû soû dzhi-vuhh-SIÂ-du.*	**Eu sou casado** *eû soû kə-ZA-du.*

PORTUGUÊS — sim ou não?

Jsem rozvedený. *sem ROZ-ve-de-nii.*	**Jsem ženatý.** *sem ZHE-na-tii.*

ČESKY — ano / ne?

ENGLISH yes or no?	That's too bad. _dhets tu beed._	I'd (still) like to get to know you better. _aîd (stil) laîk tu get tu noû yu BE-tœr._
DEUTSCH ja oder nein?	Das ist schade. _das ist SHAA-də._	Ich würde dich (trotzdem) gern besser kennenlernen. _ish VÜR-də dish (TROTS-deem) gern BE-sər KE-nən-ler-nən._
ESPAÑOL ¿sí o no?	Qué pena. _ke PE-na._	(Aún así,) me gustaría conocerte mejor. _(a-UN a-SI,) me gus-ta-RI-a ko-no-THER-te me-HHOR._
FRANÇAIS oui ou non?	C'est dommage. _se də-MAZH._	(Quand même,) j'aimerais bien te connaître un peu mieux. _(kan mem,) zhem-RE bièn tə kə-NE-tren pœ miœ̀._
ITALIANO sì o no?	Che peccato. _ke pek-KA-to._	Mi piacerebbe (lo stesso) conoscerti meglio. _mi piâ-tshe-REB-be (lo STES-so) ko-NO-sher-ti ME-lʸo._
PORTUGUÊS sim ou não?	Que pena. _ki PE-nə._	(Mesmo assim,) eu gostaria de te conhecer melhor. _(MEZ-mu ə-SIN,) eû gus-tə-RI-ə dzhi tshi ku-nʸə-SEHH me-LʸOHH._
ČESKY ano / ne?	To je škoda. _to yesh-KO-da._	(Stejně) bych tě rád lépe poznal. _(STEÎ-niè) bihh tiè raad LEE-pe POZ-nal._

Do you have an open relationship? *du yu hev ən OÛ-pən ri-LEÎ-shən-ship?*	**We [see / don't see] other people.** *wi [sii / doûnt sii] Ə-dhœr PII-pəl.*	**ENGLISH** yes or no?
Habt ihr eine offene Beziehung? *hapt I-ər AÎ-nə O-fə-nə bə-TSII-hunᵍ?*	**Wir treffen uns [auch / nicht] mit anderen Leuten.** *VI-ər TRE-fən uns [aûhh / nisht] mit AN-də-rən LOÎ-tən.*	**DEUTSCH** ja oder nein?
¿Sois una pareja abierta? *soîs U-na pa-RE-hha a-BIÊR-ta?*	**[Salimos / No salimos] con otra gente.** *[sa-LI-mos / no sa-LI-mos] kon O-tra HHEN-te.*	**ESPAÑOL** ¿sí o no?
Vous êtes un couple libéré? *vuz et eⁿ KU-plə li-be-RE?*	**Nous [voyons / voyons pas] d'autres gens.** *nu [vuâ-YOⁿ / vuâ-YOⁿ pa] DO-trə zhaⁿ.*	**FRANÇAIS** oui ou non?
Siete una coppia aperta? *SIÊ-te U-na KOP-piâ a-PER-ta?*	**[Ci vediamo anche / Non ci vediamo] con altre persone.** *[tshi ve-DIÂ-mo AN-ke / non tshi ve-DIÂ-mo] kon AL-tre per-SO-ne.*	**ITALIANO** si o no?
Vocês têm um relacionamento aberto? *vo-SES teⁿ uⁿ hhe-lə-siô-nə-MEⁿ-tu ə-BEHH-tu?*	**Nós [saímos / não saímos] com outras pessoas.** *nos [sə-I-mus / naûⁿ sə-I-mus] koⁿ OÛ-trəs pe-SO-əs.*	**PORTUGUÊS** sim ou não?
Máte volný vztah? *MAA-te VOL-niif-stah?*	**[Máme / Nemáme] volný vztah.** *[MAA-me / NE-maa-me] VOL-niif-stah.*	**ČESKY** ano / ne?

ENGLISH threesomes	Are [you / you guys] into threesomes? *ar [yu / yu gaîz] IN-tu* <u>*THRII*</u>*-səmz?*	I'm into [threesomes / group sex]. *aîm IN-tu [*<u>*THRII*</u>*-səmz / grup seks].*
DEUTSCH dreier	[Stehst du / Steht ihr] auf Dreier? *[*<u>*shteî*</u>*st du /* <u>*shteî*</u>*t ļ-ər] aûf DRA-yər?*	Ich steh auf [Dreier / Gruppensex]. *ish* <u>*shteî*</u> *aûf [DRA-yər / GRU-pen-seks].*
ESPAÑOL tríos	¿[Haces / Hacéis] tríos? *[A-*<u>*thes*</u> */ a-*<u>*THEÍS*</u>*] TRI-os?*	Me gustan [los tríos / las orgías]. *me GUS-tan [los TRI-os / las or-*<u>*HHI*</u>*-as].*
FRANÇAIS à trois	Ça [t'arrive / vous arrive] de faire l'amour à trois? *sa [ta-RIV / vuz a-RIV] də fer la-MUR a truâ?*	J'aime les [plans à trois / partouzes]. <u>*zh*</u>*em le [pla*ⁿ *a truâ / par-TUZ].*
ITALIANO triangoli	[Ti / Vi] piace far sesso a tre? *[ti / vi] PIÂ-*<u>*tshe*</u> *far SES-so a tre?*	Mi piacciono [i triangoli / le orgie]. *mi PIÂT-tsho-no [i tri-AN-go-li / le OR-*<u>*dzhe*</u>*].*
PORTUGUÊS sexo a três	[Você curte / Vocês curtem] ménage? *[vo-SE KU*<u>*HH*</u>*-tshi / vo-SES KU*<u>*HH*</u>*-te*ⁿ*] me-NA*<u>*ZH*</u>*?*	Eu gosto de [ménage / suruba]. *eû GOS-tu dzhi [me-NA*<u>*ZH*</u> */ su-RU-bə].*
ČESKY na trojku	[Chodíš / Chodíte] na trojku? *[*<u>*HHO*</u>*-diish /* <u>*HHO*</u>*-dii-te] na TROÎ-ku?*	[Chodím na trojku / Mám rád grupáč]. *[*<u>*HHO*</u>*-diim na TROÎ-ku / maam raad GRU-paa*<u>*tsh*</u>*].*

[I've / We've] never done that. *[aîv / wiiv] NE-vœr dən <u>dh</u>et.*	**But [I'll / we'll] try it.** *bət [aîl / wiil] traî it.*	**ENGLISH** threesomes
[Ich habe / Wir haben] das noch nie gemacht. *[ish HAA-bə / VI-ər HAA-bən] das no<u>hh</u> nii gə-MA<u>HH</u>T.*	**Aber [ich kann / wir können] es ausprobieren.** *A-bər [ish kan / VI-ər KŒ-nən] es AUS-pro-BII-rən.*	**DEUTSCH** dreier
Nunca lo [he / hemos] hecho. *NUN-ka lo [e / E-mos] E-<u>tsh</u>o.*	**Pero [me / nos] gustaría probar.** *PE-ro [me / nos] gus-ta-RI-a pro-BAR.*	**ESPAÑOL** tríos
Ça [m'est / nous est] jamais arrivé. *sa [me / nuz e] <u>zh</u>a-ME a-ri-VE.*	**Mais [je vais / on va] essayer.** *me [<u>zh</u>ə ve / oⁿ va] e-se-YE.*	**FRANÇAIS** à trois
Non [l'ho / l'abbiamo] mai fatto. *non [lo / lab-BIÂ-mo] maî FAT-to.*	**Ma ci [posso / possiamo] provare.** *ma <u>tsh</u>i [POS-so / pos-SIÂ-mo] pro-VA-re.*	**ITALIANO** triangoli
[Eu nunca fiz / Nós nunca fizemos] isto. *[eû NUᴺ-kə fiz / nos NUᴺ-kə fi-ZE-mus] IS-tu.*	**Mas [eu tentarei / nós tentaremos].** *məs [eû teⁿ-tə-REÎ / nos teⁿ-tə-RE-mus].*	**PORTUGUÊS** sexo a três
To [jsem v životě nedělal / jsme v životě nedělali]. *to [i-SEM V-<u>ZH</u>I-vo-tiê NE-diê-lal / i-SME V-<u>ZH</u>I-vo-tiê NE-diê-la-li].*	**Ale [zkusím / zkusíme] to.** *A-le [SKU-siim / SKU-sii-me] to.*	**ČESKY** na trojku

ENGLISH — invitations

Want to go to [another bar / a disco]?
want tu goû tu [ə-NE-dhœr bar / ə DIS-koû]?

How about a drink at [my / your] place?
haû ə-BAÛT ə drink et [maî / yœr] pleîs?

DEUTSCH — einladen

Gehen wir in eine [andere Bar / Diskothek]?
GEÎ-ən VI-ər in AÎ-nə [AN-də-rə bar / dis-ko-TEÎK]?

Hast du Lust auf einen Drink bei [mir / dir]?
hast du lust aûf AÎ-nən drink baî [MI-ər / DI-ər]?

ESPAÑOL — te invito

¿Vamos a [otro bar / una discoteca]?
BA-mos a [O-tro bar / U-na dis-ko-TE-ka]?

¿Vamos a tomar una copa a [mi / tu] casa?
BA-mos a to-MAR U-na KO-pa a [mi / tu] KA-sa?

FRANÇAIS — invitations

On va dans [un autre bar / une boîte]?
oⁿ va daⁿz [en O-trə bar / ün buât]?

Tu veux boire quelque chose chez [moi / toi]?
tü vœ buâr kel-kə shoz she [muâ / tuâ]?

ITALIANO — inviti

Andiamo in [un altro bar / una discoteca]?
an-DIÂ-mo in [un AL-tro bar / U-na dis-ko-TE-ka]?

Andiamo a bere qualcosa da [me / te]?
an-DIÂ-mo a BE-re kuâl-KO-za da [me / te]?

PORTUGUÊS — convites

Vamos a [outro bar / uma discoteca]?
VA-mus ə [OÛ-tru bahh / U-mə dzhis-ku-TE-kə]?

Quer tomar um drinque [lá em / na sua] casa?
kehh tu-MAR uⁿ drink [la eⁿ / nə SU-ə] KA-zə?

ČESKY — zvu tě

Chceš jít [do jiného baru / na diskotéku]?
hhə-TSESH yiit [do yi-NEE-ho BA-ru / na DIS-ko-tee-ku]?

Chceš jít [ke mně / k tobě] na panáka?
hhə-TSESH yiit [kem-NIÊ / kə-TO-biê] na PA-naa-ka?

I want to [go to bed / make love / have sex] with you. *aî want tu [goû tu bed / meîk ləv / hev seks] widh yu.*	[Want to go? / Let's go!] *[want tu goû? / lets goû!]*	**ENGLISH** invitations
Ich möchte mit dir [ins Bett gehen / schlafen / schlafen]. *ish MŒSH-tə mit DI-ər [ins bet GE-ən / SHLA-fən / SHLA-fen].*	[Gehen wir? / Gehen wir!] *[GEÎ-ən VI-ər? / GEÎ-ən VI-ər!]*	**DEUTSCH** einladen
Quiero [acostarme / hacer el amor / follar] contigo. *KIÊ-ro [a-kos-TAR-me / a-THER el a-MOR / fo-LYAR] kon-TI-go.*	[¿Vamos? / ¡Vámonos!] *[BA-mos? / BA-mo-nos!]*	**ESPAÑOL** te invito
Je voudrais [coucher / faire l'amour / baiser] avec toi. *zhə vu-DRE [ku-SHE / fer la-MUR / be-ZE] a-VEK tuâ.*	[On y va? / Allons-y!] *[on i va? / a-lon-ZI!]*	**FRANÇAIS** invitations
Vorrei [andare a letto / far l'amore / far sesso] con te. *vo-RREÎ [an-DA-re a LET-to / far la-MO-re / far SES-so] kon te.*	[Andiamo? / Dai, andiamo!] *[an-DIÂ-mo? / daî, an-DIÂ-mo!]*	**ITALIANO** inviti
Eu quero [ir pra cama / fazer amor / trepar] com você. *eû KE-ru [ihh prə KA-mə / fə-ZER ə-MOHH / tre-PAHH] kon vo-SE.*	[Vamos? / Vamos!] *[VA-mus? / VA-mus!]*	**PORTUGUÊS** convites
Chci se s tebou [vyspat / milovat / souložit]. *hhə-TSI ses TE-boù [VIS-pat / MI-lo-vat / SO-loû-zhit].*	[Pojd'me? / Pojd'me!] *[POÎDZH-me? / POÎDZH-me!]*	**ČESKY** zvu tě

ENGLISH *no, thanks*	I'd love to, (but I can't). *aîd ləv tu, (bət aî kent).*	Let's get to know each other better first. *lets get tu noû iitsh Ə-dhœr BE-tœr fœrst.*
DEUTSCH *nein, danke*	Ich würde gerne, (aber ich kann nicht). *ish VÜR-də GER-nə, (A-bər ish kan nisht).*	Laß uns erst besser kennen-lernen. *las uns erst BE-sər KE-nən-ler-nən.*
ESPAÑOL *no, gracias*	Me encantaría, (pero no puedo). *me en-kan-ta-RI-a, (PE-ro no PUÊ-dho).*	Vamos a esperar a conocernos mejor. *BA-mos a es-pe-RAR a ko-no-THER-nos me-HHOR.*
FRANÇAIS *non, merci*	J'aimerais bien, (mais je peux pas). *zhem-RE biên, (me zhə pœ pa).*	Faisons d'abord connaissance. *fe-ZON da-BƏR kə-ne-SANS.*
ITALIANO *no, grazie*	Mi piacerebbe molto, (ma non posso). *mi piâ-tshe-REB-be MOL-to, (ma non POS-so).*	Conosciamoci meglio prima. *ko-no-SHIÂ-mo-tshi ME-lʸo PRI-ma.*
PORTUGUÊS *não, obrigado*	Eu gostaria, (mas não posso). *eû gus-tə-RI-ə, (məs naûⁿ PO-su).*	Vamos nos conhecer melhor primeiro. *VA-mus nus ku-nʸe-SEHH me-LʸOHH pri-MEÎ-ru.*
ČESKY *ne, díky*	Rád bych, (ale nemůžu). *raad bihh, (A-le NE-muu-zhu).*	Musíme se nejdříve lépe poznat. *MU-sii-me se NEÎD-zhii-ve LEE-pe POZ-nat.*

Some other time. səm Ə-<u>dh</u>œr taîm.	**I have to go.** aî hev tu goû.	**ENGLISH** no, thanks
Ein anderes Mal. aîn AN-də-rəs maal.	**Ich muß gehen.** <u>ish</u> mus GEÎ-ən.	**DEUTSCH** nein, danke
Otro día. O-tro <u>DH</u>I-a.	**Tengo que irme.** TEN-go ke IR-me.	**ESPAÑOL** no, gracias
Une autre fois. ün O-trə fuâ.	**Il faut que j'y aille.** il fok <u>zh</u>i aî.	**FRANÇAIS** non, merci
Un'altra volta. un-AL-tra VOL-ta.	**Devo andare.** DE-vo an-DA-re.	**ITALIANO** no, grazie
Outra hora. OÛ-trə O-rə.	**Eu tenho que ir.** eû TE-nʸu ki <u>ihh</u>.	**PORTUGUÊS** não, obrigado
Někdy jindy. NIÊG-di YIN-di.	**Musím jít.** MU-siim yiit.	**ČESKY** ne, díky

ENGLISH no, thanks	I'm waiting for my boyfriend. _aîm WEÎ-ting fœr maî BOÎ-frend._	I'm busy. _aîm BI-zi._
DEUTSCH nein, danke	Ich warte auf meinen Freund. _<u>ish</u> VAR-tə aûf MAÎ-nən froînt._	Ich habe keine Zeit. _<u>ish</u> HAA-bə KAÎ-nə tsaît._
ESPAÑOL no, gracias	Estoy esperando a mi novio. _es-TOÎ es-pe-RAN-do a mi NO-biô._	No tengo tiempo. _no TEN-go TIÊM-po._
FRANÇAIS non, merci	J'attends mon copain. _<u>zh</u>a-TAᴺ moⁿ kə-PEᴺ._	J'ai pas le temps. _<u>zh</u>e pal taⁿ._
ITALIANO no, grazie	Sto aspettando il mio fidanzato. _sto as-pet-TAN-do il MI-o fi-dan-DZA-to._	Non ho tempo. _non o TEM-po._
PORTUGUÊS não, obrigado	Estou esperando meu namorado. _is-TOÛ es-pe-RAᴺ-du meû nə-mu-RA-du._	Não tenho tempo agora. _naûⁿ TE-nyu TEᴺ-pu ə-GO-rə._
ČESKY ne, díky	Čekám na svého kluka. _<u>TSHE</u>-kaam na SFEE-ho KLU-ka._	Nemám čas. _NE-maam <u>tsh</u>as._

You're not my type. *yœr nat maî taîp.*	**Leave me alone!** *liiv mi ə-LOÚN!*	**ENGLISH** no, thanks
Du bist nicht mein Typ. *du bist ni<u>sh</u>t maîn tüp.*	**Laß mich in Ruhe!** *las mi<u>sh</u> in RUU-ə!*	**DEUTSCH** nein, danke
No eres mi tipo. *no E-res mi TI-po.*	**¡Déjame en paz!** *DE-<u>hh</u>a-me en pa<u>th</u>!*	**ESPAÑOL** no, gracias
Tu es pas mon genre. *tü e pa mon <u>zha</u>nr.*	**Fous-moi la paix!** *fu-MUÂ la pe!*	**FRANÇAIS** non, merci
Non sei il mio tipo. *non seî il MI-o TI-po.*	**Lasciami in pace!** *LA-<u>sha</u>-mi in PA-tshe!*	**ITALIANO** no, grazie
Você não é o meu tipo. *vo-SE naûn e u meû <u>TSH</u>I-pu.*	**Me deixe em paz!** *mi DEÎ-<u>shi</u> en paz!*	**PORTUGUÊS** não, obrigado
Nejsi můj typ. *NEÎ-si MUU-i tip.*	**Nech mě na pokoji!** *ne<u>hh</u> miě na PO-ko-yi!*	**ČESKY** ne, díky

ENGLISH no, thanks	**Get lost!** *get last!*	**Fuck off!** *fək af!*
DEUTSCH nein, danke	**Hau ab!** *haû ap!*	**Verpiß dich!** *fer-PIS di<u>sh</u>!*
ESPAÑOL no, gracias	**¡Lárgate!** *LAR-ga-te!*	**¡Vete a tomar por culo!** *BE-te a to-MAR por KU-lo!*
FRANÇAIS non, merci	**Casse-toi!** *kas-TUÂ!*	**Va te faire foutre!** *vat fer FU-trə!*
ITALIANO no, grazie	**Vattene!** *VAT-te-ne!*	**Vaffan culo!** *VAF-fan KU-lo!*
PORTUGUÊS não, obrigado	**Cai fora!** *kaî FO-rə!*	**Vai se foder!** *vaî si fu-DE<u>HH</u>!*
ČESKY ne, díky	**Ztrat' se!** *strat<u>sh</u> se!*	**Jdi do prdele!** *i-DI do PƏR-de-le!*

Where do you live? *WE-œr du yu liv?*	**Where are you staying?** *WE-œr ar yu STE-yin⁹?*

ENGLISH lodging

Wo wohnst du? *voo voonst du?*	**Wo wohnst du hier?** *voo voonst du HI-ər?*

DEUTSCH unterkunft

¿Dónde vives? *DON-de BI-bes?*	**¿En qué hotel estás?** *en ke o-TEL es-TAS?*

ESPAÑOL alojamiento

Où tu habites? *u tü a-BIT?*	**Où est-ce que tu loges?** *u es kə tü ləzh?*

FRANÇAIS logement

Dove abiti? *DO-ve A-bi-ti?*	**Dove alloggi?** *DO-ve al-LOD-dzhi?*

ITALIANO alloggio

Onde você mora? *Oᴺ-dzhi vo-SE MO-rə?*	**Onde você está hospedado?** *Oᴺ-dzhi vo-SE is-TA us-pe-DA-du?*

PORTUGUÊS hospedagem

Kde bydlíš? *gə-DE BID-liish?*	**Kde tady bydlíš?** *gə-DE TA-di BID-liish?*

ČESKY nocleh

ENGLISH lodging	I'm at the _____ Hotel. *aîm et <u>dhə</u> _____ hoû-TEL.*	I'm at a [friend's / girlfriend's] place. *aîm et ə [frendz / GŒR-əl-frendz] pleîs.*
DEUTSCH unterkunft	Ich wohne im Hotel _____. *<u>ish</u> VOO-nə im ho-TEL _____.*	Ich wohne bei [einem Freund / einer Freundin]. *<u>ish</u> VOO-nə baî [AÎ-nəm froînt / AÎ-nər FROÎN-dən].*
ESPAÑOL alojamiento	Estoy en el Hotel _____. *es-TOÎ en el o-TEL _____.*	Estoy en casa de [un amigo / una amiga]. *es-TOÎ en KA-sa <u>dhe</u> [un a-MI-go / U-na a-MI-ga].*
FRANÇAIS logement	Je suis à l'Hôtel _____. *<u>zh</u>ə süîz a lo-TEL _____.*	Je suis chez [un ami / une amie]. *<u>zh</u>ə süî <u>she</u> [eⁿ a-MI / ün a-MI].*
ITALIANO alloggio	Io sto all'albergo _____. *I-o sto al-lal-BER-go _____.*	Sto da [un amico / un'amica]. *sto da [un a-MI-ko / u-na-MI-ka].*
PORTUGUÊS hospedagem	Eu estou no Hotel _____. *eû is-TOÛ nu u-TEL _____.*	Eu estou na casa de [um amigo / uma amiga]. *eû is-TOÛ nə KA-zə <u>dzhi</u> [uⁿ ə-MI-gu / U-mə ə-MI-gə].*
ČESKY nocleh	Bydlím v Hotelu _____. *BID-liimf HO-te-lu _____.*	Bydlím u [přítele / přítelkyně]. *BID-liim u [PSHII-te-le / PSHII-tel-ki-niê].*

I'm staying with relatives. *aîm STE-yin^g widh RE-lə-tivz.*	**I [can / can't] have guests.** *aî [ken / kent] hev gests.*	**ENGLISH** lodging
Ich wohne bei Verwandten. *ish VOO-nə baî fer-VAN-tən.*	**Ich kann [jemanden / niemanden] mitbringen.** *ish kan [YE-man-dən / NII-man-dən] MIT-brin^g-ən.*	**DEUTSCH** unterkunft
Estoy en casa de unos parientes. *es-TOÎ en KA-sa dhe U-nos pa-RIÊN-tes.*	**[Puedo / No puedo] tener visitas.** *[PUÊ-dho / no PUÊ-dho] te-NER bi-SI-tas.*	**ESPAÑOL** alojamiento
Je suis chez des parents à moi. *zhə süî she de pa-RA^N a muâ.*	**Je peux [recevoir / recevoir personne].** *zhə pœ [rə-sə-VUÂR / rə-sə-VUÂR per-SƏN].*	**FRANÇAIS** logement
Sto da parenti. *sto da pa-REN-ti.*	**[Posso / Non posso] avere ospiti.** *[POS-so / non POS-so] a-VE-re OS-pi-ti.*	**ITALIANO** alloggio
Eu estou na casa dos meus parentes. *eû is-TOÛ nə KA-zə dus meûs pə-RE^N-tshis.*	**Eu [posso / não posso] receber visitas.** *eû [PO-su / naûⁿ PO-su] hhe-se-BEHH vi-ZI-təs.*	**PORTUGUÊS** hospedagem
Bydlím u příbuzných. *BID-liim u PSHII-buz-niihh.*	**[Můžu / Nemůžu] si vzít někoho k sobě.** *[MUU-zhu / NE-muu-zhu] si vziit NIÊ-ko-hok SO-biê.*	**ČESKY** nocleh

ENGLISH *drunk driving*	[I'm / You're] drunk. *[aîm / yœr] drənk.*	[I'd / You'd] better not drive. *[aîd / yud] BE-tœr nat draîv.*
DEUTSCH *betrunken*	[Ich bin / Du bist] betrunken. *[ish bin / du bist] bə-TRUN-kən.*	[Ich sollte / Du solltest] lieber nicht fahren. *[ish ZOL-tə / du ZOL-təst] LII-bər nisht FAA-rən.*
ESPAÑOL *si bebes...*	[Estoy / Estás] borracho. *[es-TOÎ / es-TAS] bo-RRA-tsho.*	Mejor que no [conduzca / conduzcas]. *me-HHOR ke no [kon-DUTH-ka / kon-DUTH-kas].*
FRANÇAIS *conduire?*	[J'ai / Tu as] trop bu. *[zhe / tü a] tro bü.*	[Je / Tu] ferais mieux de pas conduire. *[zhə / tü] fə-RE miœd pa kon-DÜÎR.*
ITALIANO *guidare?*	[Sono / Sei] ubriaco. *[SO-no / seî] u-BRIÂ-ko.*	Meglio che [io / tu] non guidi. *ME-lʸo ke [I-o / tu] non GUÎ-di.*
PORTUGUÊS *de carro?*	[Eu estou / Você está] bêbado. *[eû is-TOÛ / vo-SE is-TA] BE-bə-du.*	É melhor [eu / você] não dirigir. *e me-LʸOR [eû / vo-SE] naûn dzhi-ri-ZHIHH.*
ČESKY *autem?*	[Jsem / Jsi] opilý. *[sem / si] O-pi-lii.*	Raději [nebudu řídit / neřiď]. *RA-diê-yi [NE-bu-dur ZHII-dit / NER-zhidzh].*

I [can / can't] drive.
aî [ken / kent] draîv.

Let's take a taxi.
lets teîk ə TEK-si.

ENGLISH
drunk driving

Ich [kann / kann nicht] fahren.
ish [kan / kan nisht] FAA-rən.

Laß uns ein Taxi nehmen.
las uns aîn TAK-si NEÎ-mən.

DEUTSCH
betrunken

[Puedo / No puedo] conducir.
*[PUÊ-dho / no PUÊ-dho]
kon-du-THIR.*

Vamos a coger un taxi.
BA-mos a ko-HHER un TAK-si.

ESPAÑOL
si bebes...

**Je [suis / suis pas] en état
de conduire.**
*zhə [süî / süî pa] an e-TAD
koⁿ-DÜÎR.*

On prend un taxi.
oⁿ praⁿ eⁿ tak-SI.

FRANÇAIS
conduire?

[Posso / Non posso] guidare.
*[POS-so / non POS-so]
guî-DA-re.*

Prendiamo un taxi.
pren-DIÂ-mo un TAK-si.

ITALIANO
guidare?

**Eu [posso / não posso]
dirigir.**
*eû [PO-su / naûⁿ PO-su]
dzhi-ri-ZHIHH.*

Vamos pegar um táxi.
VA-mus pe-GAR uⁿ TAK-si.

PORTUGUÊS
de carro?

[Můžu / Nemůžu] řídit.
*[MUU-zhu / NE-muu-zhu]
ZHII-dit.*

Vezměme si taxi.
VEZ-miê-me si TAK-si.

ČESKY
autem?

ENGLISH
see you soon

I'd like to see you again.
aîd laîk tu si yu ə-GEN.

Do you have a business card?
du yu hev ə BIZ-nes kard?

DEUTSCH
bis bald!

Ich möchte dich gern wiedersehen.
ish MŒSH-tə dish gern VII-dər-zeîn.

Hast du eine Visitenkarte?
hast du AÎ-nə vi-ZII-tən-kar-tə?

ESPAÑOL
¡nos vemos!

Me gustaría volverte a ver.
me gus-ta-RI-a bol-BER-te a ber.

¿Tienes una tarjeta de visita?
TIÊ-nes U-na tar-HHE-ta dhe bi-SI-ta?

FRANÇAIS
à bientôt!

J'aimerais bien te revoir.
zhem-RE biên tə rə-VUÂR.

Tu as une carte de visite?
tü a ün kart də vi-ZIT?

ITALIANO
a presto!

Vorrei rivederti.
vo-RREÎ ri-ve-DER-ti.

Hai un biglietto da visita?
aî un bi-LYET-to da VI-zi-ta?

PORTUGUÊS
até mais!

Eu gostaria de te ver outra vez.
eû gus-tə-RI-ə dzhi tshi ver OU-trə vez.

Você tem um cartão seu?
vo-SE teⁿ uⁿ kəhh-TAÛⁿ seú?

ČESKY
uvidíme se!

Doufám, že tě ještě uvidím.
DOÛ-faam, zhe tiê YESH-tiê u-VI-diim.

Máš vizitku?
maash VI-zit-ku?

Can I have your [phone number / address]?
ken aî hev yœr [foûn NƏM-bœr / ə-DRES]?

Here's my [phone number / address].
HI-œrz maî [foûn NƏM-bœr / ə-DRES].

ENGLISH — see you soon

Kann ich deine [Telefonnummer / Adresse] haben?
kan ish DAÎ-nə [te-le-FOON-nu-mər / a-DRE-sə] HAA-bən?

Hier ist meine [Telefonnummer / Adresse].
HI-ər ist MAÎ-nə [te-le-FOON-nu-mər / a-DRE-sə].

DEUTSCH — bis bald!

¿Me das tu [número de teléfono / dirección]?
me dhas tu [NU-me-ro dhe te-LE-fo-no / dhi-rek-THIÔN]?

Toma mi [número de teléfono / dirección].
TO-ma mi [NU-me-ro dhe te-LE-fo-no / dhi-rek-THIÔN].

ESPAÑOL — ¡nos vemos!

Je peux avoir ton [numéro de téléphone / adresse]?
zhə pœ a-VUÂR toⁿ [nu-me-ROD te-le-FƏN / a-DRES]?

Voici mon [numéro de téléphone / adresse].
vuâ-SI moⁿ [nu-me-ROD te-le-FƏN / a-DRES].

FRANÇAIS — à bientôt!

Mi dai il tuo [numero di telefono / indirizzo]?
mi daî il TU-o [NU-me-ro di te-LE-fo-no / in-di-RIT-tso]?

Ecco il mio [numero di telefono / indirizzo].
EK-ko il MI-o [NU-me-ro di te-LE-fo-no / in-di-RIT-tso].

ITALIANO — a presto!

Você pode me dar o seu [telefone / endereço]?
vo-SE PO-dzhi mi dar u seû [te-le-FO-ni / eⁿ-de-RE-su]?

Aqui está o meu [telefone / endereço].
ə-KI is-TA u meû [te-le-FO-ni / eⁿ-de-RE-su].

PORTUGUÊS — até mais!

Dáš mi [svůj telefon / svoji adresu]?
daash mi [SFUU-i TE-le-fon / SFO-yi A-dre-su]?

Tady je [můj telefon / moje adresa].
TA-di ye [MUU-i TE-le-fon / MO-ye A-dre-sa].

ČESKY — uvidíme se!

ENGLISH
see you soon

Call me at [home / work].
kol mi et [houm / work].

Please be discreet.
pliiz bi dis-KRIIT.

DEUTSCH
bis bald!

Ruf mich [zu Hause / bei der Arbeit] an.
ruuf mish [tsu HAÛ-zə / baî der AR-baît] an.

Bitte, sei diskret.
BI-tə, zaî dis-KRET.

ESPAÑOL
¡nos vemos!

Llámame [a casa / al trabajo].
LYA-ma-me [a KA-sa / al tra-BA-hho].

Por favor, sé discreto.
por fa-BOR, se dhis-KRE-to.

FRANÇAIS
à bientôt!

Appelle-moi [à la maison / au travail].
a-pel-MUÂ [a la me-ZOᴺ / o tra-VAÎ].

Sois discret, s'il te plaît.
suâ dis-KRE, sil tə ple.

ITALIANO
a presto!

Chiamami [a casa / al lavoro].
KIÂ-ma-mi [a KA-za / al la-VO-ro].

Per favore, sii discreto.
per fa-VO-re, sii dis-KRE-to.

PORTUGUÊS
até mais!

Me ligue [em casa / no trabalho].
mi LI-gi [eⁿ KA-zə / nu trə-BA-ʎu].

Por favor, seja discreto.
puhh fə-VOHH, SE-zhə dzhis-KRE-tu.

ČESKY
uvidíme se!

Zavolej mi [domů / do práce].
ZA-vo-leî mi [DO-muu / do PRAA-tse].

Prosím, buď diskrétní.
PRO-siim, budzh dis-KREET-nii.

You can leave me a message.	**I have an answering machine.**
yu ken liiv mi ə ME-sedzh.	*aî hev ən EN-sœ-ring mə-SHIIN.*

ENGLISH — see you soon

Du kannst eine Nachricht für mich hinterlassen.	**Ich habe einen Anrufbeant- worter.**
du kanst AÎ-nə NAHH-risht für mish HIN-tər-la-sən.	*ish HAA-bə AÎ-nən AN-ruf-bə- ant-vor-tər.*

DEUTSCH — bis bald!

Déjame un mensaje.	**Tengo contestador.**
DE-hha-me un men-SA-hhe.	*TEN-go kon-tes-ta-DHOR.*

ESPAÑOL — ¡nos vemos!

Laisse-moi un message.	**J'ai un répondeur.**
les-MUÂ eⁿ me-SAZH.	*zhe eⁿ re-poⁿ-DŒR.*

FRANÇAIS — à bientôt!

Lasciami un messaggio.	**Ho la segreteria.**
LA-sha-mi un mes-SAD-dzho.	*o la se-gre-te-RI-a.*

ITALIANO — a presto!

Deixe uma mensagem para mim.	**Eu tenho uma secretária eletrônica.**
DEÎ-shi U-mə meⁿ-SA-zheⁿ PA-rə miⁿ.	*eû TE-nʸu U-mə se-kre-TA-riâ e-le-TRO-ni-kə.*

PORTUGUÊS — até mais!

Nech mi vzkaz!	**Mám záznamník.**
nehh mif-SKAZ!	*maam ZAAZ-nam-niik.*

ČESKY — uvidíme se!

ENGLISH on the phone	**Hello!** *hə-LOÛ!*	**Is _____ there, please?** *iz _____ DHE-œr, pliiz?*	
DEUTSCH am telefon	**Hallo!** *HA-lo!*	**Ist _____ da, bitte?** *ist _____ da, BI-tə?*	
ESPAÑOL al teléfono	**¡Diga!** *DI-ga!*	**¿Está _____, por favor?** *es-TA _____, por fa-BOR?*	
FRANÇAIS au téléphone	**Allô!** *a-LO!*	**Je peux parler à _____, s'il vous plaît?** *zhə pœ par-LE a _____, sil vu ple?*	
ITALIANO al telefono	**Pronto!** *PRON-to!*	**Per favore, c'è _____?** *per fa-VO-re, tshe _____?*	
PORTUGUÊS ao telefone	**Alô!** *ə-LO!*	**O _____ está, por favor?** *o _____ is-TA, puhh fə-VOHH?*	
ČESKY po telefonu	**Prosím!** *PRO-siim!*	**Je tam _____, prosím?** *ye tam _____, PRO-siim?*	

This is _____. *<u>dh</u>is iz _____.*	**Just a moment, please.** *dzhəst ə MOÛ-ment, pliiz.*	**ENGLISH** on the phone
Hier ist _____. *HI-ər ist _____.*	**Moment, bitte.** *mo-MENT, BI-tə.*	**DEUTSCH** am telefon
Soy _____. *soî _____.*	**Un momento, por favor.** *un mo-MEN-to, por fa-BOR.*	**ESPAÑOL** al teléfono
C'est _____. *se _____.*	**Un moment, s'il vous plaît.** *eⁿ mə-MAᴺ, sil vu ple.*	**FRANÇAIS** au téléphone
Sono _____. *SO-no _____.*	**Un attimo, prego.** *un AT-timo, PRE-go.*	**ITALIANO** al telefono
É o _____. *e o _____.*	**Um momento, por favor.** *uⁿ mo-MEᴺ-tu, puhh fə-VOHH.*	**PORTUGUÊS** ao telefone
Tady _____. *TA-di _____.*	**Malý moment, prosím.** *MA-lii MO-ment, PRO-siim.*	**ČESKY** po telefonu

ENGLISH / on the phone	He's not here. *hiiz nat HI-œr.*	[Call / I'll call] back later. *[kol / aîl kol] bek LEÎ-tœr.*
DEUTSCH / am telefon	Er ist nicht da. *E-ər ist nisht da.*	[Rufen Sie / Ich rufe] später nochmal an. *[RUU-fən zii / ish RUU-fə] SHPEÎ-tər NOHH-maal an.*
ESPAÑOL / al teléfono	Él no está. *el no es-TA.*	[Llame / Llamaré] más tarde. *[LYA-me / lYa-ma-RE] mas TAR-de.*
FRANÇAIS / au téléphone	Il n'est pas là. *il ne pa la.*	[Essayez / J'essaierai] plus tard. *[e-se-YE / zhe-se-ə-RE] plü tar.*
ITALIANO / al telefono	Lui non c'è. *LU-i non tshe.*	[Richiami / Richiamo] più tardi. *[ri-KIÂ-mi / ri-KIÂ-mo] più TAR-di.*
PORTUGUÊS / ao telefone	Ele não está. *E-li naûⁿ is-TA.*	[Chame / Eu chamo] mais tarde. *[SHA-mi / eû SHA-mu] maîs TAHH-dzhi.*
ČESKY / po telefonu	On tady není. *on TA-di NE-nii.*	[Zavolejte / Zavolám] později. *[ZA-vo-leî-te / ZA-vo-laam] POZ-diê-yi.*

Are you free [today / tomorrow (night)]? *ar yu frii [tu-DEÎ / tu-MA-roû (naît)]?*	**... on [Saturday / Sunday / Monday / Tuesday]?** *... an [SA-tœr-deî / SƏN-deî / MƏN-deî / TUUZ-deî]?*

ENGLISH dates

Hast du [heute / morgen (abend)] etwas vor? *hast du [HOÎ-tə / MOR-gən (AA-bənt)] ET-vas for?*	**... [Samstag / Sonntag / Montag / Dienstag] etwas vor?** *... [ZAMS-taak / ZON-taak / MON-taak / DIINS-taak] ET-vas for?*

DEUTSCH das date

¿Estás libre [hoy / mañana (por la noche)]? *es-TAS LI-bre [oî / ma-NYA-na (por la NO-tshe)]?*	**... el [sábado / domingo / lunes / martes]?** *... el [SA-ba-dho / do-MIN-go / LU-nes / MAR-tes]?*

ESPAÑOL citas

Tu es libre [aujourd'hui / demain (soir)]? *tü e libr [o-zhur-DÜÏ / də-MEN (suâr)]?*	**... [samedi / dimanche / lundi / mardi]?** *... [sam-DI / di-MANSH / len-DI / mar-DI]?*

FRANÇAIS rendez-vous

Hai da fare [oggi / domani (sera)]? *haî da FA-re [OD-dzhi / do-MA-ni (SE-ra)]?*	**... [sabato / domenica / lunedì / martedì]?** *... [SA-ba-to / do-ME-ni-ka / lu-ne-DI / mar-te-DI]?*

ITALIANO usciamo?

Você tem compromisso pra [hoje / amanhã (à noite)]? *vo-SE ten kon-pru-MI-su prə [O-zhi / ə-mə-NYAN (a NOÎ-tshi)]?*	**... [sábado / domingo / segunda / terça]?** *... [SA-ba-du / du-MIN-gu / sẽ-GUN-də / TEHH-sə]?*

PORTUGUÊS encontros

Máš [dnes / zítra (večer)] volno? *maash [də-NES / ZII-tra (VE-tsher)] VOL-no?*	**... [v sobotu / v neděli / v pondělí / v úterý] volno?** *... [F-SO-bo-tu / V-NE-diê-li / F-PON-diê-lii / V-UU-te-rii] VOL-no?*

ČESKY schůzky

ENGLISH dates	I'm free on [Wednesday / Thursday / Friday]. *aîm frî an [WENZ-deî / THŒRZ-deî / FRAÎ-deî].*	Want to go for a walk? *want tu goû fœr ə wok?*
DEUTSCH das date	Ich habe [Mittwoch / Donnerstag / Freitag] nichts vor. *ish HAA-be [MIT-vohh / DO-nərs-taak / FRAÎ-taak] nishts for.*	Willst du spazierengehen? *vilst du shpa-TSII-rən-geî-ən?*
ESPAÑOL citas	Estoy libre el [miércoles / jueves / viernes]. *es-TOÎ LI-bre el [MIÊR-ko-les / HHUÊ-bes / BIÊR-nes].*	¿Quieres dar un paseo? *KIÊ-res dar un pa-SE-o?*
FRANÇAIS rendez-vous	Je suis libre [mercredi / jeudi / vendredi]. *zhə süî LI-brə [mer-krə-DI / zhœ-DI / van-drə-DI].*	Tu veux faire un tour? *tü vœ fer en tur?*
ITALIANO usciamo?	Non ho da fare [mercoledì / giovedì / venerdì]. *non o da FA-re [mer-ko-le-DI / dzho-ve-DI / ve-ner-DI].*	Facciamo quattro passi? *fat-TSHÂ-mo KUÂT-tro PAS-si?*
PORTUGUÊS encontros	Eu não tenho compromisso pra [quarta / quinta / sexta]. *eû naûn TE-nyu kon-pro-MI-su prə [KUÂHH-tə / KIN-tə / SES-tə].*	Você quer dar uma caminhada? *vo-SE kehh dar U-mə kə-mi-NYA-də?*
ČESKY schůzky	Mám [ve středu / ve čtvrtek / v pátek] volno. *maam [ves-tər-ZHE-du / vetsh-tə-VƏR-tek / F-PAA-tek] VOL-no.*	Chceš jít na procházku? *hhə-TSESH yiit na PRO-hhaas-ku?*

Want to go for a [drink / cup of coffee]? *want tu goû fœr ə [drink / kəp əf KA-fi]?*	**Would you like to go to dinner with me?** *wud yu laîk tu goû tu DI-nœr widh mi?*	**ENGLISH** dates
Willst du einen [Drink / Kaffee] trinken gehen? *vilst du AÎ-nən [drink / ka-FEÎ] TRIN-kən GEÎ-ən?*	**Willst du mit mir essen gehen?** *vilst du mit MI-ər E-sən GEÎ-ən?*	**DEUTSCH** das date
¿Quieres ir a tomar [una copa / un café]? *KIÊ-res ir a to-MAR [U-na KO-pa / un ka-FE]?*	**¿Quieres ir a cenar conmigo?** *KIÊ-res ir a the-NAR kon-MI-go?*	**ESPAÑOL** citas
Tu veux aller [boire quelque chose / prendre un café]? *tü vœ a-LE [buâr KEL-kə shoz / PRAN-dren ka-FE]?*	**Tu veux aller au resto avec moi?** *tü vœ a-LE o res-TO a-VEK muâ?*	**FRANÇAIS** rendez-vous
Vuoi andare a [bere qualcosa / prendere un caffè]? *VUÔ-i an-DA-re a [BE-re kuâl-KO-za / PREN-de-re un kaf-FE]?*	**Vuoi venire a cena con me?** *VUÔ-i ve-NI-re a TSHE-na kon me?*	**ITALIANO** usciamo?
Você quer tomar um [drinque / cafezinho]? *vo-SE kehh tu-MAR un [drink / kə-fe-ZI-nʸu]?*	**Você gostaria de ir jantar fora comigo?** *vo-SE gus-tə-RI-ə dzhi ihh zhan-TAHH FO-rə ko-MI-gu?*	**PORTUGUÊS** encontros
Chceš jít na [panáka / kávu]? *hhə-TSESH yiit na [PA-naa-ka / KAA-vu]?*	**Chceš jít se mnou na večeři?** *hhə-TSESH yiit sem-NOÛ na VE-tsher-zhi?*	**ČESKY** schůzky

ENGLISH dates	Do you want to go to a [movie / show] with me? *du yu want tu goû tu ə [MUU-vi / <u>shoû</u>] widh mi?*	Let's go [dancing / to the beach / to a party]. *lets goû [DEEN-sin^g / tu <u>dh</u>ə biit<u>sh</u> / tu ə PAR-ti].*
DEUTSCH das date	Willst du mit mir ins [Kino / Theater] gehen? *vilst du mit MI-ər ins [KI-no / te-A-tər] GEÎ-ən?*	Gehen wir [tanzen / zum Strand / auf eine Party]! *GEÎ-ən VI-ər [TAN-tsən / tsum <u>sh</u>trant / aûf AÎ-nə PAR-ti]!*
ESPAÑOL citas	¿Quieres ir al [cine / teatro] conmigo? *KIÊ-res ir al [<u>THI</u>-ne / te-A-tro] kon-MI-go?*	Vamos a [bailar / la playa / una fiesta]. *BA-mos a [baî-LAR / la PLA-ya / U-na FIÉS-ta].*
FRANÇAIS rendez-vous	Tu veux aller au [ciné / théâtre] avec moi? *tü vœ a-LE o [si-NE / te-A-trə] a-VEK muâ?*	Allons [en boîte / à la plage / à une fête]. *a-LO^N [aⁿ buât / a la pla<u>zh</u> / a ün fet].*
ITALIANO usciamo?	Vuoi venire [al cinema / a teatro] con me? *VUÔ-i ve-NI-re [al <u>TSHI</u>-ne-ma / a te-A-tro] kon me?*	Andiamo [a ballare / alla spiaggia / ad una festa]. *an-DIÂ-mo [a bal-LA-re / AL-la SPIÂD-d<u>zh</u>a / ad U-na FES-ta].*
PORTUGUÊS encontros	Você gostaria de ir [ao cinema / a um show] comigo? *vo-SE gus-tə-RI-ə <u>dzh</u>i ir [aû si-NE-mə / a uⁿ <u>sh</u>oû] ko-MI-gu?*	Vamos [dançar / à praia / a uma festa]. *VA-mus [daⁿ-SA<u>HH</u> / a PRA-yə / ə U-mə FES-tə].*
ČESKY schůzky	Chceš jít se mnou do [kina / divadla]? *<u>hh</u>ə-TSE<u>SH</u> yiit sem-NOÛ do [KI-na / DI-vad-la]?*	Pojd'me [si zatancovat / na pláž / na párty]! *POÎD<u>ZH</u>-me [si za-TAN-tso-vat / na plaa<u>sh</u> / na PAAR-ti]!*

I want to go to [a concert / the opera]. *aî want tu goû tu [ə KAN-sœrt / dhi A-pə-rə].*	It's my treat. *its maî triit.*	**ENGLISH** dates
Ich will in [ein Konzert / die Oper] gehen. *ish vil in [aîn kon-TSERT / di OO-pər] GEÎ-ən.*	Das geht auf meine Rechnung. *das geît aûf MAÎ-nə RESH-nunᵍ.*	**DEUTSCH** das date
Quiero ir a [un concierto / la ópera]. *KIÊ-ro ir a [un kon-THIÊR-to / la O-pe-ra].*	Te invito yo. *te in-BI-to yo.*	**ESPAÑOL** citas
Je veux aller à [un concert / l'opéra]. *zhə vœ a-LE a [eⁿ koⁿ-SER / lo-pe-RA].*	Je t'invite. *zhə teⁿ-VIT.*	**FRANÇAIS** rendez-vous
Voglio andare [ad un concerto / all'opera]. *VO-lʸo an-DA-re [ad un kon-TSHER-to / al-LO-pe-ra].*	Offro io. *OF-fro I-o.*	**ITALIANO** usciamo?
Eu quero ir [a um concerto / à ópera]. *eû KE-ru ir [ə uⁿ koⁿ-SEHH-tu / a O-pe-rə].*	É por minha conta. *e puhh MI-nʸə KONⁿ-tə.*	**PORTUGUÊS** encontros
Chci jít na [koncert / operu]. *hhə-TSI yiit na [KON-tsert / O-pe-ru].*	Zvu tě. *zvu tiê.*	**ČESKY** schůzky

ENGLISH dates	We can meet [here / there]. *wii ken miit [HI-œr / DHE-œr].*	We can meet at [the hotel / your place / my place]. *wii ken miit et [dhə hoù-TEL / yœr pleîs / maî pleîs].*
DEUTSCH das date	Wir können uns [hier / dort] treffen. *VI-ər KŒ-nən uns [HI-ər / dort] TRE-fən.*	Wir können uns [im Hotel / bei dir / bei mir] treffen. *VI-ər KŒ-nən uns [im ho-TEL / baî DI-ər / baî MI-ər] TRE-fən.*
ESPAÑOL citas	Nos vemos [aquí / allí]. *nos BE-mos [a-KI / a-L^YI].*	Nos vemos en [el hotel / tu casa / mi casa]. *nos BE-mos en [el o-TEL / tu KA-sa / mi KA-sa].*
FRANÇAIS rendez-vous	On se retrouve [ici / là-bas]. *o^n sə rə-TRUV [i-SI / la-BA].*	On se retrouve [à l'hôtel / chez toi / chez moi]. *o^n sə rə-TRUV [a lo-TEL / she tuâ / she muâ].*
ITALIANO usciamo?	Ci vediamo [qui / là]. *tshi ve-DIÂ-mo [kuî / la].*	Ci vediamo [all'albergo / da te / da me]. *tshi ve-DIÂ-mo [al-lal-BER-go / da te / da me].*
PORTUGUÊS encontros	Nos encontramos [aqui / aí]. *nus e^n-ko^n-TRA-mus [ə-KI / ə-I].*	Nos encontramos [no hotel / na sua casa / na minha casa]. *nus e^n-ko^n-TRA-mus [nu u-TEL / nə SU-ə KA-zə / nə MI-n^yə KA-zə].*
ČESKY schůzky	Setkáme se [tady / tam]. *SET-kaa-me se [TA-di / tam].*	Setkáme se [v hotelu / u tebe / u mne]. *SET-kaa-me se [F-HO-te-lu / u TE-be / um-NE].*

(I'm sorry,) I can't make it. *(aîm SA-ri,) aî kent meîk it.*	Sorry I'm late. *SA-ri aîm leît.*	**ENGLISH** excuses
(Tut mir leid, aber) ich kann nicht kommen. *(tut MI-ər laît, A-bər) ish kan nisht KO-mən.*	Entschuldige, daß ich zu spät komme. *en-TSHUL-di-gə, das ish tsu shpeît KO-mə.*	**DEUTSCH** ausreden
(Lo siento, pero) no puedo venir. *(lo SIÊN-to, PE-ro) no PUÊ-dho be-NIR.*	Perdona el retraso. *per-DO-na el rre-TRA-so.*	**ESPAÑOL** excusas
(Désolé, mais) je peux pas y aller. *(de-zə-LE, me) zhə pœ pa i a-LE.*	Désolé d'être en retard. *de-zə-LE DE-tran rə-TAR.*	**FRANÇAIS** excuses
(Mi dispiace, ma) non posso venire. *(mi dis-PIÂ-tshe, ma) non POS-so ve-NI-re.*	Scusa il ritardo. *SKU-za il ri-TAR-do.*	**ITALIANO** scuse
(Desculpe-me, mas) eu não posso ir. *(dis-KUL-pi-mi, məs) eû naûn PO-su ihh.*	Desculpe pelo atraso. *dis-KUL-pi PE-lu ə-TRA-zu.*	**PORTUGUÊS** desculpas
(Bohužel) nemůžu přijít. *(BO-hu-zhel) NE-muu-zhu PSHI-yiit.*	Omlouvám se, že jdu pozdě. *OM-loû-vaam se, zhe i-DU POZ-diê.*	**ČESKY** omluvy

ENGLISH gifts	[This / This gift] is for you. *[dhis / dhis gift] iz fœr yu.*	It's so beautiful! *its soû BIÚ-ti-fəl!*
DEUTSCH geschenke	[Das / Dieses Geschenk] ist für dich. *[das / DII-zəs gə-SHENK] ist für dish.*	Das ist sehr schön! *das ist ZE-ər shœn!*
ESPAÑOL regalos	[Esto / Este regalo] es para ti. *[ES-to / ES-te rre-GA-lo] es PA-ra ti.*	¡Qué bonito! *ke bo-NI-to!*
FRANÇAIS cadeaux	[C'est / Ce cadeau est] pour toi. *[se / sə ka-DO e] pur tuâ.*	C'est très joli! *se tre zhə-LI!*
ITALIANO regali	[Questo / Questo regalo] è per te. *[KUÊS-to / KUÊS-to re-GA-lo] e per te.*	È bellissimo! *e bel-LIS-si-mo!*
PORTUGUÊS presentes	[Isto / Este presente] é para você. *[IS-tu / ES-ti pre-ZEN-tshi] e PA-rə vo-SE.*	É muito lindo! *e MUÎᴺ-tu LIᴺ-du!*
ČESKY dárky	[Tohle / Tenhle dárek] je pro tebe. *[TO-hle / TEN-hle DAA-rek] ye pro TE-be.*	To je tak krásné! *to ye tak KRAAS-nee!*

(Thanks, but) I can't accept. *(thenks, bət) aî kent ək-SEPT.*	**I insist.** *aî in-SIST.*	**ENGLISH** gifts
(Danke, aber) ich kann das nicht annehmen. *(DAN-kə, A-bər) ish kan das nisht AN-neî-mən.*	**Ich bestehe darauf.** *ish bəsh-TEÎ-ə da-RAÛF.*	**DEUTSCH** geschenke
(Gracias, pero) no lo puedo aceptar. *(GRA-thiâs, PE-ro) no lo PUÉ-dho a-thep-TAR.*	**Insisto.** *in-SIS-to.*	**ESPAÑOL** regalos
(Merci, mais) je peux pas l'accepter. *(mer-SI, me) zhə pœ pa lak-sep-TE.*	**Si, j'insiste.** *si, zhen-SIST.*	**FRANÇAIS** cadeaux
(Grazie, ma) non lo posso accettare. *(GRA-tsiê, ma) non lo POS-so at-tshet-TA-re.*	**Insisto.** *in-SIS-to.*	**ITALIANO** regali
(Obrigado, mas) eu não posso aceitar. *(o-bri-GA-du, məs) eû naûn PO-su a-seî-TAHH.*	**Eu insisto.** *eû in-SIS-tu.*	**PORTUGUÊS** presentes
(Díky, ale) nemůžu to přijmout. *(DII-ki, A-le) NE-muu-zhu to PSHI-mout.*	**Trvám na tom.** *TƏR-vaam na tom.*	**ČESKY** dárky

ENGLISH good night	**(Thanks,) I had a great time.** *(thenks,) aî hed ə greît taîm.*	**Let's go to [my / your] place.** *lets goû tu [maî / yœr] pleîs.*
DEUTSCH gute nacht	**(Danke,) es hat mir sehr gefallen.** *(DAN-kə,) es hat MI-ər ZE-ər gə-FA-lən.*	**Wir können zu [mir / dir] gehen.** *VI-ər KŒ-nən tsu [MI-ər / DI-ər] GEÎ-ən.*
ESPAÑOL al final...	**(Gracias,) me lo he pasado muy bien.** *(GRA-<u>thi</u>âs,) me lo e pa-SA-<u>dho</u> muî biên.*	**Vamos a [mi / tu] casa.** *BA-mos a [mi / tu] KA-sa.*
FRANÇAIS bonne nuit	**(Merci,) c'était super.** *(mer-SI,) se-TE sü-PER.*	**Allons chez [moi / toi].** *a-LO^N <u>she</u> [muâ / tuâ].*
ITALIANO buona notte	**(Grazie,) mi sono proprio divertito.** *(GRA-tsiê,) mi SO-no PRO-priô di-ver-TI-to.*	**Andiamo da [me / te].** *an-DIÂ-mo da [me / te].*
PORTUGUÊS boa noite	**(Obrigado,) eu me diverti muito.** *(o-bri-GA-du,) eû mi di-ve<u>hh</u>-<u>TSH</u>I MUÎ^N-tu.*	**Vamos à [minha / sua] casa.** *VA-mus a [MI-n^yə / SU-ə] KA-zə.*
ČESKY dobrou noc	**(Díky,) bylo to báječné.** *(DII-ki,) BI-lo to BAA-ye<u>tsh</u>-nee.*	**Pojd'me [ke mně / k tobě].** *POÎ<u>DZH</u>-me [kem-NIÊ / kə-TO-biê].*

I should go [home / back to the hotel]. *aî shud goû [hoûm / bek tu dhə hoû-TEL].*	I'll take you home. *aîl teîk yu hoûm.*	**ENGLISH** good night
Ich muß jetzt [nach Hause / ins Hotel] gehen. *ish mus yetst [nahh HAÛ-zə / ins ho-TEL] GEÎ-ən.*	Ich bringe dich nach Hause. *ish BRING-ə dish nahh HAÛ-zə.*	**DEUTSCH** gute nacht
Tengo que volver [a casa / al hotel]. *TEN-go ke bol-BER [a KA-sa / al o-TEL].*	Te llevo a casa. *te LYE-bo a KA-sa.*	**ESPAÑOL** al final...
Il faut que je rentre à [la maison / l'hôtel]. *il fok zhə RAN-tra [la me-ZON / lo-TEL].*	Je te raccompagne. *zhə tə ra-kon-PANY.*	**FRANÇAIS** bonne nuit
Dovrei tornare [a casa / all'albergo]. *do-VREÎ tor-NA-re [a KA-za / al-lal-BER-go].*	Ti porto a casa. *ti POR-to a KA-za.*	**ITALIANO** buona notte
Eu deveria ir para [casa / o hotel]. *eû de-ve-RI-ə ihh PA-rə [KA-zə / u u-TEL].*	Eu levo você pra casa. *eû LE-vu vo-SE prə KA-zə.*	**PORTUGUÊS** boa noite
Měl bych jít [domů / do hotelu]. *miêl bihh yiit [DO-muu / do HO-te-lu].*	Zavezu tě domů. *ZA-ve-zu tiê DO-muu.*	**ČESKY** dobrou noc

good night | ENGLISH

[May I / Want to] come in?
[meî aî / want tu] kəm in?

(I'm sorry,) tonight I can't.
(aîm SA-ri,) tu-NAÎT aî kent.

gute nacht | DEUTSCH

[Darf ich / Willst du] hereinkommen?
[darf ish / vilst du] her-AÎN-ko-mən?

(Es tut mir leid,) heute Nacht kann ich nicht.
(es tut MI-ər laît,) HOÎ-tə nahht kan ish nisht.

al final... | ESPAÑOL

¿[Puedo / Quieres] entrar?
[PUÊ-dho / KIÊ-res] en-TRAR?

(Lo siento,) hoy no puedo.
(lo SIÉN-to,) oî no PUÊ-dho.

bonne nuit | FRANÇAIS

[Je peux / Tu veux] entrer?
[zhə pœ / tü vœ] aⁿ-TRE?

(Désolé,) ce soir je peux pas.
(de-zə-LE,) sə suâr zhə pœ pa.

buona notte | ITALIANO

[Posso / Vuoi] entrare?
[POS-so / VUÒ-i] en-TRA-re?

(Mi dispiace,) stasera non posso.
(mi dis-PIÂ-tshe,) sta-SE-ra non POS-so.

boa noite | PORTUGUÊS

[Posso / Você quer] entrar?
[PO-su / vo-SE ker] eⁿ-TRAHH?

(Desculpe,) essa noite eu não posso.
(dis-KUL-pi,) E-sə NOÎ-tshi eû naûⁿ PO-su.

dobrou noc | ČESKY

[Můžu / Chceš] jít dovnitř?
[MUU-zhu / hhə-TSESH] yiit DOV-nitrsh?

(Bohužel) dnes večer nemůžu.
(BO-hu-zhel) də-NES VE-tsher NE-muu-zhu.

I'll call you [tomorrow / soon].	How about a (goodnight) kiss?
aîl kol yu [tu-MA-roù / sun].	*haù ə-BAÛT ə (GUD-naît) kis?*

ENGLISH good night

Ich werde dich [morgen / bald] anrufen.	Wie wär's mit einem (Gute-Nacht-) Kuß?
ish VER-də dish [MOR-gən / balt] AN-ruu-fən.	*vi vers mit AÎ-nəm (GUU-tə-nahht-) kus?*

DEUTSCH gute nacht

Te llamo [mañana / pronto].	¿Me das un beso (de despedida)?
te LᵞA-mo [ma-NᵞA-na / PRON-to].	*me dhas un BE-so (dhe dhes-pe-DHI-dha)?*

ESPAÑOL al final...

Je t'appellerai [demain / bientôt].	Un petit bisou (pour la nuit)?
zhə ta-pə-lə-re [də-meⁿ / bièⁿ-TO].	*eⁿ pəti bi-ZU (pur la nüî)?*

FRANÇAIS bonne nuit

Ti chiamerò [domani / presto].	Che ne dici di un bacio (della buona notte)?
ti kiâ-me-RO [do-MA-ni / PRES-to].	*ke ne DI-tshi di un BA-tsho (DEL-la BUÔ-na NOT-te)?*

ITALIANO buona notte

Eu te ligo [amanhã / em breve].	Que tal um beijinho (de boa noite)?
eû tshi LI-gu [ə-mə-NᵞAⁿ / eⁿ BRE-vi].	*ki tal uⁿ beî-ZHI-nᵞu (dzhi boâ NOÎ-tshi)?*

PORTUGUÊS boa noite

Zavolám ti [zítra / brzo].	Co takhle pusu (na dobrou noc)?
ZA-vo-laam ti [ZII-tra / BƏR-zo].	*tso TAK-hle PU-su (na DO-broù nots)?*

ČESKY dobrou noc

ENGLISH — preferences

Let's go to the bedroom.
lets goû tu <u>dh</u>ə BED-rum.

What are you into?
wət ar yu IN-tu?

DEUTSCH — vorlieben

Gehen wir ins Schlafzimmer.
GEÎ-ən VI-ər ins <u>SHL</u>AF-tsi-mər.

Was magst du?
vas makst du?

ESPAÑOL — gustos

Vamos a la cama.
BA-mos a la KA-ma.

¿Qué te gusta hacer?
ke te GUS-ta a-<u>THER</u>?

FRANÇAIS — préférences

On va dans la chambre?
oⁿ va daⁿ la <u>SHA</u>ⁿ-brə?

Qu'est-ce que tu aimes faire?
kes kə tü em fer?

ITALIANO — gusti

Andiamo in camera.
an-DIÂ-mo in KA-me-ra.

Cosa ti piace fare?
KO-za ti PIÂ-<u>tshe</u> FA-re?

PORTUGUÊS — preferências

Vamos para o quarto.
VA-mus PA-rə u KUÂ<u>HH</u>-tu.

O que você gosta de fazer?
*u ki vo-SE GOS-tə <u>dzhi</u>
fə-ZE<u>HH</u>?*

ČESKY — přednosti

Pojd'me do ložnice.
PO<u>Î</u>DZH-me do LOZH-ni-tse.

Jak to děláš rád?
yak to DIÊ-laa<u>sh</u> raat?

I'm only into safe sex.
aîm OUN-li IN-tu seîf seks.
☞ HEALTH, P. 248

Do you suck?
du yu sək?

ENGLISH preferences

Ich mache nur Safer-Sex.
ish MA-hhə nuur SEÎ-fər-SEKS.
☞ GESUNDHEIT, S. 248

Bläst du gern?
blest du gern?

DEUTSCH vorlieben

Sólo hago sexo seguro.
SO-lo A-go SEK-so se-GU-ro.
☞ SALUD, PÁG. 248

¿Te gusta chupar?
te GUS-ta tshu-PAR?

ESPAÑOL gustos

Je pratique que le safe sex.
zhə pra-TIK kə lə seîf seks.
☞ SANTÉ, P. 248

Tu aimes sucer, toi?
tü em sü-SE, tuâ?

FRANÇAIS préférences

Faccio solo sesso sicuro.
FAT-tsho SO-lo SES-so si-KU-ro.
☞ SALUTE, P. 248

Ti piace succhiarlo?
ti PIÂ-tshe suk-KIÂR-lo?

ITALIANO gusti

Eu só faço sexo seguro.
eû so FA-su SEK-su si-GU-ru.
☞ SAÚDE, PÁG. 248

Você chupa?
vo-SE SHU-pə?

PORTUGUÊS preferências

Dělám jenom bezpečný sex.
DIÉ-laam YE-nom bes-PETSH-nii seks.
☞ ZDRAVÍ, STR. 248

Kouříš?
KOÚR-zhiish?

ČESKY přednosti

ENGLISH preferences	I [love / don't like] to suck. *aî [ləv / doûnt laîk] tu sək.*	I love to get sucked. *aî ləv tu get səkt.*
DEUTSCH vorlieben	Ich [blase / blase nicht] gern. *ish [BLAA-zə / BLAA-zə nisht] gern.*	Ich lasse mir gern einen blasen. *ish LA-sə MI-ər gern AÎ-nən BLAA-zən.*
ESPAÑOL gustos	[Me / No me] gusta chupar. *[me / no me] GUS-ta tshu-par.*	Me encanta que me la chupen. *me en-KAN-ta ke me la TSHU-pen.*
FRANÇAIS préférences	Moi, [j'aime / j'aime pas] sucer. *muâ, [zhem / zhem pa] sü-SE.*	J'adore me faire sucer. *zha-DƏR mə fer sü-SE.*
ITALIANO gusti	[Mi / Non mi] piace succhiarlo. *[mi / non mi] PIÂ-tshe suk-KIÂR-lo.*	Mi piace farmelo succhiare. *mi PIÂ-tshe FAR-me-lo suk-KIÂ-re.*
PORTUGUÊS preferências	Eu [gosto / não gosto] de chupar. *eû [GOS-tu / naûⁿ GOS-tu] dzhi shu-PAHH.*	Eu gosto de uma boa chupetinha. *eû GOS-tu dzhi U-mə boâ shu-pe-TSHI-nʸə.*
ČESKY přednosti	[Rád / Nerad] kouřím. *[raat / NE-rat] KOÛR-zhiim.*	Rád se nechám vykouřit. *raat se NE-hhaam vi-KOÛR-zhit.*

I [love / don't like] to fuck.
aî [ləv / doûnt laîk] tu fək.

Do you like to get fucked?
du yu laîk tu get fəkt?

ENGLISH preferences

Ich [steh / steh nicht] auf ficken.
ish [shteî / shteî nisht] aûf FI-kən.

Läßt du dich gerne ficken?
leest du dish GER-nə FI-kən?

DEUTSCH vorlieben

[Me / No me] gusta follar.
[me / no me] GUS-ta fo-LYAR.

¿Te gusta que te follen?
te GUS-ta ke te FO-lyen?

ESPAÑOL gustos

[J'aime / j'aime pas] enculer.
[zhem / zhem pa] an-kü-LE.

Tu aimes te faire enculer?
tü em tə fer an-kü-LE?

FRANÇAIS préférences

[Mi / Non mi] piace scopare.
[mi / non mi] PIÂ-tshe sko-PA-re.

Ti piace prenderlo?
ti PIÂ-tshe PREN-der-lo?

ITALIANO gusti

Eu [gosto / não gosto] de comer.
eû [GOS-tu / naûn GOS-tu] dzhi ku-MEHH.

Você gosta de dar?
vo-SE GOS-tə dzhi dahh?

PORTUGUÊS preferências

[Rád / Nerad] mrdám.
[raad / NE-rad] MƏR-daam.

Necháváš se rád mrdat?
ne-HHAA-vaash se raad MƏR-dat?

ČESKY přednosti

ENGLISH preferences	I [love / don't like] to get fucked. *aî [ləv / doûnt laîk] tu get fəkt.*	I (don't) like it rough. *aî (doûnt) laîk it rəf.*
DEUTSCH vorlieben	Ich lasse mich [gerne / nicht gerne] ficken. *ish LA-sə mish [GER-nə / nisht GER-nə] FI-kən.*	Ich steh (nicht) auf harten Sex. *ish shteî (nisht) aûf HAR-tən seks.*
ESPAÑOL gustos	[Me / No me] gusta que me follen. *[me / no me] GUS-ta ke me FO-lⁱen.*	(No) me gusta el sexo duro. *(no) me GUS-ta el SEK-so DHU-ro.*
FRANÇAIS préférences	[J'adore / J'aime pas] me faire enculer. *[zha-DƏR / zhem pa] mə fer aⁿ-kü-LE.*	J'aime (pas) les plans hard. *zhem (pa) le plaⁿ ard.*
ITALIANO gusti	[Mi / Non mi] piace prenderlo. *[mi / non mi] PIÂ-tshe PREN-der-lo.*	(Non) mi piace il sesso hard. *(non) mi PIÂ-tshe il SES-so ard.*
PORTUGUÊS preferências	Eu [gosto / não gosto] de dar. *eû [GOS-tu / naûⁿ GOS-tu] dzhi dahh.*	Eu (não) gosto de sexo bruto. *eû (naûⁿ) GOS-tu dzhi SEK-su BRU-tu.*
ČESKY přednosti	[Rád se nechám / Nenechám se] mrdat. *[raat se NE-hhaam / NE-ne-hhaam se] MƏR-dat.*	(Ne) mám to rád na tvrdo. *(ne) maam to raad nat-VƏR-do.*

I'm (not) into S & M. *aîm (nat) IN-tu es ənd em.*	**I'm (not) into threesomes.** *aîm (nat) IN-tu <u>THR</u>II-səmz.*	**ENGLISH** preferences
Ich steh (nicht) auf S/M. *i<u>sh</u> <u>sh</u>teî (ni<u>sh</u>t) aûf es-em.*	**Ich steh (nicht) auf Dreier.** *i<u>sh</u> <u>sh</u>teî (ni<u>sh</u>t) aûf DRA-yər.*	**DEUTSCH** vorlieben
(No) me gusta el sadomasoquismo. *(no) me GUS-ta el sa-<u>dho</u>-ma-so-KIS-mo.*	**(No) me gustan los tríos.** *(no) me GUS-tan los TRI-os.*	**ESPAÑOL** gustos
J'aime (pas) les plans SM. *<u>zh</u>em (pa) le plaⁿ es-em.*	**J'aime (pas) les plans à trois.** *<u>zh</u>em (pa) le plaⁿ a truâ.*	**FRANÇAIS** préferences
(Non) mi piace il sadomaso. *(non) mi PIÂ-<u>tshe</u> il sa-do-MA-zo.*	**(Non) mi piacciono i triangoli.** *(non) mi PIÂT-<u>tsho</u>-no i TRIÂN-go-li.*	**ITALIANO** gusti
Eu (não) gosto de sadomasoquismo. *eû (naûⁿ) GOS-tu <u>dzhi</u> sə-du-mə-zu-KIZ-mu.*	**Eu (não) gosto de ménage.** *eû (naûⁿ) GOS-tu <u>dzhi</u> me-NA<u>ZH</u>.*	**PORTUGUÊS** preferências
(Ne) líbí se mi sadomaso. *(ne) LII-bii se mi SA-do-ma-so.*	**(Ne) chodím na trojku.** *(ne) <u>HH</u>O-diim na TROÎ-ku.*	**ČESKY** přednosti

ENGLISH preferences

Are you into group sex?
ar yu IN-tu grup seks?

[I'd / We'd] rather not.
[aîd / wiid] RE-dhœr nat.

DEUTSCH vorlieben

Stehst du auf Gruppensex?
shteîst du aûf GRU-pən-seks?

[Ich will / Wir wollen] das lieber nicht.
[ish vil / VI-ər VO-lən] das LII-bər nisht.

ESPAÑOL gustos

¿Te gustan las orgías?
te GUS-tan las or-HHI-as?

[Prefiero / Preferimos] que no.
[pre-FIÊ-ro / pre-fe-RI-mos] ke no.

FRANÇAIS preferences

Tu aimes les partouzes?
tü em le par-TUZ?

Ça [m'intéresse / nous intéresse] pas.
sa [men-te-RES / nuz en-te-RES] pa.

ITALIANO gusti

Ti piacciono le orgie?
ti PIÂT-tsho-no le OR-dzhe?

[Preferirei / Preferiremmo] di no.
[pre-fe-ri-REÎ / pre-fe-ri-REM-mo] di no.

PORTUGUÊS preferências

Você gosta de suruba?
vo-SE GOS-tə dzhi su-RU-bə?

[Eu prefiro / Nós preferimos] não fazer isto.
[eû pre-FI-ru / nos pre-fe-RI-mus] naûn fə-ZER IS-tu.

ČESKY přednosti

Máš rád grupáč?
maash raad GRU-paatsh?

[Radši *(s)* / Radši *(pl)*] ne.
[RAAT-shi / RAAT-shi] ne.

[I / We] don't do that. *[aî / wii] doûnt du dhet.*	**[I've / We've] never done that.** *[aîv / wiiv] NE-vœr dən dhet.*	**ENGLISH** preferences
[Ich mache / Wir machen] das nicht. *[ish MA-hhə / VI-ər MA-hhən] das nisht.*	**[Ich habe / Wir haben] das noch nie gemacht.** *[ish HAA-bə / VI-ər HAA-bən] das nohh nii gə-MAHHT.*	**DEUTSCH** vorlieben
Eso no lo [hago / hacemos]. *E-so no lo [A-go / a-THE-mos].*	**No [he / hemos] hecho eso nunca.** *no [e / E-mos] E-tsho E-so NUN-ka.*	**ESPAÑOL** gustos
[Je fais / Nous faisons] pas ça. *[zhə fe / nu fe-ZON] pa sa.*	**[J'ai / On n'a] jamais fait ça.** *[zhe / on na] zha-ME fe sa.*	**FRANÇAIS** préférences
Non [faccio / facciamo] quello. *non [FAT-tsho / fat-TSHA-mo] KUÉL-lo.*	**Non [l'ho / l'abbiamo] mai fatto.** *non [lo / lab-BIÂ-mo] maî FAT-to.*	**ITALIANO** gusti
[Eu não faço / Nós não fazemos] isto. *[eû naûn FA-su / nos naûn fə-ZE-mus] IS-tu.*	**[Eu nunca fiz / Nós nunca fizemos] isto.** *[eû NUN-kə fiz / nos NUN-kə fi-ZE-mus] IS-tu.*	**PORTUGUÊS** preferências
To [nedělám / neděláme]. *to [NE-diê-laam / NE-diê-laa-me].*	**To [jsem v životě nedělal / jsme v životě nedělali].** *to [i-SEM V-ZHI-vo-tiê NE-diê-lal / i-SME V-ZHI-vo-tiê NE-diê-la-li].*	**ČESKY** přednosti

ENGLISH preferences

But [I'll / we'll] try it.
bət [aîl / wiil] traî it.

That's not safe.
dhets nat seîf.

DEUTSCH vorlieben

Aber [ich werde / wir werden] es mal ausprobieren.
A-bər [ish VER-də / VI-ər VER-dən] es maal AÛS-pro-bii-rən.

Das ist nicht sicher.
das ist nisht ZI-shər.

ESPAÑOL gustos

Pero lo [probaré / probaremos].
PE-ro lo [pro-ba-RE / pro-ba-RE-mos].

Eso es peligroso.
E-so es pe-li-GRO-so.

FRANÇAIS préférences

Mais [je veux / on va] essayer.
me [zhə vœ / on va] e-se-YE.

C'est pas très safe.
se pa tre seîf.

ITALIANO gusti

Ma ci [posso / possiamo] provare.
ma tshi [POS-so / pos-SIÂ-mo] pro-VA-re.

Quello non è sicuro.
KUÊL-lo non e si-KU-ro.

PORTUGUÊS preferências

Mas [eu vou / nós vamos] tentar.
məs [eû voû / nos VA-mus] ten-TAHH.

Isto não é seguro.
IS-tu naûn e si-GU-ru.

ČESKY přednosti

Ale [zkusím / zkusíme] to.
A-le [SKU-siim / SKU-sii-me] to.

To není bezpečné.
to NE-nii bes-PETSH-nee.

Are you top or bottom?
ar yu tap œr BA-təm?

I'm (always) top.
aîm (OL-weîz) tap.

ENGLISH
preferences

Bist du aktiv oder passiv?
bist du ak-TIIF OO-dər pa-SIIF?

Ich bin (immer) aktiv.
ish bin (I-mər) ak-TIIF.

DEUTSCH
vorlieben

¿Eres activo o pasivo?
E-res ak-TI-bo o pa-SI-bo?

Soy (siempre) activo.
soî (SIÊM-pre) ak-TI-bo.

ESPAÑOL
gustos

Tu es actif ou passif?
tü ez ak-TIF u pa-SIF?

Je suis (seulement) actif.
zhə süî (sœl-MAᴺ) ak-TIF.

FRANÇAIS
préférences

Sei attivo o passivo?
seî at-TI-vo o pas-SI-vo?

Sono (sempre) attivo.
SO-no (SEM-pre) at-TI-vo.

ITALIANO
gusti

Você é ativo ou passivo?
vo-SE e ə-TSHI-vu oû pə-SI-vu?

Eu sou (sempre) ativo.
eû soû (SEᴺ-pri) ə-TSHI-vu.

PORTUGUÊS
preferências

Mrdáš nebo se necháš?
MƏR-daash NE-bo se NE-hhaash?

(Vždycky) mrdám.
(vəzh-DITS-ki) MƏR-daam.

ČESKY
přednosti

ENGLISH preferences	**I'm (usually) bottom.** *aîm (YU-zhuâ-li) BA-təm.*	**I'm flexible.** *aîm FLEK-si-bəl.*
DEUTSCH vorlieben	**Ich bin (normalerweise) passiv.** *ish bin (nor-MAA-lər-vaî-zə) pa-SIIF.*	**Ich bin flexibel.** *ish bin flek-SII-bəl.*
ESPAÑOL gustos	**(Normalmente) soy pasivo.** *(nor-mal-MEN-te) soî pa-SI-bo.*	**Hago de todo.** *A-go dhe TO-dho.*
FRANÇAIS préférences	**Je suis (en général) passif.** *zhə süî (an zhe-ne-RAL) pa-SIF.*	**Je fais les deux.** *zhə fe le dœ.*
ITALIANO gusti	**(Normalmente) sono passivo.** *(nor-mal-MEN-te) SO-no pas-SI-vo.*	**Faccio di tutto.** *FAT-tsho di TUT-to.*
PORTUGUÊS preferências	**Eu sou (normalmente) passivo.** *eû soû (nohh-məl-MEN-tshi) pə-SI-vu.*	**Eu sou flexível.** *eû soû flek-SI-vel.*
ČESKY přednosti	**(Obyčejně) se nechám.** *(O-bi-tsheî-niê) se NE-hhaam.*	**Dělám obojí.** *DIÊ-laam O-bo-yii.*

I want to kiss you. *aî want tu kis yu.*	**Kiss me.** *kis mi.*

ENGLISH — kiss me

Ich möchte dich gern küssen. *i<u>sh</u> MŒ<u>SH</u>-tə di<u>sh</u> gern KÜ-sən.*	**Küß mich!** *küs mi<u>sh</u>!*

DEUTSCH — küssen

Quiero besarte. *KIÊ-ro be-SAR-te.*	**Bésame.** *BE-sa-me.*

ESPAÑOL — bésame

Je veux t'embrasser. *<u>zh</u>ə vœ taⁿ-bra-SE.*	**Embrasse-moi.** *aⁿ-bras-MUÂ.*

FRANÇAIS — bisous

Voglio baciarti. *VO-lʸo ba-<u>TSH</u>AR-ti.*	**Baciami.** *BA-<u>tsh</u>a-mi.*

ITALIANO — baci

Eu quero te beijar. *eû KE-ru <u>tsh</u>i beî-<u>ZH</u>AHH.*	**Me beija.** *mi BEÎ-<u>zh</u>ə.*

PORTUGUÊS — me beija

Chci tě líbat. *<u>hh</u>ə-TSI tié LII-bat.*	**Líbej mě!** *LII-beî miê!*

ČESKY — líbej mě

ENGLISH *wait!*	**Wait!** *weît!*	**[Not so fast / Stop]!** *[nat soû fest / stap]!*	
DEUTSCH *warte!*	**Warte!** *VAR-tə!*	**[Nicht so schnell / Hör auf]!** *[nisht zoo shnel / hœr aûf]!*	
ESPAÑOL *¡espera!*	**¡Espera!** *es-PE-ra!*	**¡[No tan deprisa / Para]!** *[no tan de-PRI-sa / PA-ra]!*	
FRANÇAIS *attends!*	**Attends!** *a-TAᴺ!*	**[Pas si vite / Arrête]!** *[pa si vit / a-RET]!*	
ITALIANO *aspetta!*	**Aspetta!** *as-PET-ta!*	**[Non così veloce / Fermati]!** *[non ko-ZI ve-LO-tshe / FER-ma-ti]!*	
PORTUGUÊS *espere!*	**Espere!** *is-PE-ri!*	**[Não tão depressa / Pare]!** *[naûⁿ taûⁿ dzhi-PRE-sə / PA-ri]!*	
ČESKY *počkej!*	**Počkej!** *POTSH-keî!*	**[Ne tak rychle / Přestaň]!** *[ne tak RIHH-le / PSHES-tanʸ]!*	

What's wrong? *wəts ronᵍ?*	**I'm (not) ready.** *aîm (nat) RE-di.*	**ENGLISH** wait!
Stimmt etwas nicht? *shtimt ET-vas ni<u>sh</u>t?*	**Ich bin (noch nicht) so weit.** *i<u>sh</u> bin (no<u>hh</u> ni<u>sh</u>t) zoo vaît.*	**DEUTSCH** warte!
¿Qué te pasa? *ke te PA-sa?*	**(No) estoy listo.** *(no) es-TOÎ LIS-to.*	**ESPAÑOL** ¡espera!
Qu'est-ce qui va pas? *kes ki va pa?*	**Je suis (pas) prêt.** *<u>zh</u>ə süî (pa) pre.*	**FRANÇAIS** attends!
Cosa c'è? *KO-za <u>tsh</u>e?*	**(Non) sono pronto.** *(non) SO-no PRON-to.*	**ITALIANO** aspetta!
O que é que há? *u ki e ki a?*	**Eu (não) estou pronto.** *eû (naûⁿ) is-TOÛ PROᴺ-tu.*	**PORTUGUÊS** espere!
Co se děje? *tso se DIÊ-ye?*	**(Ne) jsem připravený.** *(neî) sem p<u>sh</u>i-PRA-ve-nii.*	**ČESKY** počkej!

ENGLISH — wait!

I have to go to the [toilet / bathroom].
aî hev tu goû tu dhə [TOÎ-let / BEETH-rum].

I [can't / don't like that].
aî [kent / doûnt laîk dhet].

DEUTSCH — warte!

Ich muß [auf die Toilette / ins Badezimmer] gehen.
ish mus [aûf di tuâ-LE-tə / ins BAA-də-tsi-mər] GEÎ-ən.

Ich [kann / mag das] nicht.
ish [kan / maak das] nisht.

ESPAÑOL — ¡espera!

Tengo que ir al [baño *(WC)* / baño].
TEN-go ke ir al [BA-nʸo / BA-nʸo].

No [puedo / me gusta eso].
no [PUÈ-dho / me GUS-ta E-so].

FRANÇAIS — attends!

Je dois aller [aux toilettes / à la salle de bain].
zhə duâ a-LE [o tuâ-LET / a la sal də beⁿ].

[Je peux pas / J'aime pas ça].
[zhə pœ pa / zhem pa sa].

ITALIANO — aspetta!

Devo andare in [bagno *(WC)* / bagno].
DE-vo an-DA-re in [BA-nʸo / BA-nʸo].

Non [posso / mi piace quello].
non [POS-so / mi PIÂ-tshe KUÉL-lo].

PORTUGUÊS — espere!

Eu tenho que ir ao [banheiro *(WC)* / banheiro].
eû TE-nʸu ki ir aû [bə-NʸEÎ-ru / bə-NʸEÎ-ru].

Eu não [posso / gosto disto].
eû naûⁿ [PO-su / GOS-tu DIS-tu].

ČESKY — počkej!

Musím [na záchod / do koupelny].
MU-siim [na ZAA-hhot / do KOÛ-pel-ni].

[Nemůžu / To se mi nelíbí].
[NE-muu-zhu / to se mi NE-lii-bii].

We'll go slow, OK? *wiil goû sloû, oû-KEÎ?*	**Not tonight, (I have a headache).** *nat tu-NAIT, (aî hev ə HE-deîk).*	**ENGLISH** *wait!*
Wir machen es langsam, okay? *VI-ər MA-hhən es LANG-zam, o-KEÎ?*	**Nicht heute Nacht, (ich habe Kopfschmerzen).** *nisht HOÎ-tə nahht, (ish HAA-bə KOPF-shmer-tsən).*	**DEUTSCH** *warte!*
Vamos despacito, ¿vale? *BA-mos des-pa-THI-to, BA-le?*	**Esta noche no, (me duele la cabeza).** *ES-ta NO-tshe no, (me DHUÊ-le la ka-BE-tha).*	**ESPAÑOL** *¡espera!*
On va y aller doucement, OK? *oⁿ va i a-LE dus-MAN, o-KE?*	**Pas ce soir, (j'ai mal à la tête).** *pa sə suâr, (zhe mal a la tet).*	**FRANÇAIS** *attends!*
Andiamoci piano, OK? *an-DIÂ-mo-tshi PIÂ-no, o-KEÎ?*	**Stasera no, (ho mal di testa).** *sta-SE-ra no, (o mal di TES-ta).*	**ITALIANO** *aspetta!*
Nós vamos devagar, tá bem? *nos VA-mus di-və-GAHH, ta beⁿ?*	**Essa noite não, (eu tenho dor de cabeça).** *E-sə NOÎ-tshi naûⁿ, (eû TE-nʸu dor dzhi kə-BE-sə).*	**PORTUGUÊS** *espere!*
Půjdeme na to pomalu, jo? *PUUÎ-de-me na to PO-ma-lu, yo?*	**Dneska večer ne, (bolí mě hlava).** *də-NES-ka VE-tsher ne, (BO-lii miê HLA-va].*	**ČESKY** *počkej!*

ENGLISH touch me	**Take [my / your] clothes off.** *teîk [maî / yœr] kloûz af.*	**Hold me.** *hoûld mi.*	
DEUTSCH anfassen	**Zieh [mich / dich] aus!** *tsii [mish / dish] aûs!*	**Halt mich fest!** *halt mish fest!*	
ESPAÑOL acaríciame	**[Desnúdame / Desnúdate].** *[des-NU-dha-me / des-NU-dha-te].*	**Abrázame.** *a-BRA-tha-me.*	
FRANÇAIS touche-moi	**[Déshabille-moi / Déshabille-toi].** *[de-za-bi-yə-MUÂ / de-za-bi-yə-TUÂ].*	**Prends-moi dans tes bras.** *praⁿ-MUÂ daⁿ te bra.*	
ITALIANO toccami	**[Spogliami / Spogliati].** *[SPO-lʸa-mi / SPO-lʸa-ti].*	**Abbracciami.** *ab-BRAT-tsha-mi.*	
PORTUGUÊS me toca	**Tire [minha / sua] roupa.** *TSHI-ri [MI-nʸə / SU-ə] HHOÛ-pə.*	**Me abrace.** *mi ə-BRA-si.*	
ČESKY dotýkat se	**Svlékni [mě / se]!** *SFLEEK-ni [miê / se]!*	**Obímej mě!** *O-bii-meî miê!*	

Touch me [here / there / down there]. *tətsh mi [HI-œr / DHE-œr / daûn DHE-œr].*	**[Tickle / Don't tickle] me.** *[TI-kəl / doûnt TI-kəl] mi.*	**ENGLISH** touch me
Faß mich [hier / da / da unten] an! *fas mish [HI-ər / da / da UN-tən] an!*	**Kitzel [mich / mich nicht]!** *KI-tsəl [mish / mish nisht]!*	**DEUTSCH** anfassen
Tócame [aquí / ahí / por ahí abajo]. *TO-ka-me [a-KI / a-I / por a-I a-BA-hho].*	**[Hazme / No me hagas] cosquillas.** *[ATH-me / no me A-gas] kos-KI-lyas.*	**ESPAÑOL** acaríciame
Touche-moi [ici / là / là en bas]. *tush-MUÂ [i-SI / la / la aⁿ-BA].*	**[Chatouille-moi / Me chatouille pas].** *[sha-tuî-yə-MUÂ / mə sha-TUÎ-yə pa].*	**FRANÇAIS** touche-moi
Toccami [qui / là / là in basso]. *TOK-ka-mi [kuî / la / la in BAS-so].*	**[Fammi / Non farmi il] solletico.** *[FAM-mi / non FAR-mi il] sol-LE-ti-ko.*	**ITALIANO** toccami
Passe a mão [aqui / ali / aqui embaixo]. *PA-si ə maûⁿ [ə-KI / ə-LI / ə-KI eⁿ-BAÎ-shu].*	**[Me / Não me] faça cócegas.** *[mi / naûⁿ mi] FA-sə KO-si-gəs.*	**PORTUGUÊS** me toca
Dotýkej se mne [tady / tam / tam dole]! *do-TII-keî sem-NE [TA-di / tam / tam DO-le]!*	**[Lechtej / Nelechtej] mě!** *[LEHH-teî / NE-lehh-teî] miê!*	**ČESKY** dotýkat se

ENGLISH — touch me

Play with [me / yourself].
pleî widh [mi / yœr-SELF].

Play with my [cock / balls].
pleî widh maî [kak / bolz].

DEUTSCH — anfassen

Spiel mit [mir / dir]!
SHPI-əl mit [MI-ər / DI-ər]!

Spiel mit [meinem Schwanz / meinen Eiern]!
SHPI-əl mit [MAÎ-nəm shvants / MAÎ-nən AÎ-ərn]!

ESPAÑOL — acaríciame

[Tócamela / Tócatela].
[TO-ka-me-la / TO-ka-te-la].

Tócame [la polla / los huevos].
TO-ka-me [la PO-lʸa / los WE-bos].

FRANÇAIS — touche-moi

[Branle-moi / Branle-toi].
[braⁿ-lə-MUÂ / braⁿ-lə-TUÂ].

Caresse-moi [la bite / les couilles].
ka-res-MUÂ [la bit / le KUÎ-yə].

ITALIANO — toccami

[Toccamelo / Toccatelo].
[TOK-ka-me-lo / TOK-ka-te-lo].

Toccami [il cazzo / le palle].
TOK-ka-mi [il KAT-tso / le PAL-le].

PORTUGUÊS — me toca

[Me / Se] masturbe.
[mi / si] məs-TUHH-bi.

Pegue no meu [pau / saco].
PE-gi nu meû [paû / SA-ku].

ČESKY — dotýkat se

Hraj si [se mnou / se sebou]!
hraî si [sem-NOÛ / se SE-boû]!

Hraj si s [mým čurákem / mýma koulema]!
hraî sis [miim TSHU-raa-kem / MII-ma KOÛ-le-ma]!

[Beat me off / Wank me (Br)]! *[biit mi af / wenk mi]!*	**Play with my [nipples / butt].** *pleî widh maî [NI-pəlz / bət].*	**ENGLISH** touch me
Hol mir einen runter! *hol MI-ər AÎ-nən RUN-tər!*	**Geh an [meine Nippel / meinen Hintern]!** *geî an [MAÎ-nə NI-pəl / an MAÎ-nən HIN-tərn]!*	**DEUTSCH** anfassen
¡Hazme una paja! *ATH-me U-na PA-hha!*	**Tócame [los pezones / el culo].** *TO-ka-me [los pe-THO-nes / el KU-lo].*	**ESPAÑOL** acaríciame
Branle-moi! *bran-lə-MUÂ!*	**Caresse-moi [les tétons / le cul].** *ka-res-MUÂ [le te-TON / lə kü].*	**FRANÇAIS** touche-moi
Fammi una sega! *FAM-mi U-na SE-ga!*	**Toccami [i capezzoli / il culo].** *TOK-ka-mi [i ka-PET-tso-li / il KU-lo].*	**ITALIANO** toccami
Me bate uma punheta! *mi BA-tshi U-mə pu-NYE-tə!*	**Pegue [nos meus bicos / na minha bunda].** *PE-gi [nus meûs BI-kus / nə MI-nyə BUN-də].*	**PORTUGUÊS** me toca
Vyhoň mě! *VI-hony miê!*	**Hraj si s [mejma bradavkama / mým zadkem]!** *hraî sis [MEÎ-ma BRA-daf-ka-ma / miim ZAT-kem]!*	**ČESKY** dotýkat se

ENGLISH fingers	**Put your finger inside me.** *put yœr FIN-gœr in-SAÎD mi.*	**Put your finger up my ass.** *put yœr FIN-gœr əp maî ees.*
DEUTSCH finger	**Steck deinen Finger in mich!** *shtek DAÎ-nən FIN^G-ər in mish!*	**Steck deinen Finger in meinen Arsch!** *shtek DAÎ-nən FIN^G-ər in MAÎ-nən arsh!*
ESPAÑOL dedos	**Méteme el dedo.** *ME-te-me el DE-dho.*	**Méteme el dedo en el culo.** *ME-te-me el DE-dho en el KU-lo.*
FRANÇAIS doigts	**Mets-moi un doigt.** *me-MUÂ eⁿ duâ.*	**Mets-moi un doigt dans le cul.** *me-MUÂ eⁿ duâ daⁿ lə kü.*
ITALIANO dita	**Mettimi un dito dentro.** *MET-ti-mi un DI-to DEN-tro.*	**Mettimi un dito nel culo.** *MET-ti-mi un DI-to nel KU-lo.*
PORTUGUÊS dedos	**Põe seu dedo dentro de mim.** *poîⁿ seû DE-du DEⁿ-tru dzhi miⁿ.*	**Põe seu dedo no meu cu.** *poîⁿ seû DE-du nu meû ku.*
ČESKY prsty	**Strč mi prst dovnitř!** *stərtsh mi pərst DOV-ni-tərsh!*	**Strč mi prst do prdele!** *stərtsh mi pərst do PƏR-de-le!*

[More / Not so many]!
[MO-œr / nat soû ME-ni]!

Watch your nails!
watsh yœr neîlz!

ENGLISH fingers

[Mehr / Nicht so viele]!
[ME-ər / nisht zoo FII-lə]!

Paß auf deine Nägel auf!
pas aûf DAÎ-nə NEÎ-gəl aûf!

DEUTSCH finger

¡[Más / No tantos]!
[mas / no TAN-tos]!

¡Cuidado con las uñas!
kuî-DHA-dho kon la U-nyas!

ESPAÑOL dedos

[Encore plus / Moins]!
[an-KÊR plü / muên]!

Attention les ongles!
a-tan-SIÔN lez ON-glə!

FRANÇAIS doigts

[Ancora / Non così tante]!
[an-KO-ra / non ko-ZI TAN-te]!

Attenzione alle unghie!
at-ten-TSIÔ-ne AL-le UN-giê!

ITALIANO dita

[Mais / Não tantos]!
[maîs / naûn TAN-tus]!

Cuidado com suas unhas!
kuî-DA-du kon SU-əs U-nyəs!

PORTUGUÊS dedos

[Víc prstů / Ne tolik]!
[viits PƏRS-tuu / ne TO-lik]!

Pozor na nehty!
PO-zor na NEH-ti!

ČESKY prsty

ENGLISH / mouth

[Lick / Bite / Suck] me!
[lik / baît / sək] mi!

Don't give me a [hickey / lovebite *(Br)*]!
doûnt giv mi ə [HI-ki / LƏV-baît]!

DEUTSCH / mund

[Leck mich / Beiß mich / Blas mir einen]!
[lek mi<u>sh</u> / baîs mi<u>sh</u> / blaaz MI-ər AÎ-nən]!

Mach mir keinen Knutschfleck!
ma<u>hh</u> MI-ər KAÎ-nən kə-NU<u>TSH</u>-flek!

ESPAÑOL / boca

¡[Lámeme / Muérdeme / Chúpamela]!
[LA-me-me / MUÊR-de-me / <u>TSH</u>U-pa-me-la]!

¡No me des un chupetón!
no me <u>dh</u>es un <u>tsh</u>u-pe-TON!

FRANÇAIS / bouche

[Lèche-moi / Mords-moi / Suce-moi]!
[le<u>sh</u>-MUÂ / mər-MUÂ / süs-MUÂ]!

Me fais pas de [suçons / sucettes *(Qb)*]!
mə fe pad [sü-SO^N / sü-SET]!

ITALIANO / bocca

[Leccami / Mordimi / Succhiami]!
[LEK-ka-mi / MOR-di-mi / SUK-kiâ-mi]!

Non mi fare un succhiotto!
non mi FA-re un suk-KIÔT-to!

PORTUGUÊS / boca

Me [lambe / morde / chupa]!
mi [LA^N-bi / MO<u>HH</u>-di / <u>SH</u>U-pə]!

Não me dê um chupão!
naûⁿ mi de uⁿ <u>sh</u>u-PAÛ^N!

ČESKY / jazykem

[Lízej / Kousej / Kuř] mě!
[LII-zeî / KOÛ-seî / ku<u>rzh</u>] miê!

Nedělej mi cucflek!
NE-diê-leî mi TSUTS-flek!

Eat my ass! *iit maî ees!*	**Suck my cock!** *sək maî kak!*	**ENGLISH** mouth
Leck meinen Arsch! *lek MAÎ-nən arsh!*	**Blas meinen Schwanz!** *blaaz MAÎ-nən shvants!*	**DEUTSCH** mund
¡Cómeme el culo! *KO-me-me el KU-lo!*	**¡Chúpame la polla!** *TSHU-pa-me la PO-lʸa!*	**ESPAÑOL** boca
Lèche-moi le cul! *lesh-MUÂL kü!*	**Suce-moi la bite!** *süs-MUÂ la bit!*	**FRANÇAIS** bouche
Leccami il culo! *LEK-ka-mi il KU-lo!*	**Succhiami il cazzo!** *SUK-kiâ-mi il KAT-tso!*	**ITALIANO** bocca
Lambe meu cu! *LAᴺ-bi meû cu!*	**Chupa meu pau!** *SHU-pə meû paû!*	**PORTUGUÊS** boca
Vylízej mi prdel! *vi-LII-zeî mi PƏR-del!*	**Kuř mi čuráka!** *kurzh mi TSHU-raa-ka!*	**ČESKY** jazykem

ENGLISH mouth	Take it in your mouth. *teîk it in yœr maûth.*	I can't. It's too big. *aî kent. its tu big.*
DEUTSCH mund	Nimm ihn in den Mund! *nim iin in deen munt!*	Ich kann nicht. Er ist zu groß. *ish kan nisht. er ist tsuu groos.*
ESPAÑOL boca	Métetela en la boca. *ME-te-te-la en la BO-ka.*	No puedo. Es demasiado grande. *no PUÊ-dho. es de-ma-SIÂ-dho GRAN-de.*
FRANÇAIS bouche	Prends-la dans la bouche. *pran-LA dan la bush.*	Je peux pas. Elle est trop grosse. *zhə pœ pa. el e tro grəs.*
ITALIANO bocca	Prendimelo in bocca. *PREN-di-me-lo in BOK-ka.*	Non posso. È troppo grande. *non POS-so. e TROP-po GRAN-de.*
PORTUGUÊS boca	Põe na sua boca. *poîn nə SU-ə BO-kə.*	Eu não posso. É grande demais. *eû naûn PO-su. e GRAN-dzhi dzhi-MAÎS.*
ČESKY Jazykem	Vem si ho do pusy! *vem si ho do PU-si!*	Nemůžu. Je moc velký. *NE-muu-zhu. ye mots VEL-kii.*

I'm gagging! *aîm GEE-ginɡ!*	**Watch your teeth!** *watsh yœr tiith!*	**ENGLISH** mouth
Ich muß kotzen! *ish mus KOT-sen!*	**Paß auf deine Zähne auf!** *pas aûf DAÎ-nə TSEÎ-nə aûf!*	**DEUTSCH** mund
¡Me ahogo! *me a-O-go!*	**¡Cuidado con los dientes!** *kuî-DHA-dho kon los DIÊN-tes!*	**ESPAÑOL** boca
J'étouffe! *zhe-TUF!*	**Attention les dents!** *a-tan-SIÔN le dan!*	**FRANÇAIS** bouche
Mi sto strozzando! *mi sto strot-TSAN-do!*	**Attenzione ai denti!** *at-ten-TSIÔ-ne aî DEN-ti!*	**ITALIANO** bocca
Estou engasgando! *is-TOÛ en-gəs-GAN-du!*	**Cuidado com seus dentes!** *kuî-DA-du kon seûs DEN-tshis!*	**PORTUGUÊS** boca
Dusím se! *DU-siim se!*	**Pozor na zuby!** *PO-zor na ZU-bi!*	**ČESKY** jazykem

ENGLISH — mouth

Lick my balls.
lik maî bolz.

Let's sixty-nine.
lets siks-ti-NAÎN.

DEUTSCH — mund

Leck meine Eier!
lek MAÎ-nə AÎ-ər!

Laß uns Neunundsechsig machen.
las uns NOÎN-unt-zek-sish MA-hhən.

ESPAÑOL — boca

Lámeme los huevos.
LA-me-me los WE-bos.

Vamos a hacer un sesenta y nueve.
BA-mos a a-THER un se-SEN-ta i NUÊ-be.

FRANÇAIS — bouche

Lèche-moi les couilles.
lesh-MUÂ le KUÎ-yə.

On fait un soixante-neuf?
oⁿ fe eⁿ suâ-zaⁿt-NŒF?

ITALIANO — bocca

Leccami le palle.
LEK-ka-mi le PAL-le.

Facciamo un sessantanove.
fat-TSHA-mo un ses-san-ta-NO-ve.

PORTUGUÊS — boca

Lambe o meu saco.
LAⁿ-bi u meû SA-ku.

Vamos fazer um meia nove.
VA-mus fə-ZER uⁿ ME-yə NO-vi.

ČESKY — jazykem

Lízej mi koule!
LII-zeî mi KOÛ-le!

Kuřme se navzájem.
KURZH-me se nav-ZAA-yem.

[Faster / Slower]!
[FEES-tœr / SLO-wœr]!

Make me come!
meîk mi kəm!

ENGLISH — mouth

[Schneller / Langsamer]!
[SHNE-lər / LANG-za-mər]!

Bring mich zum Kommen!
bring mish tsum KO-mən!

DEUTSCH — mund

¡Más [rápido / lento]!
mas [RRA-pi-dho / LEN-to]!

¡Haz que me corra!
ath ke me KO-rra!

ESPAÑOL — boca

[Plus vite / Doucement]!
[plü vit / dus-MAN]!

Fais-moi jouir!
fe-MUÂ zhuîr!

FRANÇAIS — bouche

Più [veloce / lento]!
più [ve-LO-tshe / LEN-to]!

Fammi venire!
FAM-mi ve-NI-re!

ITALIANO — bocca

Mais [depressa / devagar]!
maîs [di-PRE-sə / di-və-GAHH]!

Me faz gozar!
mi faz go-ZAHH!

PORTUGUÊS — boca

[Rychleji / Pomaleji]!
[RIHH-le-yi / PO-ma-le-yi]!

Udělej mě!
u-DIÊ-leî miê!

ČESKY — jazykem

ENGLISH mouth	**Don't make me come!** *doûnt meîk mi kəm!*	**Tell me when you're going to come.** *tel mi wen yœr GOÛ-ing tu kəm.* ☞ COMING, P. 159
DEUTSCH mund	**Bring mich nicht zum Kommen!** *bring mish nisht tsum KO-mən!*	**Sag mir, wenn du kommst!** *zaak MI-ər, ven du komst!* ☞ KOMMEN, S. 159
ESPAÑOL boca	**¡No hagas que me corra!** *no A-gas ke me KO-rra!*	**Avísame cuando te vayas a correr.** *a-BI-sa-me KUÂN-do te BA-yas a ko-RRER.* ☞ CORRERSE, PÁG. 159
FRANÇAIS bouche	**Me fais pas jouir!** *mə fe pa zhuîr!*	**Dis-moi quand tu vas jouir.** *di-MUÂ kan tü va zhuîr.* ☞ JOUIR, P. 159
ITALIANO bocca	**Non farmi venire!** *non FAR-mi ve-NI-re!*	**Dimmi quando stai per venire.** *DIM-mi KUÂN-do staî per ve-NI-re.* ☞ VENIRE, P. 159
PORTUGUÊS boca	**Não me faça gozar!** *naûn mi FA-sə go-ZAHH!*	**Me diz quando você vai gozar.** *mi diz KUÂN-du vo-SE vaî go-ZAHH.* ☞ GOZAR, PÁG. 159
ČESKY jazykem	**Nedělej mě!** *NE-diê-leî miê!*	**Řekni mi kdy budeš!** *ZHEK-ni mig-DI BU-desh!* ☞ UDĚLAT SE, STR. 159

Don't come in my mouth. *doûnt kəm in maî maûth.*	**I won't come in your mouth.** *aî woûnt kəm in yœr maûth.*	**ENGLISH** mouth
Komm nicht in meinem Mund! *kom nisht in MAÎ-nəm munt!*	**Ich werde nicht in deinem Mund kommen.** *ish VER-də nisht in DAÎ-nəm munt KO-mən.*	**DEUTSCH** mund
Córrete fuera. *KO-rre-te FUÊ-ra.*	**Me correré fuera.** *me ko-rre-RE FUÊ-ra.*	**ESPAÑOL** boca
Me jouis pas dans la bouche. *mə zhuî pa dan la bush.*	**Je jouirai pas dans ta bouche.** *zhə zhuî-RE pa dan ta bush.*	**FRANÇAIS** bouche
Non mi venire in bocca. *non mi ve-NI-re in BOK-ka.*	**Non ti verrò in bocca.** *non ti ve-RRO in BOK-ka.*	**ITALIANO** bocca
Não goze na minha boca. *naûn GO-zi nə MI-nyə BO-kə.*	**Eu não vou gozar na sua boca.** *eû naûn voû go-ZAHH nə SU-ə BO-kə.*	**PORTUGUÊS** boca
Neudělej se mi do pusy! *NE-u-diê-leî se mi do PU-si!*	**Neudělám se ti do pusy.** *NE-u-diê-laam se ti do PU-si.*	**ČESKY** jazykem

ENGLISH · condoms

Do you have [condoms / lubricant]?
du yu hev [KAN-dəmz / LU-bri-kənt]?

I have [condoms / lubricant].
aî hev [KAN-dəmz / LU-bri-kənt].

DEUTSCH · Kondome

Hast du [Kondome / Gleit-gel]?
hast du [kon-DOO-mə / GLAÎT-gel]?

Ich habe [Kondome / Gleit-gel].
ish HAA-bə [kon-DOO-mə / GLAÎT-gel].

ESPAÑOL · condones

¿Tienes [condones / lubri-cante]?
TIÊ-nes [kon-DO-nes / lu-bri-KAN-te]?

Tengo [condones / lubricante].
TEN-go [kon-DO-nes / lu-bri-KAN-te].

FRANÇAIS · capotes

Tu as [des capotes / du gel]?
tü a [de ka-PƏT / dü zhel]?

J'ai [des capotes / du gel].
zhe [de ka-PƏT / dü zhel].

ITALIANO · preservativi

Hai [dei preservativi / del lubrificante]?
aî [deî pre-zer-va-TI-vi / del lu-bri-fi-KAN-te]?

Ho [dei preservativi / del lubrificante].
o [deî pre-zer-va-TI-vi / del lu-bri-fi-KAN-te].

PORTUGUÊS · camisinhas

Você tem [camisinhas / lubrificante]?
vo-SE teⁿ [kə-mi-ZI-nʸəs / lu-bri-fi-KAⁿ-tshi]?

Eu tenho [camisinhas / lubrificante].
eû TE-nʸu [kə-mi-ZI-nʸəs / lu-bri-fi-KAⁿ-tshi].

ČESKY · kondomy

Máš [kondomy / lubrikant]?
maash [KON-do-mi / LU-bri-kant]?

Mám [kondomy / lubrikant].
maam [KON-do-mi / LU-bri-kant].

I don't have [condoms / lubricant]. *aî doûnt hev [KAN-dəmz / LU-bri-kənt].*	**Not without a condom.** *nat widh-AÜT ə KAN-dəm.*	**ENGLISH** condoms
Ich habe [keine Kondome / kein Gleitgel]. *ish HAA-bə [KAÎ-nə kon-DOO-mə / kaîn GLAÎT-gel].*	**Nicht ohne Kondom.** *nisht OO-nə kon-DOOM.*	**DEUTSCH** kondome
No tengo [condones / lubricante]. *no TEN-go [kon-DO-nes / lu-bri-KAN-te].*	**Sin condón, no.** *sin kon-DON, no.*	**ESPAÑOL** condones
J'ai pas de [capotes / gel]. *zhe pad [ka-PƏT / zhel].*	**Pas sans capote.** *pa saⁿ ka-PƏT.*	**FRANÇAIS** capotes
Non ho [dei preservativi / del lubrificante]. *non o [deî pre-zer-va-TI-vi / del lu-bri-fi-KAN-te].*	**Non senza preservativo.** *non SEN-dza pre-zer-va-TI-vo.*	**ITALIANO** preservativi
Eu não tenho [camisinhas / lubrificante]. *eû naûⁿ TE-nʸu [kə-mi-ZI-nʸəs / lu-bri-fi-KAᴺ-tshi].*	**Não sem camisinha.** *naûⁿ seⁿ kə-mi-ZI-nʸə.*	**PORTUGUÊS** camisinhas
Nemám [kondomy / lubri-kant]. *NE-maam [KON-do-mi / LU-bri-kant].*	**Ne bez kondomu.** *ne bes KON-do-mu.*	**ČESKY** kondomy

ENGLISH condoms	**Put on a condom.** *put an ə KAN-dəm.*	**Put on [some / some more] lubricant.** *put an [səm / səm MO-œr] LU-bri-kənt.*
DEUTSCH kondome	**Zieh dir ein Kondom über!** *tsii DI-ər aîn kon-DOOM Ü-ber!*	**Nimm [etwas / mehr] Gleitgel!** *nim [ET-vas / ME-ər] GLAÎT-gel!*
ESPAÑOL condones	**Ponte un condón.** *PON-te un kon-DON.*	**Hace falta [lubricante / más lubricante].** *A-the FAL-ta [lu-bri-KAN-te / mas lu-bri-KAN-te].*
FRANÇAIS capotes	**Mets une capote.** *me ün ka-PƏT.*	**[Mets / Rajoute] du gel.** *[me / ra-ZHUT] dü zhel.*
ITALIANO preservativi	**Mettiti un preservativo.** *MET-ti-ti un pre-zer-va-TI-vo.*	**Metti [del / più] lubrificante.** *MET-ti [del / più] lu-bri-fi-KAN-te.*
PORTUGUÊS camisinhas	**Põe uma camisinha.** *poî͡ʰ U-mə kə-mi-ZI-nʸə.*	**Põe [lubrificante / mais lubrificante].** *poî͡ʰ [lu-bri-fi-KAN-tshi / maîs lu-bri-fi-KAN-tshi].*
ČESKY kondomy	**Nasad' si kondom!** *NA-satsh si KON-dom!*	**Použij [lubrikant / víc lubrikantu]!** *POÚ-zhii [LU-bri-kant / viits LU-bri-kan-tu]!*

What do you want me to do?
wət du yu want mi tu du?

Anything you want.
E-ni-thingᵍ yu want.

ENGLISH intercourse

Was soll ich machen?
vas zol ish MA-hhən?

Was du willst.
vas du vilst.

DEUTSCH verkehr

¿Qué quieres que haga?
ke KIÈ-res ke A-ga?

Lo que quieras.
lo ke KIÈ-ras.

ESPAÑOL coito

Qu'est-ce que tu veux que je fasse?
kes kə tü vœ kə zhə fas?

Ce que tu veux.
skə tü vœ.

FRANÇAIS coït

Cosa vuoi che faccia?
KO-za VUÔ-i ke FAT-tsha?

Quello che vuoi.
KUÊL-lo ke VUÔ-i.

ITALIANO coito

O que você quer que eu faça?
u ki vo-SE kehh ki eû FA-sə?

O que você quiser.
u ki vo-SE ki-ZEHH.

PORTUGUÊS coito

Co chceš abych dělal?
tso hhə-TSESH A-bihh DIÊ-lal?

Cokoli chceš.
TSO-ko-li hhə-TSESH.

ČESKY pohlavní styk

ENGLISH / intercourse

I want to put it inside you.
aî want tu put it in-SAÎD yu.

Put it inside me.
put it in-SAÎD mi.

DEUTSCH / verkehr

Ich möchte ihn dir rein-schieben.
ish MŒSH-tə iin DI-ər RAÎN-shii-bən.

Schieb ihn mir rein!
shiip iin MI-ər raîn!

ESPAÑOL / coito

Quiero metértela.
KIÊ-ro me-TER-te-la.

Métemela.
ME-te-me-la.

FRANÇAIS / coït

Je veux te la mettre.
zhə vœt la ME-trə.

Mets-la moi.
me-la muâ.

ITALIANO / coito

Voglio mettertelo dentro.
VO-lʸo MET-ter-te-lo DEN-tro.

Mettimelo dentro.
MET-ti-me-lo DEN-tro.

PORTUGUÊS / coito

Eu quero meter em você.
eû KE-ru me-TER eⁿ vo-SE.

Põe o seu pau dentro de mim.
poîⁿ u seû paû DEⁿ-tru dzhi miⁿ.

ČESKY / pohlavní styk

Chci ho strčit do tebe.
hhə-TSI ho STƏR-tshit do TE-be.

Strč ho do mě!
stərtsh ho do miê!

I want to fuck [you / your ass]. *aî want tu fək [yu / yœr ees].*	**Fuck me!** *fək mi!*	**ENGLISH** intercourse
Ich will [dich / deinen Arsch] ficken. *ish vil [dish / DAÎ-nən arsh] FI-kən.*	**Fick mich!** *fik mish!*	**DEUTSCH** verkehr
Quiero [follarte / follarte por el culo]. *KIÊ-ro [fo-LYAR-te / fo-LYAR-te por el KU-lo].*	**¡Fóllame!** *FO-lYa-me!*	**ESPAÑOL** coito
Je veux [te baiser / t'enculer]. *zhə vœ [tə be-ZE / tan-kü-LE].*	**Baise-moi!** *bez-MUÂ!*	**FRANÇAIS** coït
Ti voglio [scopare / inculare]. *ti VO-lYo [sko-PA-re / in-ku-LA-re].*	**Scopami!** *SKO-pa-mi!*	**ITALIANO** coito
Eu quero [te comer / comer teu cu]. *eû KE-ru [tshi ku-MEHH / ku-MEHH teû ku].*	**Me come!** *mi KO-mi!*	**PORTUGUÊS** coito
Chci tě [mrdat / mrdat do prdele]. *hhə-TSI tiê [MƏR-dat / MƏR-dat do PƏR-de-le].*	**Omrdej mě!** *o-MƏR-deî miê!*	**ČESKY** pohlavní styk

ENGLISH intercourse	**Fuck my ass!** *fək maî ees!*	**How do you want it?** *haù du yu want it?*
DEUTSCH verkehr	**Fick meinen Arsch!** *fik MAÎ-nən ar<u>sh</u>!*	**Wie willst du es?** *vii vilst du es?*
ESPAÑOL coito	**¡Fóllame por el culo!** *FO-l^ya-me por el KU-lo!*	**¿Cómo lo hacemos?** *KO-mo lo a-<u>THE</u>-mos?*
FRANÇAIS coït	**Encule-moi!** *aⁿ-kül-MUÂ!*	**Comment tu préfères?** *kə-MA^N tü pre-FER?*
ITALIANO coito	**Inculami!** *in-KU-la-mi!*	**Come lo vuoi?** *KO-me lo VUÔ-i?*
PORTUGUÊS coito	**Come meu cu!** *KO-mi meû ku!*	**Como você quer?** *KO-mu vo-SE ke<u>hh</u>?*
ČESKY pohlavní styk	**Omrdej mě do prdele!** *o-M<u>Ə</u>R-deî miê do P<u>Ə</u>R-de-le!*	**Jak to chceš?** *yak to <u>hh</u>ə-TSE<u>SH</u>?*

Be gentle. *bi DZHEN-təl.*	**I'll be gentle.** *aîl bi DZHEN-təl.*	**ENGLISH** intercourse
Mach es vorsichtig! *mahh es for-ZISH-tish!*	**Ich werde vorsichtig sein.** *ish VER-də for-ZISH-tish zaîn.*	**DEUTSCH** verkehr
Sé tierno. *se TIÊR-no.*	**Seré tierno.** *se-RE TIÊR-no.*	**ESPAÑOL** coito
Vas-y doucement. *vaz-I dus-MAᴺ.*	**Je te ferai pas mal.** *zhə tə fə-RE pa mal.*	**FRANÇAIS** coït
Vai piano. *vaî PIÂ-no.*	**Vado piano.** *VA-do PIÂ-no.*	**ITALIANO** coito
Seja gentil. *SE-zhə zheⁿ-TSHIÛ.*	**Eu vou ser gentil.** *eû voû sehh zheⁿ-TSHIÛ.*	**PORTUGUÊS** coito
Bud' jemný! *budzh YEM-nii!*	**Budu jemný.** *BU-du YEM-nii.*	**ČESKY** pohlavní styk

ENGLISH intercourse	Fuck me hard! *fək mi hard!*	I'm going to fuck you hard! *aîm GOÚ-inᵍ tu fək yu hard!*
DEUTSCH verkehr	Mach es mir hart! *mahh es MI-ər hart!*	Ich mache es dir hart! *ish MA-hhə es DI-ər hart!*
ESPAÑOL coito	¡Fóllame duro! *FO-lʸa-me DHU-ro!*	¡Te voy a follar duro! *te boî a fo-LʸAR DU-ro!*
FRANÇAIS coït	Vas-y fort! *va-ZI fər!*	Je vais y aller fort! *zhə ve i a-LE fər!*
ITALIANO coito	Scopami di brutto! *SKO-pa-mi di BRUT-to!*	Ti scopo di brutto! *ti SKO-po di BRUT-to!*
PORTUGUÊS coito	Seja bruto! *SE-zhə BRU-tu!*	Eu vou ser bruto nessa foda! *eû voû sehh BRU-tu NE-sə FO-də!*
ČESKY pohlavní styk	Bud' tvrdej! *budzh TVƏR-deî!*	Omrdám tě na tvrdo! *o-MƏR-daam tiê nat-VƏR-do!*

Lie on your back. *laî an yœr beek.*	**Get on your stomach.** *get an yœr STƏ-mək.*	**ENGLISH** positions
Leg dich auf den Rücken! *lek di<u>sh</u> aûf deen RÜ-kən!*	**Leg dich auf den Bauch!** *lek di<u>sh</u> aûf deen baû<u>hh</u>!*	**DEUTSCH** stellungen
Ponte boca arriba. *PON-te BO-ka a-RRI-ba.*	**Ponte boca abajo.** *PON-te BO-ka a-BA-<u>hh</u>o.*	**ESPAÑOL** posturas
Mets-toi sur le dos. *me-TUÂ sür lə do.*	**Mets-toi à plat ventre.** *me-TUÂ a pla VAᴺ-trə.*	**FRANÇAIS** positions
Sdraiati sulla schiena. *ZDRA-ya-ti SUL-la SKIÊ-na.*	**Sdraiati a faccia in giù.** *ZDRA-ya-ti a FAT-<u>tsha</u> in <u>dzhu</u>.*	**ITALIANO** posizioni
Deite de costas. *DEÎ-<u>tshi</u> <u>dzhi</u> KOS-təs.*	**Deite de barriga.** *DEÎ-<u>tshi</u> <u>dzhi</u> bə-<u>HHI</u>-gə.*	**PORTUGUÊS** posições
Lehni si na záda! *LEH-ni si na ZAA-da!*	**Lehni si na břicho!** *LEH-ni si na B<u>ZHI</u>-<u>hho</u>!*	**ČESKY** polohy

ENGLISH positions	**[Turn / Bend] over.** *[tœrn / bend] OÛ-vœr.*	**Move (a little).** *muuv (ə LI-təl).*	
DEUTSCH stellungen	**[Dreh dich um / Bück dich]!** *[dreî di<u>sh</u> um / bük di<u>sh</u>]!*	**Rück (ein Stückchen)!** *rük (aîn <u>SH</u>TÜK-<u>sh</u>ən)!*	
ESPAÑOL posturas	**[Date la vuelta / Saca el culo].** *[DA-te la BUÊL-ta / SA-ka el KU-lo].*	**Échate (un poco) para allá.** *E-<u>tsh</u>a-te (un PO-ko) PA-ra a-L^Ya.*	
FRANÇAIS positions	**[Tourne-toi / Penche-toi].** *[turn-TUÂ / paⁿ<u>sh</u>-TUÂ].*	**Pousse-toi (un peu).** *pus-TUÂ (eⁿ pœ).*	
ITALIANO posizioni	**[Girati / Mettiti a novanta].** *[<u>DZHI</u>-ra-ti / MET-ti-ti a no-VAN-ta].*	**Muoviti (un po').** *MUÔ-vi-ti (un po).*	
PORTUGUÊS posições	**[Vire / Empine a bunda].** *[VI-ri / iⁿ-PI-ni ə BU^N-də].*	**Mexe (um pouco).** *ME-<u>shi</u> (uⁿ POÛ-ku).*	
ČESKY polohy	**[Otoč / Ohni] se!** *[O-to<u>tsh</u> / O-hni] se!*	**Posuň se (kousek)!** *PO-sun^y se (KOÛ-sek)!*	

Get on [top / your side]. *get an [tap / yœr saîd].*	**Get on [your knees / all fours]!** *get an [yœr niiz / ol FO-œrz]!*	**ENGLISH** positions
Leg dich auf [mich / die Seite]! *lek dish aûf [mish / di ZAÎ-tə]!*	**Geh auf [die Knie / alle Viere]!** *geî aûf [dik-NII / AL-lə FII-rə]!*	**DEUTSCH** stellungen
Ponte [encima / de lado]. *PON-te [en-THI-ma / dhe LA-dho].*	**¡Ponte [de rodillas / a cuatro patas]!** *PON-te [dhe rro-DHI-lʸas / a KUÂ-tro PA-tas]!*	**ESPAÑOL** posturas
[Viens sur moi / Mets-toi sur le côté]. *[viêⁿ sür muâ / me-TUÂ sür lə ko-TE].*	**Mets-toi [sur les genoux / à quatre pattes]!** *me-TUÂ [sür lezh-NU / a KA-trə pat]!*	**FRANÇAIS** positions
Mettiti [di sopra / sul fianco]. *MET-ti-ti [di SO-pra / sul FIÂN-ko].*	**Mettiti [in ginocchio / alla pecorina]!** *MET-ti-ti [in dzhi-NOK-kiô / AL-la pe-ko-RI-na]!*	**ITALIANO** posizioni
Fica [em cima / de lado]. *FI-kə [eⁿ SI-mə / dzhi LA-du].*	**Fica de [joelhos / quatro]!** *FI-kə dzhi [ZHUÊ-lʸus / KUÂ-tru]!*	**PORTUGUÊS** posições
Lehni si na [mě / bok]! *LEH-ni si na [miê / bok]!*	**[Klekni si / Na všechny čtyři]!** *[KLEK-ni si / naf SHEHH-nitsh TIR-zhi]!*	**ČESKY** polohy

ENGLISH positions	Get on the [bed / floor]. *get an <u>dh</u>ə [bed / FLO-œr].*	[Get your legs up / Spread your legs]. *[get yœr legz əp / spred yœr legz].*
DEUTSCH stellungen	Geh auf [das Bett / den Boden]! *geî aûf [das bet / deen BOO-dən]!*	[Heb deine Beine hoch / Spreiz deine Beine]! *[hep DAÎ-nə BAÎ-nə hohh / <u>sh</u>praîts DAÎ-nə BAÎ-nə]!*
ESPAÑOL posturas	Échate en [la cama / el suelo]. *E-<u>tsh</u>a-te en [la KA-ma / el SUÉ-lo].*	[Levanta las / Ábrete de] piernas. *[le-BAN-ta las / A-bre-te <u>dh</u>e] PIÊR-nas.*
FRANÇAIS positions	Mets-toi [sur le lit / par terre]. *me-TUÂ [sür lə li / par ter].*	[Soulève / Écarte] les jambes. *[su-LEV / e-KART] le <u>zh</u>aⁿb.*
ITALIANO posizioni	Sdraiati sul [letto / pavimento]. *ZDRA-ya-ti sul [LET-to / pa-vi-MEN-to].*	[Tira su / Apri] le gambe. *[TI-ra su / A-pri] le GAM-be.*
PORTUGUÊS posições	Fica [na cama / no chão]. *FI-kə [nə KA-mə / nu <u>sh</u>aûⁿ].*	[Levante / Abra] as pernas. *[li-VAᴺ-<u>tsh</u>i / A-brə] əs PEHH-nəs.*
ČESKY polohy	Lehni si na [postel / podla-hu]! *LEH-ni si na [POS-tel / POD-la-hu]!*	[Zvedni / Roztáhni] nohy! *[ZVED-ni / ROS-taah-ni] NO-hi!*

Move your ass [up / down]. *muv yœr ees [əp / daûn].*	**Move [up / down] (a bit).** *muv [əp / daûn] (ə bit).*	**ENGLISH** positions
Geh mit deinem Arsch [hoch / runter]! *geî mit DAÎ-nəm arsh [hohh / RUN-tər]!*	**Geh (etwas) [hoch / runter]!** *geî (ET-vas) [hohh / RUN-tər]!*	**DEUTSCH** stellungen
[Sube / Baja] el culo. *[SU-be / BA-hha] el KU-lo.*	**(Un poco) para [arriba / abajo].** *(un PO-ko) PA-ra [a-RRI-ba / a-BA-hho].*	**ESPAÑOL** posturas
[Relève / Baisse] ton cul. *[rə-LEV / bes] ton kü.*	**(Un peu) plus [haut / bas].** *(en pœ) plü [o / ba].*	**FRANÇAIS** positions
[Alza / Abbassa] il culo. *[AL-tsa / ab-BAS-sa] il KU-lo.*	**Muoviti (un po') in [su / giù].** *MUÔ-vi-ti (un po) in [su / dzhu].*	**ITALIANO** posizioni
[Levante / Abaixe] a bunda. *[li-VAN-tshi / ə-BAÎ-shi] ə BUN-də.*	**(Um pouco) mais [alto / baixo].** *(un POÛ-ku) maîs [AÛ-tu / BAÎ-shu].*	**PORTUGUÊS** posições
[Zvedni / Dej níž] prdel! *[ZVED-ni / deî niish] PƏR-del!*	**[Zvedni / Sniž] se (kousek)!** *[ZVED-ni / znish] se (KOÛ-sek)!*	**ČESKY** polohy

ENGLISH — positions

Sit on my cock.
sit an maî kak.

Let's try another way.
lets traî ə-NƏ-dhœr weî.

DEUTSCH — stellungen

Setz dich auf meinen Schwanz!
zets dish aûf MAÎ-nən shvants!

Laß es uns anders probieren.
las es uns AN-dərs pro-BII-rən.

ESPAÑOL — posturas

Siéntate en mi polla.
SIÉN-ta-te en mi PO-lʸa.

Vamos a probar otra postura.
BA-mos a pro-BAR O-tra pos-TU-ra.

FRANÇAIS — positions

Assieds-toi sur ma bite.
a-siêd-TUÂ sür ma bit.

On essaie autrement?
on e-SE o-trə-MAᴺ?

ITALIANO — posizioni

Siediti sul mio cazzo.
SIÉ-di-ti sul MI-o KAT-tso.

Cambiamo posizione.
kam-BIÂ-mo po-zi-TSIÔ-ne.

PORTUGUÊS — posições

Senta no meu pau.
SEᴺ-tə nu meû paû.

Vamos tentar de outro modo.
VA-mus teⁿ-TAHH dzhi OÛ-tru MO-du.

ČESKY — polohy

Sedni si mi na čuráka!
SED-ni si mi na TSHU-raa-ka!

Zkusme to jinak.
SKUS-me to YI-nak.

You want more? *yu want MO-œr?*	[I want more / Stop]! *[aî want MO-œr / stap]!*	**ENGLISH** moans
Willst du mehr? *vilst du ME-ər?*	[Ich will mehr / Hör auf]! *[ish vil ME-ər / hœr aûf]!*	**DEUTSCH** stöhnen
¿Quieres más? *KIÊ-res mas?*	¡[Quiero más / Para]! *[KIÊ-ro mas / PA-ra]!*	**ESPAÑOL** gemidos
Tu en veux encore? *tü aⁿ vœ aⁿ-KƏR?*	[J'en veux encore / Arrête]! *[zhaⁿ vœ aⁿ-KƏR / a-RET]!*	**FRANÇAIS** petits cris
Vuoi ancora? *VUÒ-i an-KO-ra?*	[Voglio ancora / Fermati]! *[VO-lʸo an-KO-ra / FER-ma-ti]!*	**ITALIANO** gridolini
Quer mais? *kehh maîs?*	[Eu quero mais / Pare]! *[eû KE-ru maîs / PA-ri]!*	**PORTUGUÊS** gemidos
Chceš ještě? *hhə-TSESH YESH-tiê?*	[Chci ještě / Přestaň]! *[hhə-TSI YESH-tiê / PSHES-tanʸ]!*	**ČESKY** chrochtání

ENGLISH — moans

Ram it in!
reem it in!

[Deeper / Harder / Faster]!
[DII-pœr / HAR-dœr / FEES-tœr]!

DEUTSCH — stöhnen

Stoß ihn rein!
shtos iin raîn!

[Tiefer / Härter / Schneller]!
[TII-fər / HER-tər / SHNE-lər]!

ESPAÑOL — gemidos

¡Clávamela!
KLA-ba-me-la!

¡Más [dentro / fuerte / rápido]!
mas [DEN-tro / FUÊR-te / RRA-pi-dho]!

FRANÇAIS — petits cris

Défonce-moi!
de-fons-MUÂ!

Plus [profond / fort / vite]!
plü [prə-FON / fər / vit]!

ITALIANO — gridolini

Riempimi tutto!
RIÊM-pi-mi TUT-to!

[Spingi / Più forte / Più veloce]!
[SPIN-dzhi / più FOR-te / più ve-LO-tshe]!

PORTUGUÊS — gemidos

Mete fundo!
ME-tshi FUN-du!

Mais [fundo / forte / rápido]!
maîs [FUN-du / FOHH-tshi / HHA-pi-du]!

ČESKY — chrochtání

Vraž mi ho tam!
vrazh mi ho tam!

[Hloubějc / Tvrdějc / Rychlejc]!
[HLOÛ-biê-its / TVƏR-diê-its / RIHH-leîts]!

[Slow down / Not so hard]! *[sloû daûn / nat soû hard]!*	I want your [cock / ass]. *aî want yœr [kak / ees].*	**ENGLISH** moans
[Langsamer / Vorsichtig]! *[LANG-za-mər / for-ZISH-tish]!*	Ich will deinen [Schwanz / Arsch]. *ish vil DAÎ-nən [shvants / arsh].*	**DEUTSCH** stöhnen
¡Más [lento / suave]! *mas [LEN-to / SUÂ-be]!*	Quiero tu [polla / culo]. *KIÊ-ro tu [PO-lʸa / KU-lo].*	**ESPAÑOL** gemidos
Plus [lentement / douce- ment]! *plü [lant-MAN / dus-MAN]!*	Je veux [ta bite / ton cul]. *zhə vœ [ta bit / ton kü].*	**FRANÇAIS** petits cris
[Rallenta / Più adagio]! *[ral-LEN-ta / più a-DA-dzho]!*	Voglio il tuo [cazzo / culo]. *VO-lʸo il TU-o [KAT-tso / KU-lo].*	**ITALIANO** gridolini
Mais [devagar / delicado]! *maîs [di-və-GAHH / de-li-KA-du]!*	Eu quero seu [pau / cu]. *eû KE-ru seû [paû / cu].*	**PORTUGUÊS** gemidos
[Pomalejc / Jemnějc]! *[PO-ma-leîts / YEM-niê-its]!*	Chci [tvýho čuráka / tvou prdel]. *hhə-TSI [TVII-ho TSHU-raa-ka / tvoû PƏR-del].*	**ČESKY** chrochtání

ENGLISH *moans*	**Give me your [cock / ass]!** *giv mi yœr [kak / ees]!*	**Is that good?** *iz dhet gud?*
DEUTSCH *stöhnen*	**Gib mir deinen [Schwanz / Arsch]!** *gip MI-ər DAÎ-nən [shvants / arsh]!*	**Ist das gut so?** *ist das guut zoo?*
ESPAÑOL *gemidos*	**¡Dame tu [polla / culo]!** *DA-me tu [PO-lʸa / KU-lo]!*	**¿Te gusta?** *te GUS-ta?*
FRANÇAIS *petits cris*	**Donne-moi [ta bite / ton cul]!** *dən-MUÂ [ta bit / toⁿ kü]!*	**Ça fait du bien?** *sa fe dü biêⁿ?*
ITALIANO *gridolini*	**Dammi il tuo [cazzo / culo]!** *DAM-mi il TU-o [KAT-tso / KU-lo]!*	**Così ti piace?** *ko-ZI ti PIÂ-tshe?*
PORTUGUÊS *gemidos*	**Me dê seu [pau / cu]!** *mi de seû [paû / ku]!*	**Está bom?** *is-TA boⁿ?*
ČESKY *chrochtání*	**Dej mi [tvýho čuráka / tvoji prdel]!** *deî mi [TVII-ho TSHU-raa-ka / TVO-yi PƏR-del]!*	**Je to dobrý?** *ye to DO-brii?*

(Yeah,) that's so good! *(YE-ə,) dhets soû gud!*	**[Do it / That's right]!** *[du it! / dhets raît]!*

ENGLISH moans

(Ja,) so ist es gut! *(ya,) zoo ist es guut!*	**[Mach weiter / Das ist gut]!** *[mahh VAÎ-tər / das ist guut]!*

DEUTSCH stöhnen

¡(Sí,) me gusta! *(si,) me GUS-ta!*	**¡[Hazlo / Así me gusta]!** *[ATH-lo / a-SI me GUS-ta]!*

ESPAÑOL gemidos

(Ouais,) ça fait du bien! *(we,) sa fe dü biên!*	**[Vas-y / Ouais, comme ça]!** *[va-ZI / we, kəm sa]!*

FRANÇAIS petits cris

(Sì,) così mi piace! *(si,) ko-ZI mi PIÂ-tshe!*	**[Dai / Così va bene]!** *[daî / ko-ZI va BE-ne]!*

ITALIANO gridolini

(Sim,) está muito bom! *(sin,) is-TA MUÎN-tu bon!*	**[Vai / Que gostoso]!** *[vaî / ki gos-TO-zu]!*

PORTUGUÊS gemidos

(Jo,) je to moc dobrý! *(yo,) ye to mots DO-brii!*	**[Dělej mi to / Dobře]!** *[DIÈ-leî mi to / DOB-zhe]!*

ČESKY chrochtání

ENGLISH moans	**Do that again!** *du <u>dh</u>et ə-GEN!*	**You get me so hot.** *yu get mi soû hat.*
DEUTSCH stöhnen	**Nochmal!** *NO<u>HH</u>-maal!*	**Du machst mich so an.** *du ma<u>hh</u>st mi<u>sh</u> zoo an.*
ESPAÑOL gemidos	**¡Hazlo otra vez!** *A<u>TH</u>-lo O-tra be<u>th</u>!*	**Me estás poniendo muy caliente.** *me es-TAS po-NIÊN-do muî ka-LIÊN-te.*
FRANÇAIS petits cris	**Encore!** *aⁿ-KƏR!*	**Tu m'excites.** *tü mek-SIT.*
ITALIANO gridolini	**Ancora, ti prego!** *an-KO-ra, ti PRE-go!*	**Mi ecciti tanto.** *mi ET-<u>tsh</u>i-ti TAN-to.*
PORTUGUÊS gemidos	**Faz isso de novo!** *FAZ I-su <u>dzh</u>i NO-vu!*	**Você me dá muito tesão.** *vo-SE mi da MUÎᴺ-tu te-ZAÛᴺ.*
ČESKY chrochtání	**Ještě jednou!** *YESH-tiê YED-noû!*	**Ty mě tak vzrušuješ.** *ti miê tak vəz-RU-<u>sh</u>u-yesh.*

You're driving me wild!	**You're so tight!**
yœr DRAÎ-ving mi waîld!	*yœr soû taît!*

ENGLISH moans

Du machst mich so geil!	**Du bist so eng!**
du mahhst mish zoo gaîl!	*du bist zoo eng!*

DEUTSCH stöhnen

¡Me estás volviendo loco!	**¡Qué estrecho lo tienes!**
me es-TAS bol-BIÊN-do LO-ko!	*ke es-TRE-tsho lo TIÊ-nes!*

ESPAÑOL gemidos

Tu me rends dingue!	**Tu es très étroit!**
tüm ran deng!	*tü e trez e-TRUÂ!*

FRANÇAIS petits cris

Mi fai impazzire!	**Come ce l'hai stretto!**
mi faî im-pat-TSI-re!	*KO-me tshe laî STRET-to!*

ITALIANO gridolini

Você está me enlouquecendo!	**Você é tão apertado!**
vo-SE is-TA mi en-loû-ki-SEN-du!	*vo-SE e taûn ə-pehh-TA-du!*

PORTUGUÊS gemidos

Pěkně mi rozhicováváš!	**Jsi moc staženej!**
PIÊK-niè mi ROZ-hi-tso-vaa-vaash!	*si mots STA-zhe-neî!*

ČESKY chrochtání

ENGLISH moans	You're so hard! *yœr soû hard!*	You [animal / slut]! *yu [E-ni-məl / slət]!*
DEUTSCH stöhnen	Dein Schwanz ist so steif! *daîn <u>sh</u>vants ist zoo <u>sh</u>taîf!*	Du [Tier / Schlampe]! *du [TI-ər / <u>SH</u>LAM-pə]!*
ESPAÑOL gemidos	¡Qué dura la tienes! *ke <u>DHU</u>-ra la TIÊ-nes!*	¡Eres [un animal / una puta]! *E-res [un a-ni-MAL / U-na PU-ta]!*
FRANÇAIS petits cris	Elle est bien raide! *el e biêⁿ red!*	[Espèce d'animal / Salaud]! *[es-PES da-ni-MAL / sa-LO]!*
ITALIANO gridolini	Come ce l'hai duro! *KO-me t<u>she</u> laî DU-ro!*	Sei una [bestia / troia]! *seî U-na [BES-tià / TRO-ya]!*
PORTUGUÊS gemidos	Você é tão duro! *vo-SE e taûⁿ DU-ru!*	[Seu animal / Sua puta]! *[seû ə-ni-MAÛ / SU-ə PU-tə]!*
ČESKY chrochtání	Jsi moc tvrdej! *si mots TVƏR-deî!*	[Ty zvíře / Ty kurvo]! *[tiz-VIIR-<u>zhe</u> / ti KUR-vo]!*

I'm getting close! *aîm GE-ting kloûs!*	**I'm going to come!** *aîm GOÛ-ing tu kəm!*	**ENGLISH** coming
Ich bin kurz davor! *ish bin kurts da-FOR!*	**Ich komme gleich!** *ish KO-mə glaîsh!*	**DEUTSCH** kommen
¡Estoy llegando! *es-TOÎ lye-GAN-do!*	**¡Me voy a correr!** *me boî a ko-RRER!*	**ESPAÑOL** correrse
Je vais bientôt jouir! *zhə ve biên-TO zhuîr!*	**Je vais jouir!** *zhə ve zhuîr!*	**FRANÇAIS** jouir
Ci sono quasi! *tshi SO-no KUÂ-zi!*	**Sto per venire!** *sto per ve-NI-re!*	**ITALIANO** venire
Estou quase gozando! *is-TOÛ KUÂ-zi go-ZAN-du!*	**Eu vou gozar!** *eû voû go-ZAHH!*	**PORTUGUÊS** gozar
Už za chvíli budu! *uzh zahh-VII-li BU-du!*	**Už budu!** *uzh BU-du!*	**ČESKY** udělat se

ENGLISH coming	[Come / Don't come] inside me! *[kəm / doûnt kəm] in-SAÎD mi!*	Pull out (before you come). *pul aût (bi-FO-œr yu kəm).*
DEUTSCH kommen	[Komm / Komm nicht] in mich rein! *[kom / kom ni<u>sh</u>t] in mi<u>sh</u> raîn!*	Zieh ihn raus (bevor du kommst)! *tsii iin raûs (bə-FOR du komst)!*
ESPAÑOL correrse	¡[Córrete / No te corras] dentro! *[KO-<u>rre</u>-te / no te KO-<u>rras</u>] DEN-tro!*	Sácala (antes de correrte). *SA-ka-la (AN-tes de ko-<u>RRER</u>-te).*
FRANÇAIS jouir	[Jouis-moi / Me jouis pas] dedans! *[<u>zh</u>uî-MUÂ / mə <u>zh</u>uî pa] də-DAᴺ!*	Retire-toi (avant de jouir). *rə-tir-TUÂ (a-VAᴺD <u>zh</u>uîr).*
ITALIANO venire	[Vienimi / Non venirmi] dentro! *[VIÉ-ni-mi / non ve-NIR-mi] DEN-tro!*	Tiralo fuori (prima di venire). *TI-ra-lo FUÔ-ri (PRI-ma di ve-NI-re).*
PORTUGUÊS gozar	[Goza / Não goza] dentro de mim! *[GO-zə / naûⁿ GO-zə] DEᴺ-tru <u>dzh</u>i miⁿ!*	Tira (antes de gozar). *<u>TSHI</u>-rə (Aᴺ-<u>tsh</u>is <u>dzh</u>i go-ZA<u>HH</u>).*
ČESKY udělat se	[Udělej / Neudělej] se do mě! *[u-DIÉ-leî / NE-u-diê-leî] se do miê!*	Vytáhni ho (než se uděláš)! *vi-TAAH-ni ho (ne<u>sh</u> se u-DIÉ-laash)!*

I'm coming!
aîm KƏ-minƨ!

Did you come?
did yu kəm?

ENGLISH coming

Ich komme!
ish KO-mə!

Bist du gekommen?
bist du gə-KO-mən?

DEUTSCH kommen

¡Me estoy corriendo!
me es-TOÎ ko-RRIÊN-do!

¿Te has corrido?
te as ko-RRI-dho?

ESPAÑOL correrse

Je jouis!
zhə zhuî!

Tu as joui?
ţü a zhuî?

FRANÇAIS jouir

Vengo!
VEN-go!

Sei venuto?
seî ve-NU-to?

ITALIANO venire

Eu estou gozando!
eû is-TOÚ go-ZAᴺ-du!

Você gozou?
vo-SE go-ZOÛ?

PORTUGUÊS gozar

Už jsem!
ush sem!

Už ses udělal?
ush ses u-DIÊ-lal?

ČESKY udělat se

ENGLISH / coming

Was it good for you?
wəz it gud fœr yu?

That was [hot / great]!
dhet wəz [hat / greît]!

DEUTSCH / kommen

Hat es dir gefallen?
hat es DI-ər gə-FA-lən?

Das war [geil / toll]!
das var [gaîl / tol]!

ESPAÑOL / correrse

¿Te ha gustado?
te ha gus-TA-dho?

¡Fue [muy fuerte / estupendo]!
fue [muî FUÊR-te / es-tu-PEN-do]!

FRANÇAIS / jouir

C'était bon?
se-TE bon?

C'était [super / génial]!
se-TE [sü-PER / zhe-NIÂL]!

ITALIANO / venire

Ti è piaciuto?
ti e piâ-TSHU-to?

È stato [molto eccitante / stupendo]!
e STA-to [MOL-to et-tshi-TAN-te / stu-PEN-do]!

PORTUGUÊS / gozar

Gostou?
gos-TOÚ?

Foi [muito excitante / ótimo]!
foî [MUÎN-tu esh-si-TAN-tshi / O-tshi-mu]!

ČESKY / udělat se

Bylo to dobrý?
BI-lo to DO-brii?

Bylo to [silný / skvělý]!
BI-lo to [SIL-nii / skə-VIÊ-lii]!

That was the [best / worst] sex I've ever had.
dhet wəz dhə [best / wœrst] seks aîv E-vœr heed.

Let's do it again!
lets du it ə-GEN!

ENGLISH coming

Das war der [beste / schlechteste] Sex, den ich je hatte.
das var der [BES-tə / SHLESH-tes-tə] seks, deen ish ye HA-tə.

Laß uns das nochmal machen!
las uns das NOHH-maal MA-hhən!

DEUTSCH kommen

Ha sido el [mejor / peor] polvo de mi vida.
a SI-dho el [me-HHOR / pe-OR] POL-bo dhe mi BI-dha.

¿Lo hacemos otra vez?
lo a-THE-mos O-tra beth?

ESPAÑOL correrse

C'était la [meilleure / pire] baise de ma vie.
se-TE la [meî-YŒR / pir] bez də ma vi.

On recommence!
oⁿ rə-kə-MAⁿS!

FRANÇAIS jouir

È stata la [migliore / peggiore] scopata della mia vita.
e STA-ta la [mi-LYO-re / ped-DZHO-re] sko-PA-ta DEL-la MI-a VI-ta.

Facciamolo di nuovo!
fat-TSHA-mo-lo di NUÔ-vo!

ITALIANO venire

Esta foi a [melhor / pior] trepada que já tive.
ES-ta foî ə [me-LYOHH / piôhh] tre-PA-də ki zha TSHI-vi.

Vamos fazer de novo!
VA-mus fə-ZEHH dzhi NO-vu!

PORTUGUÊS gozar

To byl můj [nejlepší / nejhorší] mrd v životě.
to bil MUU-i [NEÎ-lep-shii / NEÎ-hor-shii] mərd və-ZHI-vo-tiê.

Udělejme to znova!
u-DIÉ-leî-me to ZNO-va!

ČESKY udělat se

ENGLISH / cleaning up	**Let's clean up.** *lets kliin əp.*	**[Want / Do you have] a towel?** *[want / du yu hev] ə TAÛ-əl?*
DEUTSCH / sich waschen	**Komm, wir waschen uns.** *kom, VI-ər VA-shən uns.*	**[Willst / Hast] du ein Handtuch?** *[vilst / hast] du aîn HANT-tuuhh?*
ESPAÑOL / ¡a lavarse!	**Vamos a lavarnos.** *BA-mos a la-BAR-nos.*	**¿[Quieres / Tienes] una toalla?** *[KIÊ-res / TIÊ-nes] U-na to-A-lʲa?*
FRANÇAIS / on se lave?	**On va se laver?** *oⁿ vas la-VE?*	**Tu [veux / as] une serviette?** *tü [vœ / a] ün ser-VIÊT?*
ITALIANO / laviamoci	**Laviamoci.** *la-VIÂ-mo-tshi.*	**[Vuoi / Hai] un asciugamano?** *[VUÔ-i / aî] un a-shu-ga-MA-no?*
PORTUGUÊS / lavar	**Vamos nos lavar.** *VA-mus nus lə-VAHH.*	**Você [quer / tem] uma toalha?** *vo-SE [ker / teⁿ] U-mə tu-A-lʲə?*
ČESKY / mýdlo a voda	**Utřeme se.** *U-tər-zhe-me se.*	**[Chceš / Máš] ručník?** *[hhə-TSESH / maash] RUTSH-niik ?*

Want to take a [shower / bath] (together)?
want tu teîk ə [SHA-wœr / beeth] (tu-GE-dhœr)?

Where's the bathroom?
WE-œrz dhə BEETH-rum?

ENGLISH cleaning up

Möchtest du (mit mir) [duschen / baden]?
MŒSH-təst du (mit MI-ər) [DU-shən / BAA-dən]?

Wo ist das Badezimmer?
voo ist das BAA-də-tsi-mər?

DEUTSCH sich waschen

¿Nos [duchamos / bañamos] (juntos)?
nos [du-TSHA-mos / ba-NYA-mos] (HHUN-tos)?

¿Dónde está el baño?
DON-de es-TA el BA-nyo?

ESPAÑOL ¡a lavarse!

On prend [une douche / un bain] (ensemble)?
on pran [ün dush / en ben] (an-SAN-blə)?

Où est la salle de bain?
u e la sal də ben?

FRANÇAIS on se lave?

Vuoi fare [una doccia / un bagno] (insieme a me)?
VUÔ-i FA-re [U-na DOT-tsha / un BA-nyo] (in-SIÊ-me a me)?

Dov'è il bagno?
do-VE il BA-nyo?

ITALIANO laviamoci

Você quer tomar um [banho / banho de banheira] (juntos)?
vo-SE kehh tu-MAR un [BA-nyu / BA-nyu dzhi bə-NYEÎ-rə] (ZHUN-tus)?

Onde é o banheiro?
ON-dzhi e u bə-NYEÎ-ru?

PORTUGUÊS lavar

Chceš se (společně) [vysprchovat / vykoupat]?
hhə-TSESH se (SPO-letsh-niê) [vis-PƏR-hho-vat / vi-KOÛ-pat]?

Kde je koupelna?
gə-DE ye KOÛ-pel-na?

ČESKY mýdlo a voda

ENGLISH groups	**Kiss [him / us].** *kis [him / əs].*	**Take his clothes off.** *teîk hiz kloûz af.*
DEUTSCH gruppen	**Küß [ihn / uns]!** *küs [iin / uns]!*	**Zieh ihn aus!** *tsii iin aûs!*
ESPAÑOL en grupo	**[Bésalo / Bésanos].** *[BE-sa-lo / BE-sa-nos].*	**Desnúdalo.** *des-NU-dha-lo.*
FRANÇAIS partouzes	**[Embrasse-le / Embrasse-nous].** *[aⁿ-bras-LƏ / aⁿ-bras-NU].*	**Déshabille-le.** *de-za-bi-yə-LƏ.*
ITALIANO in gruppo	**[Bacialo / Baciaci].** *[BA-tsha-lo / BA-tsha-tshi].*	**Spoglialo.** *SPO-lʸa-lo.*
PORTUGUÊS suruba	**Beija [ele / nós].** *BEÎ-zhə [E-li / nos].*	**Tire a roupa dele.** *TSHI-ri a HHOÛ-pə DE-li.*
ČESKY grupáč	**Líbej [ho / nás]!** *LII-beî [ho / naas]!*	**Svlékni ho!** *SFLEEK-ni ho!*

Play with his cock. *pleî widh hiz kak.*	**Put a condom on him.** *put ə KAN-dəm an him.*	**ENGLISH** groups
Spiel mit seinem Schwanz! *SHPI-əl mit ZAÎ-nəm shvants!*	**Zieh ein Kondom über seinen Schwanz!** *tsii aîn kon-DOOM Ü-bər ZAÎ-nən shvants!*	**DEUTSCH** gruppen
Tócale la polla. *TO-ka-le la PO-lʸa.*	**Ponle un condón.** *PON-le un kon-DON.*	**ESPAÑOL** en grupo
Caresse-lui la bite. *ka-res-LÜÎ la bit.*	**Mets-lui une capote.** *me-LÜÎ ün ka-PƏT.*	**FRANÇAIS** partouzes
Toccagli il cazzo. *TOK-ka-lʸi il KAT-tso.*	**Mettigli un preservativo.** *MET-ti-lʸi un pre-zer-va-TI-vo.*	**ITALIANO** in gruppo
Segura o pau dele. *si-GU-rə u paû DE-li.*	**Põe uma camisinha no pau dele.** *poîⁿ U-mə kə-mi-ZI-nʸə nu paû DE-li.*	**PORTUGUÊS** suruba
Hraj si s jeho čurákem! *hraî sis YE-ho TSHU-raa-kem!*	**Nasaď mu kondom!** *NA-sadzh mu KON-dom!*	**ČESKY** grupáč

ENGLISH groups	**Suck him!** *sək him!*	**Fuck him!** *fək him!*
DEUTSCH gruppen	**Blas ihn!** *blaaz iin!*	**Fick ihn!** *fik iin!*
ESPAÑOL en grupo	**¡Chúpasela!** *TSHU-pa-se-la!*	**¡Fóllatelo!** *FO-lʸa-te-lo!*
FRANÇAIS partouzes	**Suce-le!** *süs-LƏ!*	**Encule-le!** *aⁿ-kül-LƏ!*
ITALIANO in gruppo	**Succhiaglielo!** *SUK-kiâ-lʸe-lo!*	**Scopalo!** *SKO-pa-lo!*
PORTUGUÊS suruba	**Chupa ele!** *SHU-pə E-li!*	**Come ele!** *KO-mi E-li!*
ČESKY grupáč	**Kuř ho!** *kursh ho!*	**Omrdej ho!** *o-MƏR-deî ho!*

Get [some rope / a necktie]. *get [səm roûp / ə NEK-taî].*	**[Tie / Don't tie] me up!** *[taî / doûnt taî] mi əp!*	**ENGLISH** s&m
Hol [ein Seil / eine Krawatte]! *hool [aîn zaîl / AÎ-nə kra-VA-tə]!*	**Fessel [mich / mich nicht]!** *FE-səl [mish / mish nisht]!*	**DEUTSCH** s/m
Trae una [cuerda / corbata]. *TRA-e U-na [KUÊR-da / kor-BA-ta].*	**¡[Átame / No me ates]!** *[A-ta-me / no me A-tes]!*	**ESPAÑOL** sadomaso
Prends une [corde / cravatte]. *praⁿ ün [kərd / kra-VAT].*	**[Attache-moi / M'attache pas]!** *[a-tash-MUÂ / ma-TASH pa]!*	**FRANÇAIS** sado-maso
Prendi [della corda / una cravatta]. *PREN-di [DEL-la KOR-da / U-na kra-VAT-ta].*	**[Legami / Non legarmi]!** *[LE-ga-mi / non le-GAR-mi]!*	**ITALIANO** sm
Pegue uma [corda / gravata]. *PE-gi U-mə [KOHH-də / grə-VA-tə].*	**[Me / Não me] amarre!** *[mi / naûⁿ mi] ə-MA-hhi!*	**PORTUGUÊS** chicotes
Vezmi [nějaký provaz / kravatu]! *VEZ-mi [NIÊ-ya-kii PRO-vaz / KRA-va-tu]!*	**[Přivaž / Nepřivazuj] mě!** *[PSHI-vazh / NE-pshi-va-zuî] miê!*	**ČESKY** sadomaso

ENGLISH s&m

[Gag / Don't gag] me!
[geeg / doûnt geeg] mi!

Take the handcuffs off!
teîk dhə HEND-kəfs af!

DEUTSCH s/m

Knebel [mich / mich nicht]!
KNEÎ-bəl [mish / mish nisht]!

Nimm die Handschellen ab!
nim di HANT-she-lən ap!

ESPAÑOL sadomaso

¡[Amordázame / No me amordaces]!
[a-mor-DA-tha-me / no me a-mor-DA-thes]!

¡Quítame las esposas!
KI-ta-me las es-PO-sas!

FRANÇAIS sado-maso

[Bâillonne-moi / Me bâillonne pas]!
[baî-yən-MUÂ / mə baî-YƏN pa]!

Enlève les menottes!
aⁿ-lev le mə-NƏT!

ITALIANO sm

[Imbavagliami / Non mi imbavagliare]!
[im-ba-VA-ly̆a-mi / non mi im-ba-va-LY̆A-re]!

Togli le manette!
TO-ly̆i le ma-NET-te!

PORTUGUÊS chicotes

[Põe / Não põe] a mordaça na minha boca!
[poîⁿ / naûⁿ poîⁿ] ə muhh-DA-sə nə MI-nʸə BO-kə!

Tire as algemas!
TSHI-ri əs əl-ZHE-məs!

ČESKY sadomaso

[Dej / Nedávej] mi roubík!
[deî / NE-daa-veî] mi ROÛ-biik!

Sundej mi pouta!
SUN-deî mi POÛ-ta!

You need to be punished. *yu niid tu bi PƏ-nisht.*	**[Whip / Don't whip] me!** *[wip / doûnt wip] mi!*	**ENGLISH** s&m
Du mußt bestraft werden. *du must bəsh-TRAFT VER-dən.*	**Peitsch [mich / mich nicht]!** *païtsh [mish / mish nisht]!*	**DEUTSCH** s/m
Te hace falta un buen castigo. *te A-the FAL-ta un buên kas-TI-go.*	**¡[Azótame / No me azotes]!** *[a-THO-ta-me / no me a-THO-tes]!*	**ESPAÑOL** sadomaso
Tu as besoin d'une bonne punition. *tü a bə-ZUÊ^N dün bən pü-ni-SIÔ^N.*	**[Fouette-moi / Me fouette pas]!** *[fuêt-MUÂ / mə fuêt pa]!*	**FRANÇAIS** sado-maso
Hai bisogno di una punizione. *aî bi-ZO-nʸo di una pu-ni-TSIÔ-ne.*	**[Frustami / Non frustarmi]!** *[FRUS-ta-mi / non frus-TAR-mî]!*	**ITALIANO** sm
Você precisa ser castigado. *vo-SE pre-SI-zə sehh kəs-tshi-GA-du.*	**[Me dê umas chicotadas / Não me chicoteie]!** *[mi de U-məs shi-ku-TA-dəs / naûⁿ mi shi-ku-TE-yi]!*	**PORTUGUÊS** chicotes
Potřebuješ potrestat. *pot-RZHE-bu-yesh po-TRES-tat.*	**[Bičuj / Nebičuj] mě!** *[BI-tshuî / NE-bi-tshuî] miê!*	**ČESKY** sadomaso

ENGLISH s&m	[Spank / Don't spank] me! *[speenk / doûnt speenk] mi!*	[Hurt / Don't hurt] me! *[hœrt / doûnt hœrt] mi!*
DEUTSCH s/m	Schlag [mich / mich nicht]! *shlaak [mish / mish nisht]!*	Tu [mir / mir nicht] weh! *tu [MI-ər / MI-ər nisht] veî!*
ESPAÑOL sadomaso	¡[Pégame / No me pegues] en el culo! *[PE-ga-me / no me PE-ges] en el KU-lo!*	¡[Hazme / No me hagas] daño! *[ATH-me / no me A-gas] DA-nʸo!*
FRANÇAIS sado-maso	[Donne-moi / Me donne pas] une fessée! *[dən-MUÂ / mə dən pa] ün fə-SE!*	[Fais-moi / Me fais pas] mal! *[fe-MUÂ / mə fe pa] mal!*
ITALIANO sm	[Sculacciami / Non sculacciarmi]! *[sku-LAT-tsha-mi / non sku-lat-TSHAR-mi]!*	[Fammi / Non farmi] male! *[FAM-mi / non FAR-mi] MA-le!*
PORTUGUÊS chicotes	[Me / Não me] bate! *[mi / naûⁿ mi] BA-tshi!*	[Me / Não me] machuque! *[mi / naûⁿ mi] mə-SHU-ki!*
ČESKY sadomaso	[Naplácej / Neplácej] mi! *[na-PLAA-tseî / NE-plaa-tseî] mi!*	[Ubližuj / Neubližuj] mi! *[u-BLI-zhuî / NE-u-bli-zhuî] mi!*

Don't do that! *doûnt du <u>dh</u>et!*	**Take it out!** *teîk it aût!*	**ENGLISH** ouch!
Mach das nicht! *ma<u>hh</u> das ni<u>sh</u>t!*	**Nimm ihn raus!** *nim iin raûs!*	**DEUTSCH** au!
¡No hagas eso! *no A-gas E-so!*	**¡Sácala!** *SA-ka-la!*	**ESPAÑOL** ¡ay!
Fais pas ça! *fe pa sa!*	**Retire-toi!** *rə-tir-TUÂ!*	**FRANÇAIS** aïe!
Non lo fare! *non lo FA-re!*	**Tiralo fuori!** *TI-ra-lo FUÔ-ri!*	**ITALIANO** ahi!
Não faça isto! *naûⁿ FA-sə IS-tu!*	**Tira!** *<u>TSH</u>I-rə!*	**PORTUGUÊS** ai!
Nedělej to! *NE-diê-leî to!*	**Vytáhni ho!** *vi-TAAH-ni ho!*	**ČESKY** jejky!

ENGLISH ouch!	**Are you all right?** *ar yu ol raît?*	**You're (not) hurting me.** *yœr (nat) HŒR-ting mi.*
DEUTSCH au!	**Bist du okay?** *bist du o-KEÎ?*	**Du tust mir (nicht) weh.** *du tust MI-ər (nisht) veî.*
ESPAÑOL ¡ay!	**¿Te encuentras bien?** *te en-KUÊN-tras biên?*	**(No) me haces daño.** *(no) me A-thes DA-nyo.*
FRANÇAIS aïe!	**Ça va?** *sa va?*	**Tu me fais (pas) mal.** *tüm fe (pa) mal.*
ITALIANO ahi!	**Stai bene?** *staî BE-ne?*	**(Non) mi fai male.** *(non) mi faî MA-le.*
PORTUGUÊS ai!	**Você está bem?** *vo-SE is-TA ben?*	**Você (não) está me machucando.** *vo-SE (naûn) is-TA mi mə-shu-KAN-du.*
ČESKY jejky!	**Jsi v pořádku?** *sif por-ZHAAT-ku?*	**(Ne) bolí mě to.** *(ne) BO-lii miê to.*

[Stop / Don't stop]!	**I can't take it anymore!**	**ENGLISH** ouch!
[stap / doûnt stap]!	*aî kent teîk it e-ni-MO-œr!*	

[Hör / Hör nicht] auf!	**Ich kann nicht mehr!**	**DEUTSCH** au!
[hœr / hœr nischt] aûf!	*ish kan nischt ME-ər!*	

¡[Para / No pares]!	**¡No puedo más!**	**ESPAÑOL** ¡ay!
[PA-ra / no PA-res]!	*no PUÊ-dho mas!*	

[Arrête / N'arrête pas]!	**J'en peux plus!**	**FRANÇAIS** aïe!
[a-RET / na-RET pa]!	*zhan pœ plü!*	

[Fermati / Non ti fermare]!	**Non ne posso più!**	**ITALIANO** ahi!
[FER-ma-ti / non ti fer-MA-re]!	*non ne POS-so più!*	

[Pare / Não pare]!	**Não aguento mais!**	**PORTUGUÊS** ai!
[PA-ri / naûn PA-ri]!	*naûn a-GUÊN-tu maîs!*	

[Přestaň / Nepřestávej]!	**Už to nemůžu snést!**	**ČESKY** jejky!
[PSHES-tany / NE-pshes-taa-veî]!	*ush to NE-muu-zhu sneest!*	

ENGLISH — ouch!

You're raping me!
yœr REÎ-pinᵍ mi!

I'm going to call the police!
aîm GOÙ-inᵍ tu kol <u>dh</u>ə pə-LIIS!

DEUTSCH — au!

Du vergewaltigst mich!
du fer-gə-VAL-tikst mi<u>sh</u>!

Ich rufe die Polizei!
i<u>sh</u> RUU-fə di po-li-TSAÎ!

ESPAÑOL — ¡ay!

¡Me estás violando!
me es-TAS biô-LAN-do!

¡Voy a llamar a la policía!
boî a lʸa-MAR a la po-li-<u>TH</u>I-a!

FRANÇAIS — aïe!

Tu me violes!
tüm viôl!

J'appelle les flics!
<u>zh</u>a-PEL le flik!

ITALIANO — ahi!

Mi stai violentando!
mi staî viô-len-TAN-do!

Chiamo la polizia!
KIÂ-mo la po-li-TSI-a!

PORTUGUÊS — ai!

Você está me estuprando!
vo-SE is-TA mi es-tu-PRAᴺ-du!

Vou chamar a polícia!
voû <u>sh</u>ə-MAR ə po-LI-siâ!

ČESKY — jejky!

Znásilňuješ mě!
ZNAA-sil-nʸu-ye<u>sh</u> miê!

Zavolám policii!
ZA-vo-laam PO-li-tsii!

(I'm sorry,) I can't get it up. *(aîm SA-ri,) aî kent get it əp.*	**I'm a little [nervous / tense / tired].** *aîm ə LI-təl [NŒR-vəs / tens / taîrd].*	**ENGLISH** impotence
(Tut mir leid,) ich krieg keinen hoch. *(tut MI-ər laît,) ish kriik KAÎ-nən hoohh.*	**Ich bin ein bißchen [nervös / angespannt / müde].** *ish bin aîn BIS-shən [ner-VŒZ / AN-gəsh-pant / MÜÜ-də].*	**DEUTSCH** impotenz
(Lo siento,) no se me levanta. *(lo SIÊN-to,) no se me le-BAN-ta.*	**Estoy un poco [nervioso / tenso / cansado].** *es-TOÎ un PO-ko [ner-BIÔ-so / TEN-so / kan-SA-dho].*	**ESPAÑOL** impotencia
(Pardon,) j'arrive pas à bander. *(par-DON,) zha-RIV pa a ban-DE.*	**Je suis un peu [mal à l'aise / tendu / fatigué].** *zhə süîz en pœ [mal a lez / tan-DÜ / fa-ti-GE].*	**FRANÇAIS** impuissance
(Mi dispiace,) non mi si drizza. *(mi dis-PIÂ-tshe,) non mi si DRIT-tsa.*	**Sono un po' [nervoso / teso / stanco].** *SO-no un po [ner-VO-zo / TE-zo / STAN-ko].*	**ITALIANO** impotenza
(Desculpe-me,) não está endurecendo. *(dis-KUL-pi-mi,) naûn is-TA en-du-re-SEN-du.*	**Eu estou um pouco [nervoso / tenso / cansado].** *eû is-TOÛ un POÛ-ku [nehh-VO-zu / TEN-su / kan-SA-du].*	**PORTUGUÊS** impotência
(Promiň,) nestojí mi. *(PRO-miny,) NE-sto-yii mi.*	**Jsem trochu [nervózní / napjatý / unavený].** *sem TRO-hhu [NER-vooz-nii / NA-piâ-tii / U-na-ve-nii].*	**ČESKY** impotence

ENGLISH — impotence

I drank too much.
aî drenk tu mətsh.

It's not you.
its nat yu.

DEUTSCH — Impotenz

Ich habe zu viel getrunken.
ish HAA-bə tsuu FI-əl gə-TRUN-kən.

Es liegt nicht an dir.
es liikt nisht an DI-ər.

ESPAÑOL — Impotencia

Bebí demasiado.
be-BI dhe-ma-SIÂ-dho.

No es culpa tuya.
no es KUL-pa TU-ya.

FRANÇAIS — Impuissance

J'ai trop bu.
zhe tro bü.

C'est pas de ta faute.
se pad ta fot.

ITALIANO — impotenza

Ho bevuto troppo.
o be-VU-to TROP-po.

Non è colpa tua.
non e KOL-pa TU-a.

PORTUGUÊS — impotência

Eu bebi demais.
eû be-BI dzhi-MAÎS.

Não é você.
naúⁿ e vo-SE.

ČESKY — impotence

Moc jsem pil.
mots sem pil.

To není tvoje vina.
to NE-niit vo-ye VI-na.

No problem.
noû PRA-bləm.

We'll try again (later).
wiil traî ə-GEN (LEÎ-tœr).

Kein Problem.
kaîn pro-BLEÎM.

Wir versuchen es (später) nochmal.
VI-ər fer-ZUU-hhən es (SHPEÎ-tər) NOHH-maal.

No importa.
no im-POR-ta.

Lo intentaremos otra vez (luego).
lo in-ten-ta-RE-mos O-tra beth (LUÊ-go).

C'est pas grave.
se pa grav.

On essaiera encore (plus tard).
on e-se-yə-RA aⁿ-KƏR (plü tar).

Non importa.
non im-POR-ta.

Ci riproveremo (dopo).
tshi ri-pro-ve-RE-mo (DO-po).

Sem problemas.
seⁿ pro-BLE-məs.

Vamos tentar de novo (mais tarde).
VA-mus teⁿ-TAHH dzhi NO-vu (maîs TAHH-dzhi).

Bez problému.
bes PRO-blee-mu.

Zkusme to znovu (později).
SKUS-me toz-NO-vu (POZ-diê-yi).

stay or go? **ENGLISH**	**Want to stay over?** *want tu steî OÛ-vœr?*	**May I stay over?** *meî aî steî OÛ-vœr?*
bleibst du? **DEUTSCH**	**Willst du hierbleiben?** *vilst du HI-ər-blaî-bən?*	**Kann ich hierbleiben?** *kan ish HI-ər-blaî-bən?*
¿te quedas? **ESPAÑOL**	**¿Te gustaría quedarte?** *te gus-ta-RI-a ke-DHAR-te?*	**¿Me puedo quedar?** *me PUÊ-dho ke-DHAR?*
tu restes? **FRANÇAIS**	**Tu veux rester dormir?** *tü vœ res-TE dər-MIR?*	**Je peux rester?** *zhə pœ res-TE?*
rimani? **ITALIANO**	**Vuoi rimanere?** *VUÔ-i ri-ma-NE-re?*	**Posso rimanere?** *POS-so ri-ma-NE-re?*
pernoite? **PORTUGUÊS**	**Você quer dormir aqui?** *vo-SE kehh duhh-MIR ə-KI?*	**Posso dormir aqui?** *PO-su duhh-MIR ə-KI?*
strávíš noc? **ČESKY**	**Chceš tu strávit noc?** *hhə-TSESH tu STRAA-vit nots?*	**Mohl bych tu strávit noc?** *MO-həl bihh tu STRAA-vit nots?*

I'd love to. *aîd ləv tu.*	**I can't.** *aî kent.*	**ENGLISH** stay or go?
Ich würde gern. *ish VÜR-də gern.*	**Ich kann nicht.** *ish kan nisht.*	**DEUTSCH** bleibst du?
Me encantaría. *me en-kan-ta-RI-a.*	**No puedo.** *no PUÊ-dho.*	**ESPAÑOL** ¿te quedas?
Avec plaisir. *a-VEK ple-ZIR.*	**Je peux pas.** *zhə pœ pa.*	**FRANÇAIS** tu restes?
Mi piacerebbe molto. *mi piâ-tshe-REB-be MOL-to.*	**Non posso.** *non POS-so.*	**ITALIANO** rimani?
Eu adoraria. *eû ə-do-rə-RI-ə.*	**Não posso.** *naûn PO-su.*	**PORTUGUÊS** pernoite?
Rád bych. *raad bihh.*	**Nemůžu.** *NE-muu-zhu.*	**ČESKY** stráviš noc?

ENGLISH stay or go?	[I'd / You'd] better go. *[aîd / yud] BE-tœr goû.*	[Please call me / I'll call you] a taxi. *[pliiz kol mi / aîl kol yu] ə TEK-si.*
DEUTSCH bleibst du?	Ich glaube, [ich muß / du solltest] jetzt gehen. *ish GLAÛ-bə, [ish mus / du ZOL-təst] yetst GEÎ-ən.*	[Bitte bestell mir / Ich bestelle dir] ein Taxi. *[BI-tə bəsh-TEL MI-ər / ish bəsh-TE-lə DI-ər] aîn TAK-si.*
ESPAÑOL ¿te quedas?	Mejor que [me vaya / te vayas]. *me-HHOR ke [me BA-ya / te BA-yas].*	[Por favor, llámame / Te llamo] un taxi. *[por fa-BOR, LYA-ma-me / te LYA-mo] un TAK-si.*
FRANÇAIS tu restes?	[Je / Tu] ferais mieux de partir. *[zhə / tü] fə-RE miœd par-TIR.*	[Appelle-moi un taxi, s'il te plaît / Je t'appelle un taxi]. *[a-pel-MUÂ eⁿ tak-SI, sil tə ple / zhə ta-PEL eⁿ tak-SI].*
ITALIANO rimani?	È meglio che [io / tu] vada. *e ME-lʸo ke [I-o / tu] VA-da.*	[Per favore, chiamami / Ti chiamo] un taxi. *[per fa-VO-re, KIÂ-ma-mi / ti KIÂ-mo] un TAK-si.*
PORTUGUÊS pernoite?	É melhor [eu / você] ir. *e me-LYOR [eû / vo-SÊ] ihh.*	[Por favor, me chame / Vou chamar] um táxi. *[puhh fə-VOHH, mi SHA-mi / voû shə-MAR] uⁿ TAK-si.*
ČESKY stráviš noc?	Raději [půjdu / běž]. *RA-diê-yi [PUU-i-du / biêsh].*	[Zavolej mi prosím / Zavolám ti] taxíka. *[ZA-vo-leî mi PRO-siim / ZA-vo-laam ti] TAK-sii-ka.*

Could you drive me? *kud yu draîv mi?*	**I'll drive you.** *aîl draîv yu.*	**ENGLISH** stay or go?
Könntest du mich fahren? *KŒN-təst du mi<u>sh</u> FAA-rən?*	**Ich fahre dich.** *i<u>sh</u> FAA-rə di<u>sh</u>.*	**DEUTSCH** bleibst du?
¿Me podrías llevar? *me po-<u>DHRI</u>-as lʸe-BAR?*	**Yo te llevo.** *yo te LʸE-bo.*	**ESPAÑOL** ¿te quedas?
Tu pourrais me ramener? *tü pu-RE mə ram-NE?*	**Je te ramène.** *<u>zh</u>ə tə ra-MEN.*	**FRANÇAIS** tu restes?
Mi puoi accompagnare in macchina? *mi PUÔ-i ak-kom-pa-NʸA-re in MAK-ki-na?*	**Ti accompagno in macchina.** *ti ak-kom-PA-nʸo in MAK-ki-na.*	**ITALIANO** rimani?
Você pode me levar de carro? *vo-SE PO-<u>dzh</u>i mi le-VA<u>HH</u> <u>dzh</u>i KA-<u>hh</u>u?*	**Eu levo você de carro.** *eû LE-vu vo-SE <u>dzh</u>i KA-<u>hh</u>u.*	**PORTUGUÊS** pernoite?
Můžeš mě svézt? *MUU-<u>zh</u>esh miês-FEEST?*	**Svezu tě.** *SFE-zu tiê.*	**ČESKY** stráviš noc?

ENGLISH *bedtime*	**Are you tired?** *ar yu taîrd?*	**I'm tired.** *aîm taîrd.*	
DEUTSCH *träum süß!*	**Bist du müde?** *bist du MÜÜ-də?*	**Ich bin müde.** *i<u>sh</u> bin MÜÜ-də.*	
ESPAÑOL *¡a dormir!*	**¿Estás cansado?** *es-TAS kan-SA-<u>dho</u>?*	**Estoy cansado.** *es-TOÎ kan-SA-<u>dho</u>.*	
FRANÇAIS *au dodo*	**Tu es fatigué?** *tü e fa-ti-GE?*	**Je suis fatigué.** *<u>zh</u>ə süî fa-ti-GE.*	
ITALIANO *far la nanna*	**Sei stanco?** *seî STAN-ko?*	**Sono stanco.** *SO-no STAN-ko.*	
PORTUGUÊS *a dormir*	**Você está cansado?** *vo-SE is-TA kaⁿ-SA-du?*	**Eu estou cansado.** *eû is-TOÛ kaⁿ-SA-du.*	
ČESKY *hezké sny*	**Jsi unavený?** *si U-na-ve-nii?*	**Jsem unavený.** *sem U-na-ve-nii.*	

Let's go to sleep. *lets goû tu sliip.*	**Sweet dreams!** *swiit driimz!*	**ENGLISH**	bedtime
Laß uns schlafen gehen. *las uns <u>SH</u>LAA-fən GEÎ-ən.*	**Träum süß!** *troîm züüs!*	**DEUTSCH**	träum süß!
Vamos a dormir. *BA-mos a <u>dh</u>or-MIR.*	**¡Que sueñes con los angelitos!** *ke SUÊ-nʸes kon los an-<u>hh</u>e-LI-tos!*	**ESPAÑOL**	¡a dormir!
Allez, au dodo. *a-LE, o do-DO.*	**Fais de beaux rêves!** *fed-bo rev!*	**FRANÇAIS**	au dodo
Andiamo a dormire. *an-DIÂ-mo a dor-MI-re.*	**Sogni d'oro!** *SO-nʸi DO-ro!*	**ITALIANO**	far la nanna
Vamos dormir. *VA-mus du<u>hh</u>-MI<u>HH</u>.*	**Durma bem!** *DU<u>HH</u>-mə beⁿ!*	**PORTUGUÊS**	a dormir
Pojd'me spát. *POÎ<u>DZH</u>-me spaat.*	**Hezké sny!** *HES-kee sni!*	**ČESKY**	hezké sny

ENGLISH *morning!*	**Did you sleep well?** *did yu sliip wel?*	**What's your name, again?** *wəts yœr neîm, ə-GEN?*
DEUTSCH *morgens*	**Hast du gut geschlafen?** *hast du guut gəsh-LAA-fən?*	**Kannst du mir nochmal sagen, wie du heißt?** *kanst du MI-ər NOHH-maal ZAA-gən, vii du haîst?*
ESPAÑOL *¡buenos días!*	**¿Dormiste bien?** *dor-MIS-te biên?*	**¿Perdona, cómo te llamabas?** *per-DO-na, KO-mo te lya-MA-bas?*
FRANÇAIS *bonjour!*	**Tu as bien dormi?** *tü a biên dor-MI?*	**Tu t'appelles comment, déjà?** *tü ta-PEL kə-MAN, de-ZHA?*
ITALIANO *buon giorno!*	**Hai dormito bene?** *aî dor-MI-to BE-ne?*	**Scusa, come ti chiami?** *SKU-za, KO-me ti KIÂ-mi?*
PORTUGUÊS *bom dia!*	**Você durmiu bem?** *vo-SE duhh-MIÚ beⁿ?*	**Qual é o seu nome, mesmo?** *kuâl e u seû NO-mi, MEZ-mu?*
ČESKY *dobré ráno!*	**Vyspal jsi se dobře?** *VI-spal si se DOB-zhe?*	**Jakže se to jmenuješ?** *YAK-zhe se to i-ME-nu-yesh?*

Let's get breakfast. *lets get BREK-fest.*	**Want to spend the day together?** *want tu spend dhə deî tu-GE-dhœr?* ☞ SEE YOU SOON, P. 86	**ENGLISH** morning!
Laß uns frühstücken. *las uns FRÜÜSH-tü-kən.*	**Wollen wir heute zusammenbleiben?** *VO-lən VI-ər HOÎ-tə tsu-ZA-mən-blaî-bən?* ☞ BIS BALD! S. 86	**DEUTSCH** morgens
Vamos a desayunar. *BA-mos a dhe-sa-yu-NAR.*	**¿Te gustaría pasar el día conmigo?** *te gus-ta-RI-a pa-SAR el DI-a kon-MI-go?* ☞ ¡NOS VEMOS! PÁG. 86	**ESPAÑOL** ¡buenos días!
On va prendre le petit déjeuner. *oⁿ va PRAⁿ-drə ləp-TI de-zhœ-NE.*	**Tu veux passer la journée avec moi?** *tü vœ pa-SE la zhur-NE a-VEK muâ?* ☞ À BIENTÔT! P. 86	**FRANÇAIS** bonjour!
Facciamo colazione. *fat-TSHA-mo ko-la-TSIÔ-ne.*	**Vuoi passare la giornata insieme a me?** *VUÔ-i pas-SA-re la dzhor-NA-ta in-SIÊ-me a me?* ☞ A PRESTO! P. 86	**ITALIANO** buon giorno!
Vamos tomar o café da manhã. *VA-mus to-MAR u kə-FE də mə-NYAⁿ.*	**Gostaria de passar o dia comigo?** *gos-tə-RI-ə dzhi pə-SAR u DZHI-ə ko-MI-gu?* ☞ ATÉ MAIS! PÁG. 86	**PORTUGUÊS** bom dia!
Pojd'me se nasnídat. *POÎDZH-me se na-SNII-dat.*	**Chceš strávit den společně?** *hhə-TSESH STRAA-vit den SPO-letsh-niê?* ☞ UVIDÍME SE! STR. 86	**ČESKY** dobré ráno!

ENGLISH at the baths	**Can I come in?** *ken aî kəm in?*	**My friend, too?** *maî frend, tu?*
DEUTSCH in der sauna	**Kann ich reinkommen?** *kan ish RAÎN-ko-mən?*	**Mein Freund auch?** *maîn froînt aûhh?*
ESPAÑOL en la sauna	**¿Puedo entrar?** *PUÊ-dho en-TRAR?*	**¿Mi amigo también?** *mi a-MI-go tam-BIÊN?*
FRANÇAIS au sauna	**Je peux entrer?** *zhə pœ aⁿ-TRE?*	**Mon ami aussi?** *mon a-MI o-SI?*
ITALIANO in sauna	**Si può?** *si puô?*	**Anche il mio amico?** *AN-ke il MI-o a-MI-ko?*
PORTUGUÊS na sauna	**Eu posso entrar?** *eû PO-su eⁿ-TRAHH?*	**O meu amigo também?** *u meû ə-MI-gu taⁿ-BEᴺ?*
ČESKY v sauně	**Můžu dovnitř?** *MUU-zhu DOV-ni-tərsh?*	**I s přítelem?** *is PSHII-te-lem?*

Where are the condoms? *WE-œr ar <u>dh</u>ə KAN-dəmz?*	**At the [entrance / bar].** *et <u>dh</u>i [EN-trens / bar].*

ENGLISH — at the baths

Wo sind die Kondome? *voo zint di kon-DOO-mə?*	**[Am Eingang / An der Bar].** *[am AÎN-gan^g / an der bar].*

DEUTSCH — in der sauna

¿Dónde están los condones? *DON-de es-TAN los kon-DO-nes?*	**En [la entrada / el bar].** *en [la en-TRA-<u>dh</u>a / el bar].*

ESPAÑOL — en la sauna

Où sont les capotes? *u soⁿ le ka-PƏT?*	**[À l'entrée / Au bar].** *[a laⁿ-TRE / o bar].*

FRANÇAIS — au sauna

Dove hanno i preservativi? *DO-ve AN-no i pre-zer-va-TI-vi?*	**[All'ingresso / Al bar].** *[al-lin-GRES-so / al bar].*

ITALIANO — in sauna

Onde estão as camisinhas? *O^N-<u>dzh</u>i is-TAÛ^N əs kə-mi-ZI-n^yəs?*	**[Na entrada / No bar].** *[nə eⁿ-TRA-də / nu ba<u>hh</u>].*

PORTUGUÊS — na sauna

Kde jsou kondomy? *gə-DE i-SOÛ KON-do-my?*	**[U vchodu / U baru].** *[uv-<u>HH</u>O-du / u BA-ru].*

ČESKY — v sauně

ENGLISH — at the baths

[Wait just a minute / I'll be right back].

[weît dzhəst ə MI-nit / aîl bi raît bek].

Want to go to the [steam room / dry sauna]?

want tu goû tu dhə [stiim rum / draî SOO-nə]?

DEUTSCH — in der sauna

[Warte einen Moment / Ich komme gleich zurück].

[VAR-tə AÎ-nən mo-MENT / ish KO-mə glaîsh tsu-RÜK].

Kommst du mit in die [Dampfsauna / Trocken-sauna]?

komst du mit in di [DAMPF-zaû-na / TRO-kən-zaû-na]?

ESPAÑOL — en la sauna

[Espera un minuto / Vuelvo enseguida].

[es-PE-ra un mi-NU-to / BUÊL-bo en-se-GI-dha].

¿Vamos [al baño turco / a la sauna finlandesa]?

BA-mos [al BA-nyo TUR-ko / a la SAÛ-na fin-lan-DE-sa]?

FRANÇAIS — au sauna

[Attends un peu / J'arrive].

[a-TAN en pœ / zha-RIV].

On va dans le [hammam / sauna]?

on va dan lə [a-MAM / so-NA]?

ITALIANO — in sauna

[Aspetta un attimo / Torno subito].

[as-PET-ta un AT-ti-mo / TOR-no SU-bi-to].

Andiamo [nel bagno turco / nella sauna]?

an-DIÂ-mo [nel BA-nyo TUR-ko / NEL-la SAÛ-na]?

PORTUGUÊS — na sauna

[Espere um momento / Já volto].

[is-PE-ri un mo-MEN-tu / zha VOL-tu].

Vamos [ao vapor / à sauna sêca]?

VA-mus [aû və-POHH / a SAÛ-nə SE-kə]?

ČESKY — v sauně

[Počkej minutku / Hned jsem zpátky].

[POTSH-keî MI-nut-ku / hnet sem SPAAT-ki].

Chceš jít do [páry / sauny]?

hhə-TSESH yiit do [PAA-ri / SAÛ-ni]?

Want to go to the [jacuzzi / bar]? *want tu goû tu <u>dhə</u> [<u>dzh</u>ə-KU-zi / bar]?*	**Let's go to [my / your / a] room.** *lets goû tu [maî / yœr / ə] rum.*	**ENGLISH** at the baths
Kommst du mit [in den Whirlpool / an die Bar]? *komst du mit [in deen VƏR-əl-puul / an di bar]?*	**Gehen wir in [meine / deine / eine] Kabine.** *GEÎ-ən VI-ər in [MAÎ-nə / DAÎ-nə / AÎ-nə] ka-BII-nə.*	**DEUTSCH** in der sauna
¿Vamos al [jacuzzi / bar]? *BA-mos al [<u>hh</u>a-KU-<u>thi</u> / bar]?*	**Vamos a [mi / tu / una] cabina.** *BA-mos a [mi / tu / U-na] ka-BI-na.*	**ESPAÑOL** en la sauna
On va [dans le jacuzzi / au bar]? *oⁿ va [daⁿ lə <u>zh</u>a-kü-ZI / o bar]?*	**On va dans [ma / ta / une] cabine?** *oⁿ va daⁿ [ma / ta / ün] ka-BIN?*	**FRANÇAIS** au sauna
Andiamo [all'idromassaggio / al bar]? *an-DIÀ-mo [al-li-dro-mas-SAD-<u>dzh</u>o / al bar]?*	**Andiamo [nella mia / nella tua / in una] cabina.** *an-DIÀ-mo [NEL-la MI-a / NEL-la TU-a / in U-na] ka-BI-na.*	**ITALIANO** in sauna
Vamos ao [jacuzzi / bar]? *VA-mus aû [<u>zh</u>a-KU-zi / ba<u>hh</u>]?*	**Vamos [no meu / no teu / num] quarto.** *VA-mus [nu meû / nu teû / nuⁿ] KUÀ<u>HH</u>-tu.*	**PORTUGUÊS** na sauna
Chceš jít do [vířivého bazénu / baru]? *<u>hh</u>ə-TSESH yiit do [VIIR-<u>zh</u>i-vee-ho ba-ZEE-nu / BA-ru]?*	**Pojď'me [do mé / do té / do] kabinky.** *POÎ<u>DZH</u>-me [do mee / do tee / do] KA-bin-ki.*	**ČESKY** v sauně

ENGLISH — compliments

I like [you / you guys] (a lot).
aî laîk [yu / yu gaîz] (ə lat).

You're so intelligent.
yœr soû in-TE-li-dzhent.

DEUTSCH — komplimente

Ich mag [dich / euch] (sehr).
ish maak [dish / oîhh] (ZE-ər).

Du bist sehr intelligent.
du bist ZE-ər in-te-li-GENT.

ESPAÑOL — cumplidos

Me [gustas / gustáis] (mucho).
me [GUS-tas / gus-TAÎS] (MU-tsho).

Eres muy inteligente.
E-res muî in-te-li-HHEN-te.

FRANÇAIS — compliments

[Tu me plais / Vous me plaisez] (beaucoup).
[tüm ple / vum ple-ZE] (bo-KU).

Tu es très intelligent.
tü e trez eⁿ-te-li-zhaⁿ.

ITALIANO — complimenti

Mi [piaci / piacete] (molto).
mi [PIÂ-tshi / piâ-TSHE-te] (MOL-to).

Sei molto intelligente.
seî MOL-to in-tel-li-DZHEN-te.

PORTUGUÊS — elogios

Eu gosto de [você / vocês] (a beça).
eû GOS-tu dzhi [vo-SE / vo-SES] (ə BE-sə).

Você é muito inteligente.
vo-SE e MUÎⁿ-tu iⁿ-te-li-ZHEⁿ-tshi.

ČESKY — lichotky

Mám [tě / vás] (moc) rád.
maam [tiê / vaas] (mots) raat.

Jsi tak inteligentní.
si tak IN-te-li-gent-nii.

I love your [mind / style].
aî ləv yœr [maînd / staîl].

You're so classy.
yœr soû KLEE-si.

ENGLISH compliments

Ich mag [wie du denkst / deine Art].
ish maak [vii du denkst / DAÎ-nə art].

Du hast wirklich Klasse.
du hast VI-ər-kli̱sh KLA-sə.

DEUTSCH komplimente

Me encanta tu forma de [pensar / ser].
me en-KAN-ta tu FOR-ma dhe [pen-SAR / ser].

Tienes mucha clase.
TIÊ-nes MU-tsha KLA-se.

ESPAÑOL cumplidos

J'aime [ce que tu as dans la tête / ton genre].
zhem [skə tü a dan la tet / ton ZHAN-rə].

Tu as beaucoup de classe.
tü a bo-KUD klas.

FRANÇAIS compliments

Mi piace molto il tuo modo di [pensare / essere].
mi PIÂ-tshe MOL-to il TU-o MO-do di [pen-SA-re / ES-se-re].

Hai molta classe.
aî MOL-ta KLAS-se.

ITALIANO complimenti

Eu adoro [sua inteligência / seu jeito].
eû ə-DO-ru [SU-ə in-te-li-ZHEN-siâ / seû ZHEÎ-tu].

Você é muito refinado.
vo-SE e MUÎN-tu hhe-fi-NA-du.

PORTUGUÊS elogios

Moc se mi líbí [tvé myšlení / tvůj styl].
mots se mi LII-bii [tvee MISH-le-nii / TVUU-i stil].

Jsi prostě třída.
si PROS-tiê TRZHII-da.

ČESKY lichotky

ENGLISH — compliments

You're (very) [sweet / nice].
yœr (VE-ri) [swiit / naîs].

You're so much fun.
yœr soû mətsh fən.

DEUTSCH — komplimente

Du bist (sehr) [süß / nett].
du bist (ZE-ər) [züüs / net].

Mit dir macht es sehr viel Spaß.
mit DI-ər mahht es ZE-ər FI-əl shpas.

ESPAÑOL — cumplidos

Eres (muy) [dulce / simpático].
E-res (muî) [DHUL-the / sim-PA-ti-ko].

Eres muy divertido.
E-res muî dhi-ber-TI-dho.

FRANÇAIS — compliments

Tu es (très) [gentil / sympa].
tü e (tre) [zhaⁿ-TI / seⁿ-PA].

On délire bien avec toi.
oⁿ de-LIR biêⁿ a-VEK tuâ.

ITALIANO — complimenti

Sei (molto) [dolce / simpatico].
seî (MOL-to) [DOL-tshe / sim-PA-ti-ko].

Sei molto divertente.
seî MOL-to di-ver-TEN-te.

PORTUGUÊS — elogios

Você é (muito) [gentil / simpático].
vo-SE e (MUÎⁿ-tu) [zheⁿ-TSHIÛ / siⁿ-PA-tshi-ku].

Você é muito divertido.
vo-SE e MUÎⁿ-tu dzhi-vehh-TSHI-du.

ČESKY — lichotky

Jsi (velmi) [sladký / sympatický].
si (VEL-mi) [SLAT-kii / SIM-pa-tit-skii].

Je s tebou taková legrace.
yes TE-boû TA-ko-vaa LE-gra-tse.

You're (very) funny. *yœr (VE-ri) FƏ-ni.*	**You have a great [sense of humor / smile].** *yu hev ə greît [sens əv HIÛ-mœr / smaîl].*	**ENGLISH** compliments
Du bist (sehr) lustig. *du bist (ZE-ər) LUS-ti<u>sh</u>.*	**Du hast [einen tollen Sinn für Humor / ein tolles Lächeln].** *du hast [AÎ-nən TO-lən zin für hu-MOR / aîn TO-ləs LE-<u>sh</u>əln].*	**DEUTSCH** komplimente
Eres (muy) gracioso. *E-res (muî) gra-<u>THI</u>Ô-so.*	**Tienes [un gran sentido del humor / una sonrisa fantástica].** *TIÊ-nes [un gran sen-TI-<u>dho</u> <u>dh</u>el u-MOR / U-na son-<u>RRI</u>-sa fan-TAS-ti-ka].*	**ESPAÑOL** cumplidos
Tu es (très) marrant. *tü e (tre) ma-RA^N.*	**Tu as un super [sens de l'humour / sourire].** *tü a e^n sü-PER [sa^ns də lü-MUR / su-RIR].*	**FRANÇAIS** compliments
Sei (molto) spiritoso. *seî (MOL-to) spi-ri-TO-zo.*	**Hai un [senso dell'umorismo / sorriso] fantastico.** *aî un [SEN-so del-lu-mo-RIZ-mo / so-<u>RRI</u>-zo] fan-TAS-ti-ko.*	**ITALIANO** complimenti
Você é (muito) engraçado. *vo-SE e (MUÎ^N-tu) e^n-grə-SA-du.*	**Você tem um [senso de humor / sorriso] fantástico.** *vo-SE te^n u^n [SE^N-su <u>dzhi</u> u-MO<u>HH</u> / so-<u>HH</u>I-zu] fa^n-TAS-ti-ku.*	**PORTUGUÊS** elogios
Jsi (velmi) zábavný. *si (VEL-mi) ZAA-bav-nii.*	**Máš [výborný smysl pro humor / krásný úsměv].** *maa<u>sh</u> [VII-bor-nii SMI-səl pro HU-mor / KRAAS-nii UUS-miêf].*	**ČESKY** lichotky

ENGLISH — compliments

You're so [manly / feminine].
yœr soû [MEEN-li / FE-mi-nin].

You're so goodlooking.
yœr soû gud-LU-king.

DEUTSCH — komplimente

Du bist sehr [männlich / weiblich].
du bist ZE-ər [MEN-lish / VAÎP-lish].

Du siehst sehr gut aus.
du ziist ZE-ər guut aûs.

ESPAÑOL — cumplidos

Eres muy [hombre / femenino].
E-res muî [OM-bre / fe-me-NI-no].

Eres muy guapo.
E-res muî GUÂ-po.

FRANÇAIS — compliments

Tu es très [viril / féminin].
tü e tre [vi-RIL / fe-mi-NEⁿ].

Tu es très beau, toi.
tü e tre bo, tuâ.

ITALIANO — complimenti

Sei molto [virile / femminile].
seî MOL-to [vi-RI-le / fem-mi-NI-le].

Come sei bello.
KO-me seî BEL-lo.

PORTUGUÊS — elogios

Você é muito [masculino / feminino].
vo-SE e MUÎⁿ-tu [məs-ku-LI-nu / fe-mi-NI-nu].

Você é muito bonito.
vo-SE e MUÎⁿ-tu bu-NI-tu.

ČESKY — lichotky

Jsi tak [mužný / zženštilý].
si tak [MUZH-nii / z-ZHENSH-ti-lii].

Jsi tak hezký.
si tak HES-kii.

You're (very) cute.
yœr (VE-ri) kiût.

You're very attractive.
yœr VE-ri ə-TREK-tiv.

ENGLISH compliments

Du bist (sehr) süß.
du bist (ZE-ər) züüs.

Du bist sehr attraktiv.
du bist ZE-ər a-trak-TIIF.

DEUTSCH komplimente

Eres (muy) mono.
E-res (muî) MO-no.

Eres muy atractivo.
E-res muî a-trak-TI-bo.

ESPAÑOL cumplidos

Tu es (très) mignon.
tü e (tre) mi-NᵞOᴺ.

Tu es très séduisant.
tü e tre se-düî-ZAᴺ.

FRANÇAIS compliments

Sei (molto) carino.
seî (MOL-to) ka-RI-no.

Sei molto attraente.
seî MOL-to at-tra-EN-te.

ITALIANO complimenti

Você é (muito) bonitinho.
vo-SE e (MUÎᴺ-tu) bo-ni-<u>TSHI</u>-nᵞu.

Você é bastante atraente.
vo-SE e bəs-TAᴺ-<u>tshi</u> ə-trə-Eᴺ-<u>tshi</u>.

PORTUGUÊS elogios

Jsi (tak) pěkný.
si (tak) PIÊK-nii.

Jsi tak atraktivní.
si tak A-trak-tiv-nii.

ČESKY lichotky

ENGLISH compliments	You're so sexy. *yœr soû SEK-si.*	You're so hot. *yœr soû haat.*
DEUTSCH komplimente	Du bist sehr sexy. *du bist ZE-ər SEK-si.*	Du bist sehr geil. *du bist ZE-ər gaîl.*
ESPAÑOL cumplidos	Eres muy sexy. *E-res muî SEK-si.*	Estás buenísimo. *es-TAS buê-NI-si-mo.*
FRANÇAIS compliments	Tu es très sexy. *tü e tre sek-SI.*	Tu me branches, toi. *tüm braⁿsh, tuâ.*
ITALIANO complimenti	Sei molto sexy. *seî MOL-to SEK-si.*	Come sei bono! *KO-me seî BO-no!*
PORTUGUÊS elogios	Você é muito sexi. *vo-SE e MUÎⁿ-tu SEK-si.*	Você é muito gostoso. *vo-SE e MUÎⁿ-tu gos-TO-zu.*
ČESKY lichotky	Jsi tak sexy. *si tak SEK-si.*	Jsi tak vzrušující. *si tak vəz-RU-shu-yii-tsii.*

You've got such a great body!
yuv gat sətsh ə greît BA-di!

What [a body / muscles]!
wət [ə BA-di / MƏ-səlz]!

ENGLISH compliments

Du hast so einen tollen Körper!
du hast zoo AÎ-nən TO-lən KŒR-pər!

Du hast [einen tollen Körper / tolle Muskeln]!
du hast [AÎ-nən TO-lən KŒR-pər / TO-lə MUS-kəln]!

DEUTSCH komplimente

¡Qué cuerpazo tienes!
ke kuêr-PA-tho TIÉ-nes!

¡Qué [cuerpo / músculos]!
ke [KUÊR-po / MUS-ku-los]!

ESPAÑOL cumplidos

Tu es bien foutu, toi!
tü e biên fu-TÜ, tuâ!

[Quel corps / Quels muscles]!
[kel kər / kel MÜS-klə]!

FRANÇAIS compliments

Com'è bello il tuo corpo!
ko-ME BEL-lo il TU-o KOR-po!

Che [corpo / muscoli]!
ke [KOR-po / MUS-ko-li]!

ITALIANO complimenti

Você tem um corpão!
vo-SE teⁿ uⁿ kuhh-PAÛᴺ!

Que [corpo / músculos]!
ki [KOHH-pu / MUS-ku-lus]!

PORTUGUÊS elogios

Máš skvělé tělo!
maash skə-VIÊ-lee TIÊ-lo!

To [je tělo / jsou svaly]!
to [ye TIÊ-lo / i-SOÛ SFA-li]!

ČESKY lichotky

ENGLISH compliments	**What [arms / pecs]!** *wət [armz / peks]!*	**I like your [eyes / lips / legs].** *aî laîk yœr [aîz / lips / legz].*
DEUTSCH komplimente	**Du hast [tolle Arme / eine tolle Brust]!** *du hast [TO-lə AR-mə / AÎ-nə TO-lə brust]!*	**Ich mag deine [Augen / Lippen / Beine].** *ish maak DAÎ-nə [AÛ-gən / LI-pən / BAÎ-nə].*
ESPAÑOL cumplidos	**¡Qué [brazos / pecho]!** *ke [BRA-thos / PE-tsho]!*	**Me gustan tus [ojos / labios / piernas].** *me GUS-tan tus [O-hhos / LA-biôs / PIÊR-nas].*
FRANÇAIS compliments	**Quels [bras / pecs]!** *kel [bra / pek]!*	**J'aime [tes yeux / tes lèvres / tes jambes].** *zhem [tez yœ / te LE-vrə / te zhaⁿb].*
ITALIANO complimenti	**Che [braccia / pettorali]!** *ke [BRAT-tsha / pet-to-RA-li]!*	**Mi piacciono [i tuoi occhi / le tue labbra / le tue gambe].** *mi PIÂT-tsho-no [i TUÒ-i OK-ki / le TU-e LAB-bra / le TU-e GAM-be].*
PORTUGUÊS elogios	**Que [braços / peito]!** *ki [BRA-sus / PEÎ-tu]!*	**Eu gosto [dos seus olhos / dos seus lábios / das suas pernas].** *eû GOS-tu [dus seûs O-lʸus / dus seûs LA-biûs / dəs SU-əs PEHH-nəs].*
ČESKY lichotky	**To jsou [ruce / prsní svaly]!** *to i-SOÛ [RU-tse / PƏRS-nii SFA-li]!*	**Líbí se mi tvé [oči / rty / nohy].** *LII-bii se mit-VEE [O-tshi / ər-TI / NO-hi].*

I love your [face / hair / ass].
aî ləv yœr [feîs / heer / ees].

You have such a big cock!
yu hev sətsh ə big kak!

ENGLISH compliments

Ich liebe [dein Gesicht / deine Haare / deinen Arsch].
ish LII-bə [daîn gə-ZISHT / DAÎ-nə HAA-rə / DAÎ-nən arsh].

Du hast einen sehr großen Schwanz!
du hast AÎ-nən ZE-ər GROO-sən shvants!

DEUTSCH komplimente

Me encanta tu [cara / pelo / culo].
me en-KAN-ta tu [KA-ra / PE-lo / KU-lo].

¡Qué polla más grande tienes!
ke PO-lʸa mas GRAN-de TIÊ-nes!

ESPAÑOL cumplidos

J'adore [ta gueule / tes cheveux / ton cul].
zha-DƏR [ta gœl / tesh-VŒ / tonꞌ kü].

Qu'est-ce qu'elle est grosse, ta bite!
kes kel e gros, ta bit!

FRANÇAIS compliments

Adoro [il tuo viso / i tuoi capelli / il tuo culo].
a-DO-ro [il TU-o VI-zo / i TUÔ-i ka-PEL-li / il TU-o KU-lo].

Mamma, che cazzo!
MAM-ma, ke KAT-tso!

ITALIANO complimenti

Eu adoro [a tua cara / o teu cabelo / a tua bunda].
eû ə-DO-ru [ə TU-ə KA-rə / o teû kə-BE-lu / ə TU-ə BUᴺ-də].

Você tem um pau muito grande!
vo-SE teⁿ uⁿ paû MUÎᴺ-tu GRAᴺ-dzhi!

PORTUGUÊS elogios

Zbožňuji [tvůj obličej / tvé vlasy / tvůj zadek].
z-BOZH-nʸu-yi [TVUU-i O-bli-tsheî / tvee VLA-si / TVUU-i ZA-dek].

Máš pěkně velkýho čuráka!
maash PIÊK-niê VEL-kii-ho TSHU-raa-ka!

ČESKY lichotky

ENGLISH
compliments

I really like your (hairy) chest.
aî RI-ə-li laîk yœr (HEE-ri) tshest.

Do you like my tool?
du yu laîk maî tuul?

DEUTSCH
komplimente

Ich mag sehr deine (behaarte) Brust.
ish maak ZE-ər DAÎ-nə (bə-HAAR-tə) brust.

Magst du meinen Willi?
makst du MAÎ-nən VI-li?

ESPAÑOL
cumplidos

Me encanta tu pecho (peludo).
me en-KAN-ta tu PE-tsho (pe-LU-dho).

¿Te gusta mi verga?
te GUS-ta mi BER-ga?

FRANÇAIS
compliments

J'aime beaucoup ton torse (poilu).
zhem bo-KU tonⁿ tərs (puâ-LÜ).

Tu aimes ma verge?
tü em ma verzh?

ITALIANO
complimenti

Mi piace molto il tuo petto (peloso).
mi PIÂ-tshe MOL-to il TU-o PET-to (pe-LO-zo).

Ti piace il mio pistolino?
ti PIÂ-tshe il MI-o pis-to-LI-no?

PORTUGUÊS
elogios

Eu gosto muito do seu peito (peludo).
eû GOS-tu MUÎⁿ-tu du seû PEÎ-tu (pe-LU-du).

Você gosta da minha pica?
vo-SE GOS-tə də MI-nʸə PI-kə?

ČESKY
lichotky

Tvoje (chlupatá) hrud' se mi moc líbí.
TVO-ye (HHLU-pa-taa) hrutsh se mi mots LII-bii.

Líbí se ti moje péro?
LII-bii se ti MO-ye PEE-ro?

You're [wild in bed / a great fuck]. *yœr [waîld in bed / ə greît fək].*	**(Thanks,) you too.** *(thenks,) yu tu.*	**ENGLISH** compliments
[Du bist super im Bett / Es ist toll mit dir zu ficken]. *[du bist SU-pər im bet / es ist tol mit DI-ər tsu FI-kən].*	**(Danke,) du auch.** *(DAN-kə,) du aûhh.*	**DEUTSCH** komplimente
[Eres fabuloso en la cama / Follas bien]. *[E-res fa-bu-LO-so en la KA-ma / FO-lʸas biên].*	**(Gracias,) tú también.** *(GRA-thiâs,) tu tam-BIÊN.*	**ESPAÑOL** cumplidos
Tu [es un bon coup / baises bien]. *tü [ez eⁿ boⁿ ku / bez biêⁿ].*	**(Merci,) toi aussi.** *(mer-SI,) tuâ o-SI.*	**FRANÇAIS** compliments
Sei [grande a letto / una bella scopata]. *seî [GRAN-de a LET-to / U-na BEL-la sko-PA-ta].*	**(Grazie,) anche te.** *(GRA-tsiê,) AN-ke te.*	**ITALIANO** complimenti
Você é [muito bom de cama / uma boa foda]. *vo-SE e [MUÎⁿ-tu boⁿ dzhi KA-mə / U-mə boâ FO-də].*	**(Obrigado,) você também.** *(o-bri-GA-du,) vo-SE taⁿ-BEⁿ.*	**PORTUGUÊS** elogios
Jsi [dobrej v posteli / dobrý mrdák]. *si [DO-breî POS-te-li / DO-brii MƏR-daak].*	**(Díky,) ty taky.** *(DII-ki,) ti TA-ki.*	**ČESKY** lichotky

ENGLISH	I love you	**I love you (so much).** aî ləv yu (soû mətsh).	**(I think) I'm in love with you.** (aî think) aîm in ləv widh yu.
DEUTSCH	ich liebe dich	**Ich liebe dich (sehr).** ish LII-bə dish (ZE-ər).	**(Ich glaube,) ich bin in dich verliebt.** (ish GLAÛ-bə,) ish bin in dish fer-LIIPT.
ESPAÑOL	amor	**Te quiero (tanto).** te KIÊ-ro (TAN-to).	**(Creo que) estoy enamorado de ti.** (KRE-o ke) es-TOÎ e-na-mo-RA-dho dhe ti.
FRANÇAIS	je t'aime	**Je t'aime (beaucoup).** zhə tem (bo-KU).	**(Je crois que) je suis amoureux de toi.** (zhə kruâ kə) zhə süîz a-mu-RŒD tuâ.
ITALIANO	amore	**Ti voglio (molto) bene.** ti VO-lʸo (MOL-to) BE-ne.	**(Mi sembra che) mi sono innamorato di te.** (mi SEM-bra ke) mi SO-no in-na-mo-RA-to di te.
PORTUGUÊS	te amo	**Eu te amo (muito).** eû tshi A-mu (MUIᴺ-tu).	**(Eu acho que) estou apaixonado por você.** (eû A-shu ki) is-TOÛ ə-paî-sho-NA-du puhh vo-SE.
ČESKY	miluji tě	**(Moc) tě miluji.** (mots) tiê MI-lu-yi.	**(Myslím, že) jsem do tebe zamilován.** (MIS-liim, zheî) sem do TE-be ZA-mi-lo-vaan.

I want you.
aî want yu.

I [need / adore] you.
aî [niid / ə-DO-œr] yu.

ENGLISH — i love you

Ich will dich.
ish vil dish.

Ich [brauche dich / mag dich sehr].
ish [BRAÛ-hhə dish / maak dish ZE-ər].

DEUTSCH — ich liebe dich

Te deseo.
te dhe-SE-o.

Te [necesito / adoro].
te [ne-the-SI-to / a-DHO-ro].

ESPAÑOL — amor

J'ai envie de toi.
zhe aⁿ-VID tuâ.

[J'ai besoin de toi / Je t'adore].
[zhe bə-ZUÊᴺ də tuâ / zhə ta-DƏR].

FRANÇAIS — je t'aime

Ti voglio.
ti VO-lʸo.

[Ho bisogno di te / Ti adoro].
[o bi-ZO-nʸo di te / ti a-DO-ro].

ITALIANO — amore

Eu quero você.
eû KE-ru vo-SE.

Eu [preciso de você / te adoro].
eû [pri-SI-zu dzhi vo-SE / tshi ə-DO-ru].

PORTUGUÊS — te amo

Chci tě.
hhə-TSI tiê.

[Potřebuji / Zbožňuji] tě.
[pot-RZHE-bu-yi / ZBOZH-nʸu-yi] tiê.

ČESKY — miluji tě

ENGLISH i love you	**I can't live without you.** *aî kent liv widh-AÛT yu.*	**You make me so happy.** *yu meîk mi soû HEE-pi.*
DEUTSCH ich liebe dich	**Ich kann ohne dich nicht leben.** *ish kan OO-nə dish nisht LEÎ-bən.*	**Du machst mich sehr glücklich.** *du mahhst mish ZE-ər GLÜK-lish.*
ESPAÑOL amor	**No puedo vivir sin ti.** *no PUÊ-dho bi-BIR sin ti.*	**Me haces muy feliz.** *me A-thes muî fe-LITH.*
FRANÇAIS je t'aime	**Je peux pas me passer de toi.** *zhə pœ pam pa-SED tuâ.*	**Tu me rends très heureux.** *tüm ran trez œ-RŒ.*
ITALIANO amore	**Non posso vivere senza te.** *non POS-so VI-ve-re SEN-dza te.*	**Tu mi rendi così felice.** *tu mi REN-di ko-ZI fe-LI-tshe.*
PORTUGUÊS te amo	**Eu não posso viver sem você.** *eû naûn PO-su vi-VEHH sen vo-SE.*	**Você me faz muito feliz.** *vo-SE mi faz MUÎN-tu fe-LIZ.*
ČESKY miluji tě	**Nemůžu bez tebe žít.** *NE-muu-zhu bes TE-be zhiit.*	**Děláš mě tak šťastným.** *DIÊ-laash miê tak SHTIÂST-niim.*

I'm crazy about you.
aîm KREÎ-zi ə-BAÛT yu.

Babe.
beîb.

ENGLISH — i love you

Ich bin verrückt nach dir.
ish bin fe-RÜKT nahh DI-ər.

Kleines.
KLAÎ-nəs.

DEUTSCH — ich liebe dich

Estoy loco por ti.
es-TOÎ LO-ko por ti.

[Nene / Papi *(LA)*].
[NE-ne / PA-pi].

ESPAÑOL — amor

Je suis fou de toi.
zhə süî fud tuâ.

Chéri.
she-RI.

FRANÇAIS — je t'aime

Sono pazzo di te.
SO-no PAT-tso di te.

Tesoro.
te-ZO-ro.

ITALIANO — amore

Eu sou louco por você.
eû soû LOÛ-ku puhh vo-SE.

Tesão.
te-ZAÛᴺ.

PORTUGUÊS — te amo

Jsem do tebe blázen.
sem do TE-be BLAA-zen.

Chlapečku.
HHLA-petsh-ku.

ČESKY — miluji tě

ENGLISH / i love you	**(My) baby.** *(maî) BEI-bi.*	**(My) honey.** *(maî) HƏ-ni.*
DEUTSCH / ich liebe dich	**(Mein) Kleiner.** *(maîn) KLAÎ-nər.*	**(Mein) Schatz.** *(maîn) <u>sh</u>ats.*
ESPAÑOL / amor	**(Mi) niño.** *(mi) NI-nʸo.*	**(Mi) cariño.** *(mi) ka-RI-nʸo.*
FRANÇAIS / je t'aime	**Mon bébé.** *monbe-BE.*	**Mon chou.** *mon<u>sh</u>u.*
ITALIANO / amore	**(Mio) bambino.** *(MI-o) bam-BI-no.*	**(Mia) dolcezza.** *(MI-a) dol-<u>TSHET</u>-tsa.*
PORTUGUÊS / te amo	**(Meu) gato.** *(meû) GA-tu.*	**Meu bem.** *meû ben.*
ČESKY / miluji tě	**(Můj) chlapečku.** *(MUU-i) <u>HHLA</u>-pet<u>sh</u>-ku.*	**(Mé) zlatíčko.** *(mee) ZLA-ti<u>tsh</u>-ko.*

(My) darling. *(maî) DAR-ling.*	**(My) love.** *(maî) ləv.*	**ENGLISH** i love you
(Mein) Liebling. *(maîn) LIIP-ling.*	**(Mein) Lieber.** *(maîn) LII-bər.*	**DEUTSCH** ich liebe dich
(Mi) querido. *(mi) ke-RI-<u>dh</u>o.*	**(Mi) amor.** *(mi) a-MOR.*	**ESPAÑOL** amor
Mon cher. *mon <u>sh</u>er.*	**Mon amour.** *mon a-MUR.*	**FRANÇAIS** je t'aime
(Mio) caro. *(MI-o) KA-ro.*	**Amore (mio).** *a-MO-re (MI-o).*	**ITALIANO** amore
Meu querido. *meû ke-RI-du.*	**Meu amor.** *meû ə-MO<u>HH</u>.*	**PORTUGUÊS** te amo
(Můj) drahý. *(MUU-i) DRA-hii.*	**(Moje) lásko.** *(MO-ye) LAAS-ko.*	**ČESKY** miluji tě

ENGLISH problems	What's wrong? *wəts ron?*	Is there a problem? *iz <u>DHE</u>-ær ə PRA-bləm?*
DEUTSCH probleme	Was ist los? *vas ist loos?*	Gibt es ein Problem? *gipt es aîn pro-BLEÎM?*
ESPAÑOL problemas	¿Qué pasa? *ke PA-sa?*	¿Hay algún problema? *aî al-GUN pro-BLE-ma?*
FRANÇAIS problèmes	Qu'est-ce qu'il y a? *kes ki i a?*	Il y a un problème? *i a eⁿ prə-BLEM?*
ITALIANO problemi	Cosa succede? *KO-za sut-<u>TSHE</u>-de?*	C'è qualche problema? *<u>tshe</u> KUÁL-ke pro-BLE-ma?*
PORTUGUÊS problemas	O que é que há? *u ki e ki a?*	Tem algum problema? *teⁿ aû-GUⁿ pro-BLE-mə?*
ČESKY problémy	Co se děje? *tso se DIÊ-ye?*	Něco není v pořádku? *NIÊ-tso NE-niif por-<u>ZHAAT</u>-ku?*

Please don't fall in love with me.
pliiz doûnt fol in ləv widh mi.

I don't like you anymore.
aî doûnt laîk yu e-ni-MO-œr.

ENGLISH problems

Bitte verlieb dich nicht in mich!
BI-tə fer-LIIP dish nisht in mish!

Ich mag dich nicht mehr.
ish maak dish nisht ME-ər.

DEUTSCH probleme

Por favor, no te enamores de mí.
por fa-BOR, no te e-na-MO-res de mi.

Ya no me gustas.
ya no me GUS-tas.

ESPAÑOL problemas

Je t'en prie, tombe pas amoureux de moi.
zhə tan pri, tonb pa a-mu-RŒD muâ.

Tu me plais plus.
tüm ple plü.

FRANÇAIS problèmes

Per favore, non innamorarti di me.
per fa-VO-re, non in-na-mo-RAR-ti di me.

Non mi piaci più.
non mi PIÂ-tshi più.

ITALIANO problemi

Por favor, não se apaixone por mim.
puhh fə-VOHH, naûn si ə-paî-SHO-ni puhh min.

Eu não gosto mais de você.
eû naûn GOS-tu maîs dzhi vo-SE.

PORTUGUÊS problemas

Prosím, nezamilovávej se do mne!
PRO-siim, NE-za-mi-lo-vaa-veî se dom-NE!

Už tě nemám rád.
ush tiê NE-maam raat.

ČESKY problémy

ENGLISH problems	I don't love you. *aî doûnt ləv yu.*	I like you (very much), but this isn't working. *aî laîk yu (VE-ri mətsh), bət dhis I-zənt WŒR-kinɡ.*
DEUTSCH probleme	Ich liebe dich nicht. *ish LII-bə dish nisht.*	Ich mag dich (sehr), aber es geht nicht. *ish maak dish (ZE-ər), A-bər es geît nisht.*
ESPAÑOL problemas	No te quiero. *no te KIÊ-ro.*	Me gustas (mucho), pero esto no funciona. *me GUS-tas (MU-tsho), PE-ro ES-to no fun-THIÔ-na.*
FRANÇAIS problèmes	Je t'aime pas. *zhə tem pa.*	Tu me plais (beaucoup), mais ça marche plus. *tüm ple (bo-KU), me sa marsh plü.*
ITALIANO problemi	Non ti voglio bene. *non ti VO-lʸo BE-ne.*	Mi piaci (molto), ma non funziona. *mi PIÂ-tshi (MOL-to), ma non fun-TSIÔ-na.*
PORTUGUÊS problemas	Eu não te amo. *eû naûⁿ tshi A-mu.*	Eu gosto (muito) de você, mas não está dando certo. *eû GOS-tu (MUÎⁿ-tu) dzhi vo-SE, məs naûⁿ is-TA DAⁿ-du SEHH-tu.*
ČESKY problémy	Nemiluji tě. *NE-mi-lu-yi tiê.*	Mám tě (moc) rád, ale nešlape nám to. *maam tiê (mots) raat, A-le NESH-la-pe naam to.*

I like you (a lot), but I don't love you.
aî laîk yu (ə lat), bət aî doûnt ləv yu.

He suspects about us.
hi səs-PEKTS ə-BAÛT əs.

ENGLISH problems

Ich mag dich (sehr), aber ich liebe dich nicht.
ish maak dish (ZE-ər), A-bər ish LII-bə dish nisht.

Er verdächtigt uns.
E-ər fer-DESH-tikt uns.

DEUTSCH probleme

Me gustas (mucho), pero no te quiero.
me GUS-tas (MU-tsho), PE-ro no te KIÊ-ro.

Él sospecha lo nuestro.
el sos-PE-tsha lo NUÊS-tro.

ESPAÑOL problemas

Tu me plais (beaucoup), mais je t'aime pas.
tüm ple (bo-KU), me zhə tem pa.

Il se doute de quelque chose.
il sə dut də KEL-kə shoz.

FRANÇAIS problèmes

Mi piaci (molto), ma non ti voglio bene.
mi PIÂ-tshi (MOL-to), ma non ti VO-lʲo BE-ne.

Lui sospetta di noi.
LU-i sos-PET-ta di noî.

ITALIANO problemi

Eu gosto (muito) de você, mas eu não te amo.
eû GOS-tu (MUÎⁿ-tu) dzhi vo-SE, məs eû naûⁿ tshi A-mu.

Ele suspeita de nós.
E-li sus-PEÎ-tə dzhi nos.

PORTUGUÊS problemas

Mám tě (moc) rád, ale nemiluji tě.
maam tiê (mots) raat, A-le NE-mi-lu-yi tiê.

On něco o nás tuší.
on NIÊ-tso o naas TU-shii.

ČESKY problémy

ENGLISH problems	**He found out about us.** *hi faûnd aût ə-BAÛT əs.*	**I can't leave him.** *aî kent liiv him.*
DEUTSCH probleme	**Er hat uns entdeckt.** *E-ər hat uns ENT-dekt.*	**Ich kann ihn nicht verlassen.** *ish kan iin nisht fer-LA-sən.*
ESPAÑOL problemas	**Él se enteró de lo nuestro.** *el se en-te-RO dhe lo NUÊS-tro.*	**No puedo dejarlo.** *no PUÊ-dho dhe-HHAR-lo.*
FRANÇAIS problèmes	**Il a tout découvert sur nous.** *il a tu de-ku-VER sür nu.*	**Je peux pas le quitter.** *zhə pœ pal ki-TE.*
ITALIANO problemi	**Lui ha scoperto di noi.** *LU-i a sko-PER-to di noî.*	**Non posso lasciarlo.** *non POS-so la-SHAR-lo.*
PORTUGUÊS problemas	**Ele descobriu sobre nós.** *E-li des-ku-BRI-u SO-bri nos.*	**Eu não posso deixá-lo.** *eû naûⁿ PO-su deî-SHA-lu.*
ČESKY problémy	**On o nás ví.** *on o naas vii.*	**Nemůžu ho opustit.** *NE-muu-zhu ho o-PUS-tit.*

You're cheating on me.
yœr <u>TSH</u>II-ting an mi.

You're using me.
yœr YU-zing mi.

Du betrügst mich.
du bə-TRÜKST mi<u>sh</u>.

Du benutzt mich.
du bə-NUTST mi<u>sh</u>.

Me estás poniendo los cuernos.
me es-TAS po-NIÊN-do los KUÊR-nos.

Me estás utilizando.
me es-TAS u-ti-li-<u>TH</u>AN-do.

Tu me trompes.
tüm troⁿp.

Tu profites de moi.
tü prə-FIT də muâ.

Mi stai tradendo.
mi staî tra-DEN-do.

Mi stai usando.
mi staî u-ZAN-do.

Você está me traindo.
vo-SE is-TA mi trə-I^N-du.

Você está me usando.
vo-SE is-TA mi u-ZA^N-du.

Podvádíš mě.
pod-VAA-dii<u>sh</u> miê.

Zneužíváš mě.
ZNE-u-<u>zh</u>ii-vaa<u>zh</u> miê.

ENGLISH problems

That's not true.
dhets nat tru.

Don't be mad at me.
doûnt bi med et mi.

DEUTSCH probleme

Das ist nicht wahr.
das ist nisht vaar.

Sei nicht böse auf mich!
zaî nisht BŒ-zə aûf mish!

ESPAÑOL problemas

No es verdad.
no es ber-DHADH.

No te enfades conmigo.
no te en-FA-dhes kön-MI-go.

FRANÇAIS problèmes

C'est pas vrai.
se pa vre.

Sois pas fâché.
suâ pa fa-SHE.

ITALIANO problemi

Non è vero.
non e VE-ro.

Non essere arrabbiato con me.
non ES-se-re a-rrab-BIÂ-to kon me.

PORTUGUÊS problemas

Isto não é verdade.
IS-tu naûⁿ e vehh-DA-dzhi.

Não fique bravo comigo.
naûⁿ FI-ki BRA-vu ko-MI-gu.

ČESKY problémy

To není pravda.
to NE-nii PRAV-da.

Nebuď na mne naštvaný!
NE-budzh nam-NE NASH-tva-nii!

Calm down. *kolm daûn.*	**I want us to stay friends.** *aî want əs tu steî frendz.*	**ENGLISH** problems
Beruhig dich! *bə-RU-<u>ish</u> di<u>sh</u>!*	**Ich möchte, daß wir Freunde bleiben.** *i<u>sh</u> M<u>ŒSH</u>-tə, das VI-ər FROÎN-də BLAÎ-bən.*	**DEUTSCH** probleme
Cálmate. *KAL-ma-te.*	**Quiero que seamos amigos.** *KIÊ-ro ke se-A-mos a-MI-gos.*	**ESPAÑOL** problemas
Calme-toi. *kalm-TUÂ.*	**On peut rester copains.** *oⁿ pœ rəs-TE kə-PEᴺ.*	**FRANÇAIS** problèmes
Calmati. *KAL-ma-ti.*	**Voglio che rimaniamo amici.** *VO-ˡʸo ke ri-ma-NIÂ-mo a-MI-<u>tshi</u>.*	**ITALIANO** problemi
Acalme-se. *ə-KAÛ-mi-si.*	**Eu quero que continuemos amigos.** *eû KE-ru ki koⁿ-<u>tshi</u>-NUÊ-mus ə-MI-gus.*	**PORTUGUÊS** problemas
Uklidni se! *u-KLID-ni se!*	**Chci, abychom zůstali přátelé.** *hhə-TSI, A-bi-hhom ZUUS-ta-li PSHAA-te-lee.*	**ČESKY** problémy

ENGLISH problems	**(I'm sorry, but) it's over.** *(aîm SA-ri, bət) its OÛ-vœr.*	**I don't want to see you again.** *aî doûnt want tu si yu ə-GEN.*
DEUTSCH probleme	**(Tut mir leid, aber) es ist vorbei.** *(tut MI-ər laît, A-bər) es ist for-BAÎ.*	**Ich will dich nicht wieder-sehen.** *ish vil dish nisht VII-dər-zeîn.*
ESPAÑOL problemas	**(Lo siento, pero) se acabó.** *(lo SIÊN-to, PE-ro) se a-ka-BO.*	**No quiero volverte a ver.** *no KIÊ-ro bol-BER-te a ber.*
FRANÇAIS problèmes	**(Désolé, mais) c'est fini.** *(de-zə-LE, me) se fi-NI.*	**Je veux plus te voir.** *zhə vœ plü tə vuâr.*
ITALIANO problemi	**(Mi dispiace, ma) è tutto finito.** *(mi dis-PIÂ-tshe, ma) e TUT-to fi-NI-to.*	**Non voglio vederti più.** *non VO-lyo ve-DER-ti più.*
PORTUGUÊS problemas	**(Sinto muito, mas) acabou tudo.** *(SIN-tu MUÎN-tu, məs) ə-kə-BOÛ TU-du.*	**Eu não quero ver você de novo.** *eû naûn KE-ru vehh vo-SE dzhi NO-vu.*
ČESKY problémy	**(Lituji, ale) to je konec.** *(LI-tu-yi, A-le) to ye KO-nets.*	**Už tě nechci znovu vidět.** *ush tiê NEHH-tsi ZNO-vu VI-diêt.*

I'm sorry I ever met you! *aîm SA-ri aî E-vœr met yu!*	**I hate you.** *aî heît yu.*	**ENGLISH** problems
Es tut mir leid, daß ich dich je getroffen habe! *es tut MI-ər laît, das ish dish yee gə-TRO-fən HAA-bə!*	**Ich hasse dich.** *ish HA-sə dish.*	**DEUTSCH** probleme
¡Ojalá nunca te hubiera conocido! *o-hha-LA NUN-ka te u-BIÊ-ra ko-no-THI-dho!*	**Te odio.** *te O-dhiô.*	**ESPAÑOL** problemas
J'aurais jamais dû te rencontrer! *zho-RE zha-ME dü tə ran-kon-TRE!*	**Je te déteste.** *zhə tə de-TEST.*	**FRANÇAIS** problèmes
Magari non ci fossimo mai incontrati! *ma-GA-ri non tshi FOS-si-mo maî in-kon-TRA-ti!*	**Ti odio.** *ti O-diô.*	**ITALIANO** problemi
Eu me arrependo de ter conhecido você! *eû mi a-hhe-PEⁿ-du dzhi tehh ko-nʸe-SI-du vo-SE!*	**Eu te odeio.** *eû tshi u-DE-yu.*	**PORTUGUÊS** problemas
Lituji, že jsem tě kdy poznal! *LI-tu-yi, zheî-SEM tiêg-DI POZ-nal!*	**Nenávidím tě.** *NE-naa-vi-diim tiê.*	**ČESKY** problémy

ENGLISH — problems

Damn you!
deem yu!

Go to hell!
goû tu hel!

DEUTSCH — probleme

Hol dich der Teufel!
hol di<u>sh</u> der TOÎ-fəl!

Geh zur Hölle!
geî tsur HŒ-lə!

ESPAÑOL — problemas

¡Vete a la mierda!
BE-te a la MIÊR-da!

¡Vete al infierno!
BE-te al in-FIÊR-no!

FRANÇAIS — problèmes

Salaud!
sa-LO!

Va te faire foutre!
vat fer FU-trə!

ITALIANO — problemi

Al diavolo!
al DIÂ-vo-lo!

Va all'inferno!
va al-lin-FER-no!

PORTUGUÊS — problemas

Desgraçado!
des-grə-SA-du!

Vai pro inferno!
vaî pro ⁱn-FE<u>HH</u>-nu!

ČESKY — problémy

Jdi k čertu!
i-DIK <u>TSHER</u>-tu!

Jdi do prdele!
i-DI do PƏR-de-le!

I'm sorry.
aîm SA-ri.

You were right.
yu wœr raît.

ENGLISH — making up

Es tut mir leid.
es tut MI-ər laît.

Du hattest recht.
du HA-təst resht.

DEUTSCH — versöhnung

Lo siento.
lo SIÉN-to.

Tú tenías la razón.
tu te-NI-as la rra-THON.

ESPAÑOL — perdonar

Je suis désolé.
zhə süî de-zə-LE.

C'est toi qui avais raison.
se tuâ ki a-VE re-ZO^N.

FRANÇAIS — faire la paix

Mi dispiace.
mi dis-PIÂ-tshe.

Tu avevi ragione.
tu a-VE-vi ra-DZHO-ne.

ITALIANO — far la pace

Desculpe.
dis-KUL-pi.

Você estava certo.
vo-SE is-TA-və SEHH-tu.

PORTUGUÊS — perdoar

Je mi líto.
ye mi LII-to.

Měl jsi pravdu.
miêl si PRAV-du.

ČESKY — usmíříme se

ENGLISH *making up*	**I was wrong.** *aî wəz ronᵍ.*	**I shouldn't have said that.** *aî SHU-dənt həv sed dhet.*
DEUTSCH *versöhnung*	**Ich hatte unrecht.** *ish HA-tə UN-resht.*	**Ich hätte das nicht sagen sollen.** *ish HE-tə das nisht ZAA-gən ZO-lən.*
ESPAÑOL *perdonar*	**Yo no tenía la razón.** *yo no te-NI-a la rra-THON.*	**No debería haberte dicho eso.** *no dhe-be-RI-a a-BER-te DHI-tsho E-so.*
FRANÇAIS *faire la paix*	**C'est moi qui ai eu tort.** *se muâ ki e œ tər.*	**J'aurais pas dû dire ça.** *zho-RE pa dü dir sa.*
ITALIANO *far la pace*	**Io avevo torto.** *Io a-VE-vo TOR-to.*	**Non avrei dovuto dirlo.** *non a-VREÎ do-VU-to DIR-lo.*
PORTUGUÊS *perdoar*	**Eu estava errado.** *eû is-TA-və e-HHA-du.*	**Eu não deveria ter dito isto.** *eû naûⁿ de-ve-RI-ə tehh DYI-tu IS-tu.*
ČESKY *usmiříme se*	**Já se mýlil.** *yaa se MII-lil.*	**Neměl jsem to říkat.** *NE-miêl sem tor-ZHII-kat.*

I didn't mean it. *aî DI-dənt miin it.*	**I lost control.** *aî last kən-TROÛL.*	**ENGLISH** making up
Ich habe das nicht so gemeint. *ish HAA-bə das nisht zoo gə-MAÎNT.*	**Ich habe die Kontrolle verloren.** *ish HAA-bə di kon-TRO-lə fer-LOO-rən.*	**DEUTSCH** versöhnung
Lo dije sin querer. *lo DHI-hhe sin ke-RER.*	**Perdí el control.** *per-DI el kon-TROL.*	**ESPAÑOL** perdonar
J'ai pas voulu dire ça. *zhe pa vu-LÜ dir sa.*	**J'étais pas moi-même.** *zhe-TE pa muâ-MEM.*	**FRANÇAIS** faire la paix
Non intendevo dirlo. *non in-ten-DE-vo DIR-lo.*	**Ho perso il controllo.** *o PER-so il kon-TROL-lo.*	**ITALIANO** far la pace
Eu não quis dizer isto. *eû naûn kiz dzhi-ZER IS-tu.*	**Eu perdi o controle.** *eû pehh-DZHI u kon-TRO-li.*	**PORTUGUÊS** perdoar
Nemyslel jsem to vážně. *NE-mis-lel sem to VAAZH-niê.*	**Nekontroloval jsem se.** *NE-kon-tro-lo-val sem se.*	**ČESKY** usmíříme se

ENGLISH making up	**Can you forgive me?** *ken yu fœr-GIV mi?*	**I forgive you.** *aî fœr-GIV yu.*
DEUTSCH versöhnung	**Kannst du mir verzeihen?** *kanst du MI-ər fer-TSAÎ-ən?*	**Ich verzeih dir.** *<u>ish</u> fer-TSAÎ DI-ər.*
ESPAÑOL perdonar	**¿Me perdonas?** *me per-DO-nas?*	**Te perdono.** *te per-DO-no.*
FRANÇAIS faire la paix	**Tu me pardonnes?** *tüm par-DƏN?*	**Je te pardonne.** *<u>zh</u>ət par-DƏN.*
ITALIANO far la pace	**Puoi perdonarmi?** *PUÔ-i per-do-NAR-mi?*	**Ti perdono.** *ti per-DO-no.*
PORTUGUÊS perdoar	**Você pode me perdoar?** *vo-SE PO-<u>dzh</u>i mi pehh-DUÂ<u>HH</u>?*	**Eu te perdôo.** *eû <u>tsh</u>i pehh-DO-u.*
ČESKY usmíříme se	**Můžeš mi odpustit?** *MUU-<u>zhesh</u> mi ot-PUS-tit?*	**Odpouštím ti.** *ot-POÛ<u>SH</u>-tiim ti.*

I can't forgive you. *aî kent fœr-GIV yu.*	**Give me [another / one last] chance.** *giv mi [ə-NƏ-dhœr / wan lest] tsheens.*	**ENGLISH** *making up*
Ich kann dir nicht verzeihen. *ish kan DI-ər nisht fer-TSAÎ-ən.*	**Gib mir [noch eine / eine letzte] Chance.** *gip MI-ər [nohh AÎ-nə / AÎ-nə LETS-tə] SHAᴺ-sə.*	**DEUTSCH** *versöhnung*
No te puedo perdonar. *no te PUÊ-dho per-do-NAR.*	**Dáme [otra / una última] oportunidad.** *DA-me [O-tra / U-na UL-ti-ma] o-por-tu-ni-DHADH.*	**ESPAÑOL** *perdonar*
Je peux pas te pardonner. *zhə pœ pat par-də-NE.*	**Donne-moi [encore une / une dernière] chance.** *dən-MUÀ [aᵘ-KƏR ün / ün der-NIÊR] shaⁿs.*	**FRANÇAIS** *faire la paix*
Non ti posso perdonare. *non ti POS-so per-do-NA-re.*	**Concedimi [un'altra / un'ultima] possibilità.** *kon-TSHE-di-mi [un-AL-tra / un-UL-ti-ma] pos-si-bi-li-TA.*	**ITALIANO** *far la pace*
Eu não posso te perdoar. *eû naûⁿ PO-su tshi pehh-DUÂHH.*	**Me dê [outra / uma última] chance.** *mi de [OÛ-trə / U-mə UL-tshi-mə] SHAᴺ-si.*	**PORTUGUÊS** *perdoar*
Nemůžu ti odpustit. *NE-muu-zhu ti ot-PUS-tit.*	**Dej mi [ještě / poslední] šanci.** *deî mi [YESH-tiê / POS-led-nii] SHAN-tsi.*	**ČESKY** *usmíříme se*

ENGLISH / making up	This [is / was] your last chance. *dhis [iz / wəz] yœr lest tsheens.*	I still love you. *aî stil ləv yu.*
DEUTSCH / versöhnung	Das [ist / war] deine letzte Chance. *das [ist / var] DAÎ-nə LETS-tə SHAᴺ-sə.*	Ich liebe dich immer noch. *ish LII-bə dish I-mər nohh.*
ESPAÑOL / perdonar	Ésta [va a ser / fue] la última oportunidad. *ES-ta [ba a ser / fuê] la UL-ti-ma o-por-tu-ni-DHADH.*	Todavía te quiero. *to-dha-VI-a te KIÊ-ro.*
FRANÇAIS / faire la paix	[C'est / C'était] ta dernière chance. *[se / se-TE] ta der-NIÊR shaⁿs.*	Je t'aime quand même. *zhə tem kaⁿ mem.*
ITALIANO / far la pace	Questa [è / è stata] la tua ultima possibilità. *KUÊS-ta [e / e STA-ta] la TU-a UL-ti-ma pos-si-bi-li-TA.*	Ti amo ancora. *ti A-mo an-KO-ra.*
PORTUGUÊS / perdoar	Esta [é / foi] sua última chance. *ES-ta [e / foî] SU-ə UL-tshi-mə SHAᴺ-si.*	Eu ainda amo você. *eû ə-Iᴺ-də A-mu vo-SE.*
ČESKY / usmíříme se	To [je / byla] poslední šance. *to [ye / BI-la] POS-led-nii SHAN-tse.*	Stále tě miluji. *STAA-le tiê MI-lu-yi.*

Can we try again? *ken wi traî ə-gen?*	**Let's make up.** *lets meîk əp.*	**ENGLISH** making up
Können wir es noch einmal versuchen? *KŒ-nən VI-ər es nohh AÎN-maal fər-ZUU-hhən?*	**Komm, vertragen wir uns wieder.** *kom, fer-TRAA-gən VI-ər uns VII-dər.*	**DEUTSCH** versöhnung
¿Podemos intentarlo de nuevo? *po-DHE-mos in-ten-TAR-lo dhe NUÊ-bo?*	**Vamos a arreglarlo.** *BA-mos a a-rre-GLAR-lo.*	**ESPAÑOL** perdonar
Et si on essayait encore? *e si on e-se-YE aⁿ-KƏR?*	**On fait la paix?** *oⁿ fe la pe?*	**FRANÇAIS** faire la paix
Possiamo riprovarci? *pos-SIÂ-mo ri-pro-VAR-tshi?*	**Facciamo pace.** *fat-TSHA-mo PA-tshe.*	**ITALIANO** far la pace
Podemos tentar de novo? *pu-DE-mus teⁿ-TAHH dzhi NO-vu?*	**Vamos fazer as pazes.** *VA-mus fə-ZER əs PA-zes.*	**PORTUGUÊS** perdoar
Můžeme to zkusit znovu? *MUU-zhe-me to SKU-sit ZNO-vu?*	**Pojd'me se usmířit.** *POÎDZH-me se us-MIIR-zhit.*	**ČESKY** usmíříme se

ENGLISH — the future

What are you looking for?
wət ar yu LU-king for?

I don't know.
aî doûnt noû.

DEUTSCH — die zukunft

Wonach suchst du?
voo-NAHH zuhhst du?

Ich weiß es nicht.
ish vaîs es nisht.

ESPAÑOL — el futuro

¿Qué intenciones tienes?
ke in-ten-THIÔ-nes TIÊ-nes?

No lo sé.
no lo se.

FRANÇAIS — l'avenir

Tu cherches quoi?
tü shersh kuâ?

J'en sais rien.
zhaⁿ se riêⁿ.

ITALIANO — il futuro

Cosa cerchi?
KO-za TSHER-ki?

Non lo so.
non lo so.

PORTUGUÊS — o futuro

O que você está procurando?
u ki vo-SE is-TA pro-ku-RAⁿ-du?

Eu não sei.
eû naûⁿ seî.

ČESKY — budoucnost

Jaký vztah hledáš?
YA-kiif-stah HLE-daash?

Nevím.
NE-vim.

I'm looking for [love / just sex]. *aîm LU-king fœr [ləv / <u>dzh</u>əst seks].*	**I'm looking for a [boyfriend / sugar daddy].** *aîm LU-king fœr ə [BOÎ-frend / <u>SH</u>U-gœr DEE-di].*	**ENGLISH** the future
Ich [suche nach Liebe / will nur Sex]. *ish [ZUU-<u>hh</u>e nahh LII-bə / vil nuur zeks].*	**Ich suche nach einem [Freund / Sugar-Daddy].** *ish ZUU-<u>hh</u>ə nahh AÎ-nəm [froînt / <u>SH</u>U-gər-de-di].*	**DEUTSCH** die zukunft
Estoy buscando [amor / sólo sexo]. *es-TOÎ bus-KAN-do [a-MOR / SO-lo SEK-so].*	**Estoy buscando [novio / espónsor].** *es-TOÎ bus-KAN-do [NO-biô / es-PON-sor].*	**ESPAÑOL** el futuro
Je cherche [une relation amoureuse / que du cul]. *<u>zh</u>ə shersh [ün rə-la-siôⁿ a-mu-RŒZ / kə dü kü].*	**C'est un [copain / papa gâteau] que je cherche.** *set eⁿ [kə-PEⁿ / pa-PA ga-TO] kə <u>zh</u>ə shersh.*	**FRANÇAIS** l'avenir
Cerco [l'amore / solo sesso]. *<u>TSH</u>ER-ko [la-MO-re / SO-lo SES-so].*	**Cerco [un fidanzato / uno che mi mantenga].** *<u>TSH</u>ER-ko [un fi-dan-DZA-to / U-no ke mi man-TEN-ga].*	**ITALIANO** il futuro
Eu estou procurando [amor / apenas sexo]. *eû is-TOÛ pro-ku-RAⁿ-du [ə-MOHH / ə-PE-nəs SEK-su].*	**Eu estou procurando um [namorado / homem rico].** *eû is-TOÛ pro-ku-RAⁿ-du uⁿ [nə-mu-RA-du / O-meⁿ <u>HH</u>I-ku].*	**PORTUGUÊS** o futuro
Hledám [lásku / jenom sex]. *HLE-daam [LAAS-ku / YE-nom seks].*	**Hledám [přítele / bohatého strýčka].** *HLE-daam [PSHII-te-le / BO-ha-tee-ho STRII<u>TSH</u>-ka].*	**ČESKY** budoucnost

ENGLISH / the future	I [want / don't want] a long-term relationship. *aî [want / doûnt want] ə long-tœrm ri-LEÎ-shən-ship.*	I'm looking (mostly) for friendship. *aîm LU-king (MOÛST-li) fœr FREND-ship.*
DEUTSCH / die zukunft	Ich möchte [eine / keine] feste Beziehung. *ish MŒSH-tə [AÎ-nə / KAÎ-nə] FES-tə bə-TSII-hung.*	Ich will (lieber) eine Freund-schaft. *ish vil (LII-bər) AÎ-nə FROÎNT-shaft.*
ESPAÑOL / el futuro	[Quiero / No quiero] una relación seria. *[KIÊ-ro / no KIÊ-ro] U-na rre-la-THIÔN SE-riâ.*	Estoy buscando (más que nada) amistad. *es-TOÎ bus-KAN-do (mas ke NA-dha) a-mis-TADH.*
FRANÇAIS / l'avenir	Je [veux / veux pas] une relation sérieuse. *zhə [vœ / vœ pa] ün rə-la-siôn se-RIÊZ.*	Je cherche (surtout) un vrai copain. *zhə shersh (sür-TU) en vre kə-PEN.*
ITALIANO / il futuro	[Voglio / Non voglio] una relazione seria. *[VO-lʸo / non VO-lʸo] U-na re-la-TSIÔ-ne SE-riâ.*	Cerco (soprattutto) amicizia. *TSHER-ko (so-pra-TUT-to) a-mi-TSHI-tsiâ.*
PORTUGUÊS / o futuro	Eu [quero / não quero] um relacionamento sério. *eû [KE-ru / naûn KE-ru] un hhe-lə-siô-nə-MEN-tu SE-riû.*	Eu estou procurando (principalmente) amizade. *eû is-TOÛ pro-ku-RAN-du (prin-si-paû-MEN-tshi) ə-mi-ZA-dzhi.*
ČESKY / budoucnost	[Chci / Nechci] dlouhodobý vztah. *[hhə-TSI / NEHH-tsi] DLOÛ-ho-do-biif-stah.*	Hledám (hlavně) přátelství. *HLE-daam (HLAV-niê) PSHAA-tels-tvii.*

I'm looking for financial support. *aîm LU-king fœr faî-NEN-tshəl sə-PORT.*	**I want to live with you.** *aî want tu liv widh yu.*

ENGLISH — the future

Ich suche jemand, der mich finanziell unterstützt. *ish ZUU-hhə YE-mant, der mish fi-nan-TSIÊL UN-tər-shtütst.*	**Ich möchte mit dir leben.** *ish MŒSH-tə mit DI-ər LEÎ-bən.*

DEUTSCH — die zukunft

Estoy buscando apoyo económico. *es-TOÎ bus-KAN-do a-PO-yo e-co-NO-mi-ko.*	**Me gustaría vivir contigo.** *me gus-ta-RI-a bi-BIR kon-TI-go.*

ESPAÑOL — el futuro

Ce que je veux, c'est quelqu'un qui m'aide. *skə zhə vœ, se kel-KEN ki med.*	**Je voudrais bien habiter avec toi.** *zhə vu-DRE biên a-bi-TE a-VEK tuâ.*

FRANÇAIS — l'avenir

Cerco un sostegno economico. *TSHER-ko un sos-TE-nyo e-ko-NO-mi-ko.*	**Voglio vivere con te.** *VO-lyo VI-ve-re kon te.*

ITALIANO — il futuro

Eu estou procurando apoio financeiro. *eû is-TOÛ pro-ku-RAN-du ə-PO-yu fi-nan-SEÎ-ru.*	**Eu quero morar com você.** *eû KE-ru mu-RAHH koⁿ vo-SE.*

PORTUGUÊS — o futuro

Hledám finanční podporu. *HLE-daam FI-nantsh-nii POT-po-ru.*	**Chtěl bych s tebou bydlet.** *hhə-TIÉL bihh STE-boů BID-let.*

ČESKY — budoucnost

the future ENGLISH	**(Maybe) I could stay here.** *(MEÎ-bi) aî kud steî HI-œr.*	**We could live together in [my / your] country.** *wi kud liv tu-GE-dhœr in [maî / yœr] KƏN-tri.*	
die zukunft DEUTSCH	**Ich könnte (vielleicht) hierbleiben.** *ish KŒN-tə (fii-LAÎSHT) HI-ər-blaî-bən.*	**Wir könnten in [meinem / deinem] Land zusammen wohnen.** *VI-ər KŒN-tən in [MAÎ-nəm / DAÎ-nəm] lant tsu-ZA-mən VOO-nən.*	
el futuro ESPAÑOL	**(Quizá) pueda quedarme aquí.** *(ki-THA) PUÊ-dha ke-DHAR-me a-KI.*	**Podríamos vivir juntos en [mi / tu] país.** *po-DHRI-a-mos bi-BIR HHUN-tos en [mi / tu] pa-IS.*	
l'avenir FRANÇAIS	**Je pourrais (peut-être) rester ici.** *zhə pu-RE (pœ-TE-trə) res-TE i-SI.*	**On pourrait vivre ensemble dans [mon / ton] pays.** *oⁿ pu-RE viv-raⁿ-SAⁿ-blə daⁿ [moⁿ / toⁿ] pe-I.*	
il futuro ITALIANO	**(Forse) potrei rimanere qui.** *(FOR-se) po-TREÎ ri-ma-NE-re kuî.*	**Potremmo vivere insieme nel [mio / tuo] paese.** *po-TREM-mo VI-ve-re in-SIÊ-me nel [MI-o / TU-o] pa-E-ze.*	
o futuro PORTUGUÊS	**(Talvez) eu pudesse ficar aqui.** *(təl-VES) eû pu-DE-si fi-KAR ə-KI.*	**Nós poderíamos viver juntos no [meu / seu] país.** *nos pu-de-RI-ə-mus vi-VEHH ZHUⁿ-tus nu [meû / seû] pə-IS.*	
budoucnost ČESKY	**Mohl bych tu (možná) zůstat.** *MO-həl bihh tu (MOZH-naa) ZUUS-tat.*	**Mohli bychom [spolu v mé / spolu v té] zemi žít.** *MO-hli BI-hhom [SPO-luv mee / SPO-luf tee] ZE-mi zhiit.*	

I'd like that, (but it's too soon). *aîd laîk <u>dhet</u>, (bət its tu sun).*	**Let's get to know each other better.** *lets get tu noû ii<u>tsh</u> ə-<u>dh</u>œr BE-tœr.*

ENGLISH — the future

Die Idee gefällt mir, (aber das geht zu schnell). *di i-DEÎ gə-FELT MI-ər, (A-bər das geît tsu <u>shn</u>el).*	**Wir müssen uns erst besser kennenlernen.** *VI-ər MÜ-sən uns erst BE-sər KE-nən-ler-nən.*

DEUTSCH — die zukunft

Me gustaría, (pero es demasiado pronto). *me gus-ta-RI-a, (PE-ro es de-ma-SIÂ-<u>dh</u>o PRON-to).*	**Vamos a esperar a conocer- nos mejor.** *BA-mos a es-pe-RAR a ko-no-<u>THER</u>-nos me-<u>HH</u>OR.*

ESPAÑOL — el futuro

Ça me plairait, (mais atten- dons un peu). *sam ple-RE, (me a-taⁿ-DO^N eⁿ pœ).*	**Il faut qu'on apprenne à se connaître.** *il fo kon a-PREN as kə-NE-trə.*

FRANÇAIS — l'avenir

Mi piacerebbe, (ma è troppo presto). *mi piâ-<u>tshe</u>-REB-be, (ma e TROP-po PRES-to).*	**Conosciamoci meglio.** *ko-no-<u>SHA</u>-mo-<u>tshi</u> ME-l^yo.*

ITALIANO — il futuro

Eu gostaria disto, (mas é muito cedo). *eû gus-tə-RI-ə DIS-tu, (məs e MUÎ^N-tu SE-du).*	**Vamos nos conhecer melhor.** *VA-mus nus ko-n^ye-SE<u>HH</u> me-L^YO<u>HH</u>.*

PORTUGUÊS — o futuro

Rád bych, (ale to je příliš brzy). *raad bi<u>hh</u>, (A-le to ye P<u>SH</u>II-li<u>sh</u> BƏR-zi).*	**Nejdříve se lépe poznejme.** *NEÎD-<u>zh</u>ii-ve se LEE-pe POZ-neî-me.*

ČESKY — budoucnost

ENGLISH farewells	I've had a great time with you. *aîv hed ə greît taîm widh yu.*	I wish I didn't have to leave. *aî wish aî DI-dənt hev tu liiv.*
DEUTSCH abreisen	Ich hatte eine tolle Zeit mit dir. *ish HA-tə AÎ-nə TO-lə tsaît mit DI-ər.*	Ich wünschte, ich müßte nicht gehen. *ish VÜNSH-tə, ish MÜS-tə nisht GEÎ-ən.*
ESPAÑOL adiós	Me lo he pasado muy bien contigo. *me lo e pa-SA-dho muî bién kon-TI-go.*	Ojalá no tuviera que irme. *o-hha-LA no tu-BIÈ-ra ke IR-me.*
FRANÇAIS adieux	J'ai passé de très bons moments avec toi. *zhe pa-SE də tre bon mə-MAN a-VEK tuâ.*	Je voudrais tant rester. *zhə vu-DRE tan rəs-TE.*
ITALIANO l'addio	Sono stato molto bene con te. *SO-no STA-to MOL-to BE-ne kon te.*	Vorrei non dover partire. *vo-RREÎ non do-VER par-TI-re.*
PORTUGUÊS adeus	Eu me diverti muito com você. *eû mi dzhi-vehh-TSHI MUÎN-tu kon vo-SE.*	Eu gostaria de não ter que ir embora. *eû gus-tə-RI-ə dzhi naûn tehh ki ir en-BO-rə.*
ČESKY rozloučení	Strávil jsem s tebou báječné chvíle. *STRAA-vil sem STE-boû BAA-yetsh-neehh-VII-le.*	Nejraději bych neodjížděl. *NEÎ-ra-diê-yi bihh NE-od-yiizh-diêl.*

(Please) don't leave. *(pliiz) doûnt liiv.*	**I'll miss you (so much).** *aîl mis yu (soû mətsh).*	**ENGLISH** farewells
(Bitte) geh nicht! *(BI-tə) geî nisht!*	**Ich werde dich (sehr) vermissen.** *ish VER-də dish (ZE-ər) fer-MI-sən.*	**DEUTSCH** abreisen
(Por favor,) no te marches. *(por fa-BOR,) no te MAR-tshes.*	**Te echaré (mucho) de menos.** *te e-tsha-RE (MU-tsho) dhe ME-nos.*	**ESPAÑOL** adiós
(Je t'en prie,) t'en va pas. *(zhə tan pri,) tan va pa.*	**Tu vas (beaucoup) me manquer.** *tü va (bo-KU) mə man-KE.*	**FRANÇAIS** adieux
(Ti prego,) non partire. *(ti PRE-go,) non par-TI-re.*	**Mi mancherai (tanto).** *mi man-ke-RAÎ (TAN-to).*	**ITALIANO** l'addio
(Por favor,) não vá embora. *(puhh fə-VOHH,) naûn va en-BO-rə.*	**Eu vou sentir (muita) saudade sua.** *eû voû sen-TIHH (MUÎN-ta) saû-DA-dzhi SU-ə.*	**PORTUGUÊS** adeus
(Prosím tě,) neodcházej! *(PRO-siim tiê,) NE-od-hhaa-zeî!*	**Budeš mi (moc) chybět.** *BU-desh mi (mots) HHI-biêt.*	**ČESKY** rozloučení

ENGLISH farewells	**Don't cry.** *doûnt kraî.*	**Come visit me (soon).** *kəm VI-zit mi (sun).*
DEUTSCH abreisen	**Wein doch nicht!** *vaîn do<u>hh</u> ni<u>sh</u>t!*	**Komm mich (bald) besuchen!** *kom mi<u>sh</u> (balt) bə-ZUU-<u>hh</u>ən!*
ESPAÑOL adiós	**No llores.** *no L^YO-res.*	**Ven a verme (pronto).** *ben a BER-me (PRON-to).*
FRANÇAIS adieux	**Pleure pas.** *plœr pa.*	**Rends-moi visite (bientôt).** *raⁿ-MUÂ vi-ZIT (biêⁿ-TO).*
ITALIANO l'addio	**Non piangere.** *non PIÂN-<u>dzh</u>e-re.*	**Vieni (presto) a trovarmi.** *VIÊ-ni (PRES-to) a tro-VAR-mi.*
PORTUGUÊS adeus	**Não chore.** *naûⁿ <u>SHO</u>-ri.*	**Venha visitar-me (logo).** *VE-n^yə vi-zi-TA<u>HH</u>-mi (LO-gu).*
ČESKY rozloučení	**Nebreč!** *NE-bre<u>tsh</u>!*	**Přijed' mě (brzo) navštívit!** *PSHI-ye<u>dzh</u> miê (BƏR-zo) nav-<u>SH</u>TII-vit!*

I'll come back (soon).
aîl kəm bek (sun).

We'll write each other.
wil raît iitsh Ə-dhœr.

ENGLISH farewells

Ich komme (bald) zurück.
ish KO-mə (balt) tsu-RÜK.

Wir werden uns schreiben.
VI-ər VER-dən uns SHRAÎ-bən.

DEUTSCH abreisen

Volveré (pronto).
bol-be-RE (PRON-to).

Vamos a escribirnos.
BA-mos a es-kri-BIR-nos.

ESPAÑOL adiós

Je serai (bientôt) de retour.
zhə sə-RE (bièⁿ-TO) də rə-TUR.

On s'écrira.
oⁿ se-kri-RA.

FRANÇAIS adieux

Tornerò (presto).
tor-ne-RO (PRES-to).

Scriviamoci.
skri-VIÂ-mo-tshi.

ITALIANO l'addio

Eu voltarei (logo).
eû vul-tə-REÎ (LO-gu).

Vamos nos corresponder.
VA-mus nus ku-hhes-poⁿ-DEHH.

PORTUGUÊS adeus

Vrátím se (brzo).
VRAA-tiim se (BƏR-zo).

Budeme si psát.
BU-de-me sip-SAAT.

ČESKY rozloučení

ENGLISH farewells	We can talk on the phone (a lot). *wi kən tok an <u>dh</u>ə foûn (ə lat).*	Could you come with me to the [airport / train station]? *kud yu kəm wi<u>dh</u> mi tu <u>dh</u>i [EER-port / treîn STEÎ-<u>sh</u>ən]?*
DEUTSCH abreisen	Wir können (oft) telefonieren. *VI-ər KŒ-nən (oft) te-le-fo-NII-ren.*	Könntest du mit mir zum [Flughafen / Bahnhof] kommen? *KŒN-təst du mit MI-ər tsum [FLUUK-haa-fən / BAAN-hoof] KO-mən?*
ESPAÑOL adiós	Podemos llamarnos (a menudo). *po-<u>DHE</u>-mos lʲa-MAR-nos (a me-NU-<u>dh</u>o).*	¿Me puedes acompañar [al aeropuerto / a la estación]? *me PUÊ-<u>dh</u>es a-kom-pa-NʸAR [al a-e-ro-PUÊR-to / a la es-ta-<u>THIÔN</u>]?*
FRANÇAIS adieux	On pourra se téléphoner (souvent). *oⁿ pu-RAS te-le-fə-NE (su-VAⁿ).*	Tu peux m'accompagner à [l'aéroport / la gare]? *tü pœ ma-koⁿ-pa-NʸE a [la-e-rə-PƏR / la gar]?*
ITALIANO l'addio	Possiamo parlarci (spesso) per telefono. *pos-SIÂ-mo par-LAR-tshi (SPES-so) per te-LE-fo-no.*	Puoi accompagnarmi [all'aeroporto / alla stazione]? *PUÔ-i ak-kom-pa-NʸAR-mi [al-la-e-ro-POR-to / AL-la sta-TSIÔ-ne]?*
PORTUGUÊS adeus	Nós podemos nos falar por telefone (frequentemente). *nos po-DE-mus nus fə-LAHH puhh te-le-FO-ni (fri-kuêⁿ-<u>tsh</u>i-MEⁿ-<u>tsh</u>i).*	Você poderia ir comigo até [o aeroporto / a estação de trem]? *vo-SE po-de-RI-ə <u>ihh</u> ko-MI-gu ə-TE [u aî-ru-PO<u>HH</u>-tu / ə es-tə-SAÛⁿ <u>dzh</u>i treⁿ]?*
ČESKY rozloučení	Můžeme si (často) volat. *MUU-<u>zh</u>e-me si (<u>TSH</u>AS-to) VO-lat.*	Vyprovodíš mě na [letiště / nádraží]? *vi-PRO-vo-diish miê na [LE-ti<u>sh</u>-tiê / NAA-dra-<u>zh</u>ii]?*

Don't forget me. *doûnt fœr-GET mi.*	**I'll never forget you.** *aîl NE-vœr fœr-GET yu.*	**ENGLISH** farewells
Vergiß mich nicht! *fer-GIS mi<u>sh</u> ni<u>sh</u>t!*	**Ich werde dich niemals vergessen.** *i<u>sh</u> VER-də di<u>sh</u> NII-mals fer-GE-sən.*	**DEUTSCH** abreisen
No me olvides. *no me ol-BI-<u>dh</u>es.*	**No te olvidaré jamás.** *no te ol-bi-<u>dh</u>a-RE <u>hh</u>a-MAS.*	**ESPAÑOL** adiós
M'oublie pas. *mu-BLI pa.*	**Je t'oublierai jamais.** *<u>zh</u>ə tu-bli-ə-RE <u>zh</u>a-ME.*	**FRANÇAIS** adieux
Non dimenticarti di me. *non di-men-ti-KAR-ti di me.*	**Non ti dimenticherò mai.** *non ti di-men-ti-ke-RO maî.*	**ITALIANO** l'addio
Não se esqueça de mim. *naûⁿ si es-KE-sa <u>dzh</u>i miⁿ.*	**Eu não te esquecerei jamais.** *eû naûⁿ <u>tsh</u>i es-ki-se-REÎ <u>zh</u>ə-MAÎS.*	**PORTUGUÊS** adeus
Nezapomeň na mě! *NE-za-po-menʸ na miê!*	**Nikdy na tebe nezapomenu.** *NIG-di na TE-be NE-za-po-me-nu.*	**ČESKY** rozloučení

ENGLISH / shopping

I need [lubricated / unlubricated] condoms.
aî niid [LU-bri-keî-ted / ƏN-lu-bri-keî-ted] KAN-dəmz.

I'm looking for large condoms.
aîm LU-king fœr lardzh KAN-dəmz.

DEUTSCH / einkaufen

Ich brauche Kondome [mit / ohne] Gleitgel.
ish BRAÛ-hhə kon-DOO-mə [mit / OO-nə] GLAÎT-gel.

Ich suche große Kondome.
ish ZUU-hhə GROO-sə kon-DOO-mə.

ESPAÑOL / compras

Necesito condones [con / sin] lubricante.
ne-the-SI-to kon-DO-nes [kon / sin] lu-bri-KAN-te.

Estoy buscando condones grandes.
es-TOÎ bus-KAN-do kon-DO-nes GRAN-des.

FRANÇAIS / achats

J'ai besoin de préservatifs [lubrifiés / non lubrifiés].
zhe bə-ZUÊⁿ də pre-zer-va-TIF [lü-bri-FIÊ / noⁿ lü-bri-FIÊ].

Je voudrais des préservatifs de grande taille.
zhə vu-DRE de pre-zer-va-TIF də graⁿd taî.

ITALIANO / compere

Ho bisogno di preservativi [lubrificati / non lubrificati].
o bi-ZO-nʸo di pre-zer-va-TI-vi [lu-bri-fi-KA-ti / non lu-bri-fi-KA-ti].

Cerco dei preservativi più grandi.
TSHER-ko deî pre-zer-va-TI-vi più GRAN-di.

PORTUGUÊS / compras

Eu preciso de camisinhas [lubrificadas / não lubrificadas].
eû pri-SI-zu dzhi kə-mi-ZI-nʸas [lu-bri-fi-KA-dəs / naûⁿ lu-bri-fi-KA-dəs].

Eu estou procurando camisinhas grandes.
eû is-TOÛ pro-ku-RAⁿ-du kə-mi-ZI-nʸəs GRAⁿ-dzhis.

ČESKY / nákupy

Potřebuji kondomy [s lubrikantem / bez lubrikantu].
pot-RZHE-bu-yi KON-do-mi [SLU-bri-kan-tem / bez LU-bri-kan-tu].

Hledám velmi velké kondomy.
HLE-daam VEL-mi VEL-kee KON-do-mi.

Do you have (water-soluble) lubricant? *du yu hev (WA-tœr-SA-liû-bəl) LU-bri-kent?*	**I need a [dildo / buttplug].** *aî niid ə [DIL-doû / BƏT-pləg].*	**ENGLISH** shopping
Haben Sie (wasserlösliches) Gleitgel? *HAA-bən zii (VA-sər-lœs-li-<u>sh</u>əs) GLAÎT-gel?*	**Ich brauche einen [Dildo / Plug].** *i<u>sh</u> BRAÛ-<u>hh</u>ə AÎ-nən [DIL-do / plək].*	**DEUTSCH** einkaufen
¿Tiene un lubricante (hidrosoluble)? *TIÉ-ne un lu-bri-KAN-te (i-<u>dh</u>ro-so-LU-ble)?*	**Necesito un [consolador / tapón para el culo].** *ne-<u>the</u>-SI-to un [kon-so-la-<u>DHOR</u> / ta-PON PA-ra el KU-lo].*	**ESPAÑOL** compras
Vous avez un lubrifiant (soluble à l'eau)? *vuz a-VE eⁿ lü-bri-FIÂ^N (sə-LÜ-blə a lo)?*	**J'ai besoin d'un [godemiché / plug].** *<u>zh</u>e bə-ZUÊ^N deⁿ [gəd-mi-<u>SHE</u> / pləg].*	**FRANÇAIS** achats
Avete un lubrificante (idrosolubile)? *a-VE-te un lu-bri-fi-KAN-te (i-dro-so-LU-bi-le)?*	**Ho bisogno di un [dildo / buttplug].** *o bi-ZO-n^yo di un [DIL-do / BAT-plag].*	**ITALIANO** compere
Você tem um lubrificante (à base de água)? *vo-SE teⁿ uⁿ lu-bri-fi-KA^N-<u>tshi</u> (a BA-zi <u>dzhi</u> A-guâ)?*	**Eu preciso de um [consolo / tampão anal].** *eû pri-SI-zu <u>dzhi</u> uⁿ [koⁿ-SO-lu / taⁿ-PAÛ^N ə-NAÛ].*	**PORTUGUÊS** compras
Máte lubrikant (rozpustný ve vodě)? *MAA-te LU-bri-kant (ROS-pust-nii ve VO-diê)?*	**Potřebuji [robertek / špunt do prdele].** *pot-<u>RZHE</u>-bu-yi [RO-ber-tek / <u>shpunt do PƏR-de-le].*	**ČESKY** nákupy

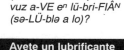

ENGLISH shopping	A [cockring / pair of chaps], please. *ə [KAK-ring / peer əv tsheps], pliiz.*	I'd like some titclamps. *aîd laîk səm tit klemps.*
DEUTSCH einkaufen	[Einen Schwanzring / Ein Paar Chaps], bitte. *[AÎ-nən SHVANTS-ring / aîn paar tshaps], BI-tə.*	Ich möchte Brustwarzen-klemmen. *ish MŒSH-tə BRUST-var-tsən-kle-mən.*
ESPAÑOL compras	Un [cockring / par de chaps], por favor. *un [KOK-ring / par de tshaps], por fa-BOR.*	Quisiera unas pinzas para pezones. *ki-SIĔ-ra U-nas PIN-thas PA-ra pe-THO-nes.*
FRANÇAIS achats	[Un cockring / des chaps], s'il vous plaît. *[eⁿ kək-RING / de shap], sil vu ple.*	Je voudrais des pinces à sein. *zhə vu-DRE de peⁿs a seⁿ.*
ITALIANO compere	Un [cockring / paio di chaps], per favore. *un [kok-RING / PA-yo di tshaps], per fa-VO-re.*	Vorrei delle pinzette per capezzoli. *vo-RREÎ DEL-le pin-DZET-te per ka-PET-tso-li.*
PORTUGUÊS compras	[Um coqueringue / Umas cal-ças de vaqueiro], por favor. *[uⁿ ko-ki-RING / U-məs KAÛ-səs dzhi və-KEÎ-ru], puhh fə-VOHH.*	Eu queria grampos de teta. *eû ke-RI-ə GRAⁿ-pus dzhi TE-tə.*
ČESKY nákupy	[Jeden kroužek na penis / Jedny kožené kalhoty], prosím. *[YE-den KROÛ-zhek na PE-nis / YED-ni KO-zhe-nee KAL-ho-ti], PRO-siim.*	Chtěl bych kolíčky na bra-davky. *hhə-TIÊL bihh KO-liitsh-ki na BRA-daf-ky.*

Where are your porn [magazines / videos]?
WE-œr ar yœr porn [me-gə-ZIINZ / VI-di-oûs]?

Do you sell any gay guides?
du yu sel E-ni geî gaîdz?

ENGLISH shopping

Wo sind die [Pornohefte / Pornovideos]?
voo zint di [POR-no-hef-tə / POR-no-vi-de-os]?

Verkaufen Sie einen Schwulenführer?
fer-KAÛ-fən zii AÎ-nən SHVU-lən-füü-rər?

DEUTSCH einkaufen

¿Dónde están [las revistas / los vídeos] porno?
DON-de es-TAN [las rre-BIS-tas / los BI-dhe-os] POR-no?

¿Tiene una guía gay?
TIÊ-ne U-na GI-a geî?

ESPAÑOL compras

Où se trouvent les [revues / vidéos] pornos?
us truv le [rə-VÜ / vi-de-O] pər-NO?

Vous vendez un guide gai?
vu van-DE en gid ge?

FRANÇAIS achats

Dove sono [le riviste / i video] porno?
DO-ve SO-no [le ri-VIS-te / i VI-de-o] POR-no?

Vendete una guida gay?
ven-DE-te U-na GUÎ-da geî?

ITALIANO compere

Onde estão [as revistas / os vídeos] pornô?
ON-dzhi is-TAÛN [əs hhe-VIS-təs / us VI-de-us] POHH-no?

Você tem uma guia para gays?
vo-SE ten U-mə GI-ə PA-rə geîs?

PORTUGUÊS compras

Kde máte porno [časopisy / videa]?
gə-DE MAA-te POR-no [TSHA-so-pi-si / VI-de-a]?

Prodáváte gay průvodce?
PRO-daa-vaa-te geî PRUU-vot-tse?

ČESKY nákupy

ENGLISH — shopping

I'll take a whip.
aîl teîk ə wip.

Some chains, please.
səm <u>tsh</u>eînz, pliiz.

DEUTSCH — einkaufen

Ich nehme eine Peitsche.
<u>ish</u> NEÎ-mə AÎ-nə PAÎ-<u>tsh</u>ə.

Ein paar Ketten, bitte.
aîn paar KE-tən, BI-tə.

ESPAÑOL — compras

Me llevo un látigo.
me L^YE-bo un LA-ti-go.

Unas cadenas, por favor.
U-nas ka-<u>DHE</u>-nas, por fa-BOR.

FRANÇAIS — achats

Je prends un fouet.
<u>zh</u>ə praⁿ eⁿ fuê.

Des chaînes, s'il vous plaît.
de <u>sh</u>en, sil vu ple.

ITALIANO — compere

Compero una frusta.
KOM-pe-ro U-na FRUS-ta.

Delle catene, per favore.
DEL-le ka-TE-ne, per fa-VO-re.

PORTUGUÊS — compras

Eu fico com um chicote.
eû FI-ku koⁿ uⁿ <u>sh</u>i-KO-<u>tsh</u>i.

Umas correntes, por favor.
U-məs ko-<u>HHE^N</u>-<u>tsh</u>is, pu<u>hh</u> fə-VO<u>HH</u>.

ČESKY — nákupy

Vezmu si bič.
VEZ-mu si bi<u>tsh</u>.

Řetězy, prosím.
<u>ZHE</u>-tiê-zi, PRO-siim.

I'd like a massage. *aîd laîk ə mə-SAZH.*	**How much will it cost?** *haû mətsh wil it kast?*	**ENGLISH** shopping
Ich möchte eine Massage. *ish MŒSH-tə AÎ-nə ma-SAA-zhə.*	**Wieviel kostet das?** *vii-FI-əl KOS-tət das?*	**DEUTSCH** einkaufen
Quisiera un masaje. *ki-SIÊ-ra un ma-SA-hhe.*	**¿Cuánto cuesta?** *KUÂN-to KUÊS-ta?*	**ESPAÑOL** compras
Je voudrais un massage. *zhə vu-DRE eⁿ ma-SAZH.*	**Combien ça coûte?** *koⁿ-BIÊⁿ sa kut?*	**FRANÇAIS** achats
Vorrei un massaggio. *vo-RREÎ un mas-SAD-dzho.*	**Quanto costa?** *KUÂN-to KOS-ta?*	**ITALIANO** compere
Eu queria uma massagem. *eû ke-RI-ə U-mə mə-SA-zheⁿ.*	**Quanto custa?** *KUÂN-tu KUS-tə?*	**PORTUGUÊS** compras
Chtěl bych masáž. *hhə-TIÉL bihh MA-saash.*	**Kolik to stojí?** *KO-lik to STO-yii?*	**ČESKY** nákupy

ENGLISH shopping	**For how long?** *fœr haû long?*	**Can you write the price down for me?** *ken yu raît dhə praîs daûn fœr mi?*
DEUTSCH einkaufen	**Für wie lange?** *für vii LANg-ə?*	**Können Sie mir den Preis aufschreiben?** *KŒ-nən zii MI-ər deen praîs AÛF-shraî-bən?*
ESPAÑOL compras	**¿Por cuánto tiempo?** *por KUÂN-to TIÊM-po?*	**¿Me puede escribir el precio?** *me PUÊ-dhe es-kri-BIR el PRE-thiô?*
FRANÇAIS achats	**Pour combien de temps?** *pur kon-BIÊN də tan?*	**Vous pouvez m'écrire le prix?** *vu pu-VE me-KRIR lə pri?*
ITALIANO compere	**Per quanto tempo?** *per KUÂN-to TEM-po?*	**Mi può scrivere il prezzo?** *mi puô SKRI-ve-re il PRET-tso?*
PORTUGUÊS compras	**Por quanto tempo?** *puhh KUÂN-tu TEN-pu?*	**Podia escrever o preço para mim?** *po-DZHI-ə es-kre-VER u PRE-su PA-rə min?*
ČESKY nákupy	**Na jak dlouho?** *na yak DLOÛ-ho?*	**Můžete mi tu cenu napsat?** *MUU-zhe-te mi tu TSE-nu NAP-sat?*

That's too expensive.
<u>dh</u>ets tu eks-PEN-siv.

I don't pay (for sex).
aî doûnt peî (fœr seks).

ENGLISH shopping

Das ist zu teuer.
das ist tsu TOÎ-ər.

Ich bezahle nicht (für Sex).
i<u>sh</u> bə-TSAA-lə ni<u>sh</u>t (für seks).

DEUTSCH einkaufen

Es demasiado caro.
es de-ma-SIÂ-<u>dh</u>o KA-ro.

Yo no pago (por follar).
yo no PA-go (por fo-L^YAR).

ESPAÑOL compras

C'est trop cher.
se tro <u>sh</u>er.

Je paie pas (pour le cul).
<u>zh</u>ə pe pa (pur lə kü).

FRANÇAIS achats

È troppo caro.
e TROP-po KA-ro.

Io non pago (per il sesso).
I-o non PA-go (per il SES-so).

ITALIANO compere

É caro demais.
e KA-ru <u>dzh</u>i-MAÎS.

Eu não pago (por sexo).
eû naûⁿ PA-gu (pu<u>hh</u> SEK-su).

PORTUGUÊS compras

Je to příliš drahé.
ye to P<u>SH</u>II-li<u>sh</u> DRA-hee.

(Za sex) neplatím.
(za seks) NE-pla-tiim.

ČESKY nákupy

ENGLISH / health	**Have you always had safe sex?** *hev yu OL-weîz hed seîf seks?*	**I always have safe sex.** *aî OL-weîz hev seîf seks.*
DEUTSCH / gesundheit	**Hast du immer Safer-Sex gemacht?** *hast du I-mər SEÎ-fər-seks gə-MAHHT?*	**Ich mache immer Safer-Sex.** *ish MA-hhə I-mər SEÎ-fər-seks.*
ESPAÑOL / salud	**¿Siempre has practicado el sexo seguro?** *SIÊM-pre as prak-ti-KA-dho el SEK-so se-GU-ro?*	**Siempre practico el sexo seguro.** *SIÊM-pre prak-TI-ko el SEK-so se-GU-ro.*
FRANÇAIS / santé	**Tu as toujours pratiqué le sexe sans risque?** *tü a tu-ZHUR pra-ti-KE lə seks saⁿ risk?*	**Je pratique toujours le sexe sans risque.** *zhə pra-TIK tu-ZHUR lə seks saⁿ risk.*
ITALIANO / salute	**Hai fatto sempre sesso sicuro?** *aî FAT-to SEM-pre SES-so si-KU-ro?*	**Faccio sempre sesso sicuro.** *FAT-tsho SEM-pre SES-so si-KU-ro.*
PORTUGUÊS / saúde	**Você sempre faz sexo seguro?** *vo-SE SEⁿ-pri faz SEK-su se-GU-ru?*	**Eu sempre faço sexo seguro.** *eû SEⁿ-pri FA-su SEK-su se-GU-ru.*
ČESKY / zdraví	**Dělal jsi to vždy bezpečně?** *DIÊ-lal si to vəzh-DI bes-PETSH-niê?*	**Vždy to dělám bezpečně.** *vəzh-DI to DIÊ-laam bes-PETSH-niê.*

I haven't always had safe sex. *aî HE-vent OL-weîz hed seîf seks.*	Have you been tested for HIV (recently)? *hev yu bin TES-ted fœr eîtsh-aî-vii (RI-sent-li)?*	**ENGLISH** health
Ich habe nicht immer Safer-Sex gemacht. *ish HAA-bə nisht I-mər SEÎ-fər-seks gə-MAHHT.*	Bist du (vor kurzem) HIV-getestet worden? *bist du (for KUR-tsəm) ha-i-faû-gə-TES-tət VOR-dən?*	**DEUTSCH** gesundheit
No siempre he practicado el sexo seguro. *no SIÊM-pre e prak-ti-KA-dho el SEK-so se-GU-ro.*	¿Te has hecho la prueba del SIDA (últimamente)? *te as E-tsho la PRUÊ-ba dhel SI-dha (UL-ti-ma-men-te)?*	**ESPAÑOL** salud
J'ai pas toujours fait du sexe sans risque. *zhe pa tu-ZHUR fe dü seks san risk.*	Tu as fait le test du SIDA (récemment)? *tü a fel test dü si-DA (re-sa-MAN)?*	**FRANÇAIS** santé
Non ho fatto sempre sesso sicuro. *non o FAT-to SEM-pre SES-so si-KU-ro.*	Hai fatto il test per l'AIDS (recentemente)? *aî FAT-to il test per laî-di-ES-se (re-tshen-te-MEN-te)?*	**ITALIANO** salute
Eu nem sempre fiz sexo seguro. *eû nen SEN-pri fiz SEK-su se-GU-ru.*	Você fez o teste de AIDS (recentemente)? *vo-SE fez u TES-tshi dzhi eîdz (hhe-sen-tshi-MEN-tshi)?*	**PORTUGUÊS** saúde
Ne vždy jsem to dělal bezpečně. *ne vəzh-DI sem to DIÊ-lal bes-PETSH-niê.*	Byl jsi (v poslední době) na testu AIDS? *bil si (F-POS-led-nii DO-biê) na TES-tu eîdz?*	**ČESKY** zdraví

ENGLISH health	I was tested (recently). *aî wəz TES-ted (RI-sent-li).*	I haven't been tested (recently). *aî HE-vent bin TES-ted (RI-sent-li).*
DEUTSCH gesundheit	Ich bin (vor kurzem) HIV-getestet worden. *ish bin (for KUR-tsəm) ha-i-faû-gə-TES-tət VOR-dən.*	Ich bin (in letzter Zeit) nicht HIV-getestet worden. *ish bin (in LETS-tər tsaît) nisht ha-i-faû-gə-TES-tət VOR-dən.*
ESPAÑOL salud	Me hice la prueba (hace poco). *me I-the la PRUÊ-ba (A-the PO-ko).*	No me he hecho la prueba (últimamente). *no me e E-tsho la PRUÊ-ba (UL-ti-ma-men-te).*
FRANÇAIS santé	J'ai fait le test (récemment). *zhe fel test (re-sa-MAᴺ).*	J'ai pas fait le test (récemment). *zhe pa fel test (re-sa-MAᴺ).*
ITALIANO salute	Ho fatto il test (recente-mente). *o FAT-to il test (re-tshen-te-MEN-te).*	Non ho fatto il test (recente-mente). *non o FAT-to il test (re-tshen-te-MEN-te).*
PORTUGUÊS saúde	Eu fiz o teste (recente-mente). *eû fiz u TES-tshi (hhe-seⁿ-tshi-MEᴺ-tshi).*	Eu não fiz o teste (recente-mente). *eû naûⁿ fiz u TES-tshi (hhe-seⁿ-tshi-MEᴺ-tshi).*
ČESKY zdraví	Byl jsem (nedávno) na testu AIDS. *bil sem (NE-daav-no) na TES-tu eîdz.*	Nebyl jsem (v poslední době) na testu AIDS. *NE-bil sem (F-POS-led-nii DO-biê) na TES-tu eîdz.*

I'm [HIV-negative / HIV-positive].
aîm [eîtsh-aî-vii-NE-gə-tiv / eîtsh-aî-vii-PA-zi-tiv].

I (don't) have AIDS.
aî (doûnt) hev eîdz.

ENGLISH health

Ich bin [HIV-negativ / HIV-positiv].
ish bin [ha-i-faû-ne-ga-TIIF / ha-i-faû-POO-zi-tiif].

Ich habe (kein) AIDS.
ish HAA-bə (kaîn) eîdz.

DEUTSCH gesundheit

Soy [seronegativo / seropositivo].
soî [se-ro-ne-ga-TI-bo / se-ro-po-si-TI-bo].

(No) tengo el SIDA.
(no) TEN-go el SI-dha.

ESPAÑOL salud

Je suis [séronégatif / séropositif].
zhə süî [se-ro-ne-ga-TIF / se-ro-po-zi-TIF].

J'ai (pas) le SIDA.
zhe (pa) lə si-DA.

FRANÇAIS santé

Sono [sieronegativo / sieropositivo].
SO-no [siê-ro-ne-ga-TI-vo / siê-ro-po-zi-TI-vo].

(Non) ho l'AIDS.
(non) o laî-di-ES-se

ITALIANO salute

Eu [não tenho / tenho] o vírus.
eû [naûn TE-nʸu / TE-nʸu] u VI-rus.

Eu (não) tenho AIDS.
eû (naûn) TE-nʸu eîdz.

PORTUGUÊS saúde

Jsem [HIV-negativní / HIV-pozitivní].
sem [HA-i-ve-NE-ga-tiv-nii / HA-i-ve-PO-zi-tiv-nii].

(Ne) mám AIDS.
(ne) maam eîdz.

ČESKY zdraví

ENGLISH health	Have you had any sexually-transmitted diseases? *hev yu hed E-ni SEK-shuê-li trens-MI-ted di-ZII-zez?*	I had gonorrhea. *aî hed ga-na-RI-ə.*
DEUTSCH gesundheit	Hattest du irgendwelche Geschlechtskrankheiten? *HA-təst du IR-gənd-vel-shə gəsh-LESH TS-krank-haî-tən?*	Ich hatte Tripper. *ish HA-tə TRI-pər.*
ESPAÑOL salud	¿Has tenido alguna enfermedad venérea? *as te-NI-dho al-GU-na en-fer-me-DHADH be-NE-re-a?*	He tenido gonorrea. *e te-NI-dho go-no-RRE-a.*
FRANÇAIS santé	Tu as déjà eu des maladies sexuelles? *tü a de-ZHA œ de ma-la-DI sek-SÜÊL?*	J'ai eu une blenno. *zhe œ ün ble-NO.*
ITALIANO salute	Hai mai avuto qualche malattia venerea? *aî maî a-VU-to KUÂL-ke ma-lat-TI-a ve-NE-re-a?*	Ho avuto lo scolo. *o a-VU-to lo SKO-lo.*
PORTUGUÊS saúde	Você já teve alguma doença venérea? *vo-SE zha TE-vi aû-GU-mə DUÊ\u207N-sə vi-NE-riâ?*	Eu tive gonorréia. *eû TSHI-vi gu-nu-HHE-yə.*
ČESKY zdraví	Měl jsi nějaké pohlavní choroby? *miêl si NIÊ-ya-kee PO-hlav-nii HHO-ro-by?*	Měl jsem kapavku. *miêl sem KA-paf-ku.*

	ENGLISH health
I (also) had syphilis. *aî (OL-soû) hed SI-fi-lis.*	(I think) I have [herpes / crabs]. *(aî think) aî hev [HŒR-piiz / kreebz].*

	DEUTSCH gesundheit
Ich hatte (auch) Syphilis. *ish HA-tə (aûhh) ZÚ-fi-lis.*	(Ich glaube,) ich habe [Herpes / Läuse]. *(ish GLAÛ-bə,) ish HAA-bə [HER-pəs / LOÎ-zə].*

	ESPAÑOL salud
He tenido sífilis (también). *e te-NI-dho SI-fi-lis (tam-BIÊN).*	(Creo que) tengo [herpes / ladillas]. *(KRE-o ke) TEN-go [ER-pes / la-DHI-lʸas].*

	FRANÇAIS santé
J'ai eu la syphilis (aussi). *zhe œ la si-fi-LIS (o-SI).*	(Je crois que) j'ai [de l'herpès / des morpions]. *(zhə kruâ kə) zhe [də ler-PES / de mər-PIÔᴺ].*

	ITALIANO salute
Ho avuto (anche) la sifilide. *o a-VU-to (AN-ke) la si-FI-li-de.*	(Mi sembra che) ho [l'herpes / le piattole]. *(mi SEM-bra ke) o [LER-pes / le PIÂT-to-le].*

	PORTUGUÊS saúde
Eu tive sífilis (também). *eû TSHI-vi SI-fi-lis (taⁿ-BEᴺ).*	(Eu acho que) tenho [herpes / chato]. *(eû A-shu ki) TE-nʸu [EHH-pis / SHA-tu].*

	ČESKY zdraví
Měl jsem (také) syfilis. *miêl sem (TA-kee) SI-fi-lis.*	(Myslím, že) mám [opar / filcky]. *(MIS-liim, zhe) maam [O-par / FILT-ski].*

ENGLISH health	**We'll be careful, okay?** *wiil bi KEER-fəl, oû-KEÎ?*	**(I like you, but) I'd rather not.** *(aî laîk yu, bət) aîd REE-dhœr nat.*
DEUTSCH gesundheit	**Wir werden vorsichtig sein, okay?** *VI-ər VER-dən for-ZISH-tish zaîn, o-KEÎ?*	**(Ich mag dich, aber) ich will lieber nicht.** *(ish maak dish, A-bər) ish vil LII-bər nisht.*
ESPAÑOL salud	**Iremos con cuidado, ¿vale?** *i-RE-mos kon kuî-DHA-dho, BA-le?*	**(Me gustas, pero) mejor lo dejamos.** *(me GUS-tas, PE-ro) me-HHOR lo dhe-HHA-mos.*
FRANÇAIS santé	**On va faire attention, OK?** *on va fer a-tan-SIÓN, o-KE?*	**(Tu me déplais pas, mais) je préfère qu'on en reste là.** *(tüm de-PLE pa, me) zhə pre-FER kon an rest la.*
ITALIANO salute	**Staremo attenti, OK?** *sta-RE-mo at-TEN-ti, o-KEÎ?*	**(Mi piaci molto, ma) meglio non far niente.** *(mi PIÂ-tshi MOL-to, ma) ME-lʸo non far NIÊN-te.*
PORTUGUÊS saúde	**Nós vamos ser bem cuidadosos, tá bom?** *nos VA-mus sehh ben kuî-da-DO-zus, ta bon?*	**(Eu gosto de você, mas) é melhor não.** *(eû GOS-tu dzhi vo-SE, məs) e me-LʸOHH naûn.*
ČESKY zdraví	**Budeme opatrní, ano?** *BU-de-me O-pa-tər-nii, A-no?*	**(Líbíš se mi, ale) raději ne.** *(LII-biish se mi, A-le) RA-diê-yi ne.*

Help! *help!*	**Call the police!** *kol dhə pə-LIIS!*	**ENGLISH** emergencies
Hilfe! *HIL-fə!*	**Ruf die Polizei!** *ruuf di po-li-TSAÎ!*	**DEUTSCH** notfälle
¡Socorro! *so-KO-<u>rr</u>o!*	**¡Llama a la policia!** *L^YA-ma a la po-li-<u>TH</u>I-a!*	**ESPAÑOL** urgencias
Au secours! *o sə-KUR!*	**Appelle la police!** *a-PEL la pə-LIS!*	**FRANÇAIS** urgences
Aiuto! *a-YU-to!*	**Chiama la polizia!** *KIÂ-ma la po-li-<u>TSI</u>-a!*	**ITALIANO** emergenze
Socorro! *su-KO-<u>hh</u>u!*	**Chama a polícia!** *<u>SH</u>A-mə ə po-LI-siâ!*	**PORTUGUÊS** emergência
Pomoc! *PO-mots!*	**Zavolej policii!** *ZA-vo-leî PO-li-tsii!*	**ČESKY** krize

ENGLISH — emergencies

(Please) take me to a hospital.
(pliiz) teîk mi tu ə HAS-pi-təl.

I've been robbed.
aîv bin rabd.

DEUTSCH — notfälle

(Bitte) bring mich ins Krankenhaus!
(BI-tə) brinᵍ mish ins KRAN-kən-haûs!

Ich bin beraubt worden.
ish bin bə-RAÛPT VOR-dən.

ESPAÑOL — urgencias

(Por favor,) llévame al hospital.
(por fa-BOR,) LʸE-ba-me al os-pi-TAL.

Me han robado.
me an rro-BA-dho.

FRANÇAIS — urgences

(S'il te plaît,) conduis-moi à l'hôpital.
(sil tə ple,) koⁿ-düî-MUÂ a lə-pi-TAL.

On m'a volé l'argent.
oⁿ ma və-LE lar-ZHAᴺ.

ITALIANO — emergenze

(Per favore,) portami in un ospedale.
(per fa-VO-re,) POR-ta-mi in un os-pe-DA-le.

Sono stato rapinato.
SO-no STA-to ra-pi-NA-to.

PORTUGUÊS — emergência

(Por favor,) leve-me ao hospital.
(puhh fa-VOHH,) LE-vi-mi aû os-pi-TAÛ.

Eu fui roubado.
eû fuî hhoû-BA-du.

ČESKY — krize

(Prosím,) odvez mě do nemocnice.
(PRO-siim,) OD-vez miê do NE-mots-ni-tse.

Byl jsem okraden.
bil sem O-kra-den.

I've been beaten. *aîv bin BII-tən.*	**I've been raped.** *aîv bin reîpt.*	**ENGLISH** emergencies
Ich bin niedergeschlagen worden. *i<u>sh</u> bin NII-dər-gə<u>sh</u>-laa-gən VOR-dən.*	**Ich bin vergewaltigt worden.** *i<u>sh</u> bin fer-gə-VAL-tikt VOR-dən.*	**DEUTSCH** notfälle
Me han pegado. *me an pe-GA-<u>dho</u>.*	**Me han violado.** *me an biô-LA-<u>dho</u>.*	**ESPAÑOL** urgencias
On m'a frappé. *oⁿ ma fra-PE.*	**On m'a violé.** *oⁿ ma viô-LE.*	**FRANÇAIS** urgences
Sono stato picchiato. *SO-no STA-to pik-KIÂ-to.*	**Sono stato violentato.** *SO-no STA-to viô-len-TA-to.*	**ITALIANO** emergenze
Eu fui espancado. *eû fuî es-paⁿ-KA-du.*	**Eu fui estuprado.** *eû fuî es-tu-PRA-du.*	**PORTUGUÊS** emergência
Byl jsem zmlácen. *bil semz-MLAA-tsen.*	**Byl jsem znásilněn.** *bil semz-NAA-sil-niên.*	**ČESKY** krize

ENGLISH countries	[I'm / We're] from _____.	the United States Great Britain (Northern) Ireland Canada Germany	
DEUTSCH länder	[Ich bin / Wir sind] aus _____.	den Vereinigten Staaten Großbritannien (Nord) Irland Kanada Deutschland	
ESPAÑOL países	[Soy / Somos] de _____.	los Estados Unidos Gran Bretaña Irlanda (del Norte) Canadá Alemania	
FRANÇAIS pays	[Je viens / Nous venons] _____.	des États-Unis de Grande Bretagne d'Irlande (du Nord) du Canada d'Allemagne	
ITALIANO paesi	[Vengo / Veniamo] _____.	dagli Stati Uniti dalla Gran Bretagna dall'Irlanda (del Nord) dal Canada dalla Germania	
PORTUGUÊS países	[Eu sou / Nós somos] _____.	dos Estados Unidos da Grã-Bretanha da Irlanda (do Norte) do Canadá da Alemanha	
ČESKY země	[Já jsem / My jsme] _____.	ze Spojených Států z Velké Britanie ze (Severního) Irska z Kanady z Německa	

		ENGLISH countries
Austria	Italy	
Switzerland	Brazil	
Spain	Portugal	
France	the Czech Republic	
Belgium	the Netherlands	

		DEUTSCH länder
Österreich	Italien	
der Schweiz	Brasilien	
Spanien	Portugal	
Frankreich	der Tschechischen Republik	
Belgien	den Niederlanden	

		ESPAÑOL países
Austria	Italia	
Suiza	Brasil	
España	Portugal	
Francia	la República Checa	
Bélgica	Holanda	

		FRANÇAIS pays
d'Autriche	d'Italie	
de Suisse	du Brésil	
d'Espagne	du Portugal	
de France	de la Republique Tchèque	
de Belgique	des Pays-Bas	

		ITALIANO paesi
dall'Austria	dall'Italia	
dalla Svizzera	dal Brasile	
dalla Spagna	dal Portogallo	
dalla Francia	dalla Repubblica Ceca	
dal Belgio	dall'Olanda	

		PORTUGUÊS países
de Áustria	da Itália	
da Suíça	do Brasil	
da Espanha	de Portugal	
da França	da República Tcheca	
da Bélgica	dos Países Baixos	

		ČESKY země
z Rakouska	z Italie	
ze Švýcarska	z Brazílie	
ze Španělska	z Portugalska	
z Francie	z [České republiky / Čech]	
z Belgie	z Nizozemska	

ENGLISH numbers	one	six	eleven
	two	seven	twelve
	three	eight	thirteen
	four	nine	fourteen
	five	ten	fifteen
DEUTSCH zahlen	♂ ein / ♀ eine	sechs	elf
	zwei	sieben	zwölf
	drei	acht	dreizehn
	vier	neun	vierzehn
	fünf	zehn	fünfzehn
ESPAÑOL números	♂ un / ♀ una	seis	once
	dos	siete	doce
	tres	ocho	trece
	cuatro	nueve	catorce
	cinco	diez	quince
FRANÇAIS numéros	♂ un / ♀ une	six	onze
	deux	sept	douze
	trois	huit	treize
	quatre	neuf	quatorze
	cinq	dix	quinze
ITALIANO numeri	♂ un, uno / ♀ una	sei	undici
	due	sette	dodici
	tre	otto	tredici
	quattro	nove	quattordici
	cinque	dieci	quindici
PORTUGUÊS números	♂ um / ♀ uma	seis	onze
	♂ dois / ♀ duas	sete	doze
	três	oito	treze
	quatro	nove	quatorze
	cinco	dez	quinze
ČESKY čísla	♂ jeden / ♀ jedna	šest	jedenáct
	♂ dva / ♀ dvě	sedm	dvanáct
	tři	osm	třináct
	čtyři	devět	čtrnáct
	pět	deset	patnáct

sixteen	twenty-one	thirty	**ENGLISH**	numbers
seventeen	twenty-three	forty		
eighteen	twenty-five	fifty		
nineteen	twenty-seven	sixty		
twenty	twenty-nine	seventy		
sechzehn	einundzwanzig	dreißig	**DEUTSCH**	zahlen
siebzehn	dreiundzwanzig	vierzig		
achtzehn	fünfundzwanzig	fünfzig		
neunzehn	siebenundzwanzig	sechzig		
zwanzig	neunundzwanzig	siebzig		
dieciséis	veintiuno	treinta	**ESPAÑOL**	números
diecisiete	veintitrés	cuarenta		
dieciocho	veinticinco	cincuenta		
diecinueve	veintisiete	sesenta		
veinte	veintinueve	setenta		
seize	vingt et un	trente	**FRANÇAIS**	numéros
dix-sept	vingt-trois	quarante		
dix-huit	vingt-cinq	cinquante		
dix-neuf	vingt-sept	soixante		
vingt	vingt-neuf	soixante-dix		
sedici	ventuno	trenta	**ITALIANO**	numeri
diciassette	ventitre	quaranta		
diciotto	venticinque	cinquanta		
diciannove	ventisette	sessanta		
venti	ventinove	settanta		
dezesseis	vinte e um	trinta	**PORTUGUÊS**	números
dezessete	vinte e três	quarenta		
dezoito	vinte e cinco	cinquenta		
dezenove	vinte e sete	sessenta		
vinte	vinte e nove	setenta		
šestnáct	dvacet jeden	třicet	**ČESKY**	čísla
sedmnáct	dvacet tři	čtyřicet		
osmnáct	dvacet pět	padesát		
devatenáct	dvacet sedm	šedesát		
dvacet	dvacet devět	sedmdesát		

WORD LIST

WÖRTER-VERZEICHNIS

VOCABULARIO

VOCAB ULAIRE

VOCABOLARIO

SLOVNÍK

VOCABU LÁRIO

ENGLISH people	bisexual, switch hitter	to be bisexual, to be bi, to be AC-DC, to swing both ways, to be a switch hitter	bottom
DEUTSCH leute	der Bisexuelle	bisexuell sein, bi sein	der Passive
ESPAÑOL gente	el bisexual, el bi	ser bisexual, darle a los dos palos, irle los dos palos, jugar en los dos campos	el pasivo
FRANÇAIS gens	le bisexuel, le bi, le berdache *(Qb)*, le bilingue *(Qb)*	être bisexuel, être bique et bouc, être jazz-tango, être au deux *(Qb)*	le passif, le mec passif, l'enculé, la planche *(Qb)*
ITALIANO gente	il bisessuale, il bisex	essere bisessuale, essere bisex, andare a corrente alternata	il passivo
PORTUGUÊS pessoas	o bissexual, o gilete	ser bissexual, cortar dos dois lados, ser gilete	o passivo
ČESKY lidé	bisexuál, kluk na obojí	být bisexuál, být na obojí	pasivní kluk, kluk který se nechá mrdat

(my) boyfriend, guy, beau ☞ LOVER, P. 275	butch, straight-acting, non-effeminate, manly	clone	**ENGLISH**	people
(mein) Freund, fester Freund ☞ GELIEBTER, S. 275	männlich, Kerl, machohaft, betont maskulin	der geklonter Typ, der Clone, der Ledertyp	**DEUTSCH**	leute
(mi) novio, amigo, pareja ☞ AMANTE, PÁG. 275	macho, masculino, chongo *(LA)*	el clon, el bigotudo, el bigotes	**ESPAÑOL**	gente
(mon) ami, mec, copain, chum *(Qb)*, faraud *(Qb)* ☞ AMANT, P. 275	macho, mec-mec, butch *(Qb)*	le clone, le mâle à moustache *(Qb)*	**FRANÇAIS**	gens
(il mio) fidanzato, amico, ragazzo, compagno ☞ AMANTE, P. 275	macho, maschile, virile	il clone	**ITALIANO**	gente
(meu) namorado, gato, caso, amigo ☞ AMANTE, PÁG. 275	bofe, masculino, não efeminado, machão	a barbie; o gay estereotípico com bigode	**PORTUGUÊS**	pessoas
(můj) přítel, kluk, milý ☞ MILENEC, STR. 275	chlapský, mužný	„klon"; gay, který se snaží vypadat podle současných gay trendů	**ČESKY**	lidé

ENGLISH people	closeted, in the closet, not out ☞ COME OUT, P. 267 & OUT, P. 276	cocksucker	cocktease, cockteaser, tease
DEUTSCH leute	versteckt, nicht offen schwul lebend ☞ COMING-OUT HABEN, S. 267 & OFFEN SCHWUL, S. 276	der Schwanzlutscher	*(NE)* einer, der anmacht und dann abblitzen läßt
ESPAÑOL gente	no abiertamente gay, escondido ☞ DECLARARSE, PÁG. 267 & ABIERTAMENTE GAY, PÁG. 276	el chupapollas, el chupapijas *(LA)*	el calientapollas
FRANÇAIS gens	coincé, fermé *(Qb)* ☞ ASSUMER, P. 267 & PAS COINCÉ, P. 276	le pompeur, le suceur (de bite), le mangeux (de queue) *(Qb)*	l'allumeur, l'aguicheur, le bandeur, l'agace pissette *(Qb)*
ITALIANO gente	nascosto, non dichiarato, velato ☞ DICHIARARSI, P. 267 & APERTAMENTE GAY, P. 276	il succhiacazzo, il ciucciacazzi, il sugaminchia	il provocatore; uno che te lo fa tirare ma poi non ci sta
PORTUGUÊS pessoas	incubado, não assumido, enrustido ☞ ASSUMIR, PÁG. 267 & ASSUMIDO, PÁG. 276	o chupador de pau	o provocador
ČESKY lidé	skrývaný ☞ OCHALIT, STR. 267 & NESKRÝVANÝ, STR. 276	*(NE)* kluk který kouří čuráky	*(NE)* kluk který ostatní dráždí sexuálně ale nenechá k ničemu dojít

come out (of the closet) ☞ OUT, P. 276	daddy	dirty old man, old lech, old goat	**ENGLISH**	people
das Coming-Out haben ☞ OFFEN SCHWUL, S. 276	der Daddy	der alte geile Typ, der alte Wüstling	**DEUTSCH**	leute
declararse, hacer pública la propia homosexualidad, blanquear *(LA)* ☞ ABIERTAMENTE GAY, PÁG. 276	el papá, el viejo	el viejo verde, el sátiro	**ESPAÑOL**	gente
assumer, sortir de l'ombre *(Qb)* ☞ PAS COINCÉ, P. 276	le papy, le motté *(Qb)*	le vieux vicelard, le vieux dégueulasse	**FRANÇAIS**	gens
dichiararsi, uscire allo scoperto, venire fuori ☞ APERTAMENTE GAY, P. 276	il papà, il babbo	il vecchio bavoso, il vecchio porco	**ITALIANO**	gente
assumir, declarar-se *(Por)* ☞ ASSUMIDO, PÁG. 276	o paisão	o velho assanhado, o velho safado, o coroa sem vergonha	**PORTUGUÊS**	pessoas
ochalit svoji homosexualitu, přestat skrývat svoji homosexualitu ☞ NESKRÝVANÝ, STR. 276	„strýček"	špinavej dědek, starý necuda	**ČESKY**	lidé

ENGLISH people	in drag ☞ TRANSVESTITE, P. 282; DRAG SHOW P. 313	dyke ☞ LESBIAN, P. 275	easy, loose (sexually) ☞ SLUTTY, P. 280
DEUTSCH leute	im Fummel, als Tunte, als Transe ☞ TRANSVESTIT, S. 282; TRAVESTIESHOW, S. 313	die Lesbe ☞ LESBE, S. 275	locker (sexuel) ☞ NUTTIG, S. 280
ESPAÑOL gente	travestido *(adj)* ☞ TRAVESTI, PÁG. 282; ESPECTÁCULO DE TRAVESTIS, PÁG. 313	la tortillera, la bollera ☞ LESBIANA, PÁG. 275	fácil, golfo ☞ PUTA, PÁG. 280
FRANÇAIS gens	travesti *(adj)* ☞ TRAVESTI, P. 282; SPECTACLE DE TRAV, P. 313	la gouine, la gousse, la less *(Qb)*, la boutche *(Qb)* ☞ LESBIENNE, P. 275	facile, qui a la cuisse légère *(Qb)* ☞ GROS COUREUR, P. 280
ITALIANO gente	travestito *(adj)* ☞ TRAVESTITO, P. 282; SPETTACOLO DI TRAVES- TITI, P. 313	la lesbica, la saffica, la saffo, la donna gay, la ciucciabrugnona ☞ LESBICA, P. 275	facile ☞ TROIA, P. 280
PORTUGUÊS pessoas	travestido, vestido de mulher ☞ TRAVESTI, PÁG. 282; SHOW DE TRAVESTI, PÁG. 313	a sapatão, a fanchona, a machona ☞ LÉSBICA, PÁG. 275	fácil ☞ PIRANHA, PÁG. 280
ČESKY lidé	*(NE)* oblečený do ženských šatů ☞ TRAVESTIE, STR. 282; TRAVESTIE SHOW, STR. 313	lesbička, lesba, lízačka ☞ LESBA, STR. 275	*(NE)* který jde s každým ☞ PROVAŘENÝ, STR. 280

escort	escort service, escort agency	fag hag, fruit fly	**ENGLISH**	people
der Callboy	der Callboyservice	die Schwulenmutti, die Tuntenmutter	**DEUTSCH**	leute
el chico de compañía	la agencia de chicos de compañía, la casa con chicos	*(NE)* una de esas chicas que siempre anda con gays, la jotera *(LA)*	**ESPAÑOL**	gente
le callboy, l'escorte *(Qb)*	l'agence de callboys, l'agence d'escortes *(Qb)*	la fille à pédés, la morue à pédés, la fille à tapettes *(Qb)*	**FRANÇAIS**	gens
l'accompagnatore	il servizio d'accompagnatori, l'agenzia d'accompagnatori	*(NE)* una che frequenta i gay, una che è amica di molti finocchi	**ITALIANO**	gente
o acompanhante	o serviço de acompanhantes, a agência de acompanhantes	*(NE)* uma mulher com muitos amigos gays	**PORTUGUÊS**	pessoas
společník, doprovod	escort servis	buzimutr	**ČESKY**	lidé

ENGLISH / people	fag, faggot, queer, homo, fairy, fruit, pansy, poof *(Br)*, poofter *(Br)* ☞ QUEEN, P. 277	gay guy, queer boy	gay, queer, bent *(Br)*
DEUTSCH / leute	der Homo, der warme Bruder, die Trine ☞ TUNTE, S. 277	der Schwule, der Gay, der Homo	♂ schwul, ♀ lesbisch
ESPAÑOL / gente	el marica, el maricón, el mariquita, el puto *(LA)*, el pájaro *(LA)*, el pato *(LA)* ☞ LOCA, PÁG. 277	el gay, el homosexual, el internacional *(LA)*, el joto *(LA)*	gay, homosexual, ♀ lesbiana
FRANÇAIS / gens	l'homo, le pédé, la folle, la tante, la chouquette, la moumoune *(Qb)*, la grande fille *(Qb)* ☞ FOLLE, P. 277	le pédé, l'homo, le gai *(Qb)*	gai, ♂ pédé, homo, folle, ♀ lesbienne
ITALIANO / gente	il frocio, il finocchio, il recchione, la checca, la cula ☞ CHECCA, P. 277	il gay	gay, ♀ lesbica
PORTUGUÊS / pessoas	a bicha, o veado, a mariquinha, a boneca, o fresco, o maricas *(Por)*, o paneleiro *(Por)* ☞ BICHA, PÁG. 277	o gay, o entendido	gay, ♂ entendido, ♀ lésbica, entendida
ČESKY / lidé	teplouš, buzerant, buzna, přihřátý ☞ TETA, STR. 277	gay, homosexuál	homosexuální, gay

golddigger, gigolo	guy, dude, boy, lad *(Br)*, chap *(Br)*, bloke *(Br)*	het, breeder ☞ HET, P. 272	**ENGLISH**	people
(NE) einer, der sich aushalten läßt	der Typ, der Kerl, der Junge	die Hete, ♂ der / ♀ die Hetero, ♂ der / ♀ die Normale ☞ HETERO, S. 272	**DEUTSCH**	leute
el cazafortunas, el interesado, el gigoló	el tipo, el tío, el chico, el muchacho, el chaval, el pibe *(LA)*	♂ el / ♀ la hétero ☞ HÉTERO, PÁG. 272	**ESPAÑOL**	gente
l'aventurier, le gigolo, le gig, le courailleur *(Qb)*	le mec, le type, le garçon, le gars *(Qb)*	l'hétéro, ♂ le / ♀ la straight *(Qb)* ☞ HÉTÉRO, P. 272	**FRANÇAIS**	gens
la marchetta, l'avventuriere, il marchettaro	il ragazzo, il tipo, il tizio	l'etero ☞ ETERO, P. 272	**ITALIANO**	gente
o caça fortuna, o gigolô, o caça-dote	o tipo, o cara, o rapaz, o sujeito, o garoto, o menino, o gajo *(Por)*	♂ o / ♀ a hetero, ♂ o / ♀ a careta ☞ HETERO, PÁG. 272	**PORTUGUÊS**	pessoas
prospěchář	kluk, chlapec, chlap, hoch	normál ☞ NORMÁLNÍ, STR. 272	**ČESKY**	lidé

ENGLISH people	het, hetero, straight *(adj)* ☞ HET, P. 271	heterosexual *(n & adj)*	homophobic
DEUTSCH leute	hetero, normal ☞ HETE, S. 271	♂ der / ♀ die Heterosexuelle *(n)*; heterosexuell *(adj)*	homophob, schwulenfeindlich
ESPAÑOL gente	hétero *(adj)* ☞ HÉTERO, PÁG. 271	♂ el / ♀ la heterosexual *(n)*; heterosexual *(adj)*	♂ homofóbico, ♀ homofóbica
FRANÇAIS gens	hétéro, straight *(Qb) (adj)* ☞ HÉTÉRO, P. 271	♂ l'hétérosexuel, ♀ l'hétérosexuelle *(n)*; ♂ hétérosexuel, ♀ hétérosexuelle *(adj)*	homophobe
ITALIANO gente	etero *(adj)* ☞ ETERO, P. 271	l'eterosessuale *(n)*; eterosessuale *(adj)*	♂ omofobico, ♀ omofobica
PORTUGUÊS pessoas	hetero, careta *(adj)* ☞ HETERO, PÁG. 271	♂ o / ♀ a heterossexual *(n)*; heterossexual *(adj)*	♂ homofóbico, ♀ homofóbica
ČESKY lidé	normální ☞ NORMÁL, P. 271	♂ heterosexuál, ♀ heterosexuálka *(n)*; heterosexuální *(adj)*	homofobní

homosexual *(n & adj)* ☞ FAG, P. 270 & QUEEN, P. 277	hung, well-hung, well-endowed, hung like a horse, big-dicked	hustler, callboy, working boy, rent boy *(Br)* ☞ PROSTITUTE, P. 277	**ENGLISH** people
♂ der / ♀ die Homo-sexuelle *(n)*; homo-sexuell *(adj)* ☞ HOMO, S. 270 & TUNTE, S. 277	gut bestückt	der Stricher, der Strich-junge, der Callboy ☞ PROSTITUIERTE, S. 277	**DEUTSCH** leute
♂ el / ♀ la homosexual *(n)*; homosexual *(adj)* ☞ MARICA, PÁG. 270 & LOCA, PÁG. 277	bien dotado, bien armado	el chapero, el chulo, el gigoló, el taxi *(LA)* ☞ PROSTITUTO, PÁG. 277	**ESPAÑOL** gente
♂ l'homosexuel, ♀ l'ho-mosexuel *(n)*; ♂ homo-sexuel, ♀ homosexu-uelle *(adj)* ☞ HOMO, P. 270 & FOLLE, P. 277	bien monté, bien membré, «BM», «TBM», bien amanché *(Qb)*, bien greillé *(Qb)*	le tapin, la pute, le gig, le gigolo, le commercial *(Qb)* ☞ PROSTITUÉ, P. 277	**FRANÇAIS** gens
l'omosessuale *(n)*; omosessuale *(adj)* ☞ FROCIO, P. 270 & CHECCA, P. 277	dotato, ben dotato, fornito	la marchetta, il marchet-taro ☞ PROSTITUTO, P. 277	**ITALIANO** gente
♂ o / ♀ a homossexual *(n)*; homossexual *(adj)* ☞ BICHA, PÁG. 270 & BICHA, PÁG. 277	bem dotado, malão, bom de mala, com uma boa moca *(Por)*	o michê, o garoto de programa, o garoto de aluguel, o chulo *(Por)* ☞ PROSTITUTO, PÁG. 277	**PORTUGUÊS** pessoas
♂ homosexuál, ♀ homosexuálka *(n)*; homosexuální *(adj)* ☞ TEPLOUŠ, STR. 270 & TETA, STR. 277	dobře vybavený, s velkým čurákem	prostitut, děvka, gigolo, kurva ☞ PROSTITUT, STR. 277	**ČESKY** lidé

ENGLISH people	kinky	leatherman, leatherguy ☞ LEATHER BAR, P. 315	lecher, lech
DEUTSCH leute	versaut, abgefahren, ausgefallen, abartig, pervers	der Ledertyp, der Ledermann ☞ LEDERBAR, S. 315	der Wüstling
ESPAÑOL gente	morboso	el hombre leather ☞ BAR LEATHER, PÁG. 315	el obseso, el vicioso, el lascivo, el sátiro
FRANÇAIS gens	cochon, lubrique, bizarre	le mec cuir, le gars au cuir *(Qb)* ☞ BAR CUIR, P. 315	l'obsedé, le libertin, le dévergondé, le débauché
ITALIANO gente	perverso, trasgressivo	il leather, l'uomo in cuoio ☞ BAR LEATHER, P. 315	il libertino
PORTUGUÊS pessoas	sacana, vicioso	*(NE)* o homem que se veste em couro ☞ BAR DE COURO, PÁG. 315	o lascívo, o insaciável, o tarado
ČESKY lidé	ujetý	koženák, leatherman ☞ LEATHER BAR, STR. 315	chlípník, prasák, obšourník

			ENGLISH people
lesbian *(n)* ☞ DYKE, P. 268	(my) lover ☞ BOYFRIEND, P. 265	masochist	

			DEUTSCH leute
die Lesbe ☞ LESBE, S. 268	(mein) Geliebter, Lover ☞ FREUND, S. 265	der Masochist, der Maso	

			ESPAÑOL gente
la lesbiana ☞ TORTILLERA, PÁG. 268	(mi) amante, novio, compañero ☞ NOVIO, PÁG. 265	el masoquista, el masoca	

			FRANÇAIS gens
la lesbienne, la «less» *(Qb)* ☞ GOUINE, P. 268	(mon) amant, copain, chum *(Qb)* ☞ AMI, P. 265	le masochiste, le maso	

			ITALIANO gente
la lesbica ☞ LESBICA, P. 268	(il mio) amante, innamorato, fidanzato ☞ FIDANZATO, P. 265	il masochista	

			PORTUGUÊS pessoas
a lésbica ☞ SAPATÃO, PÁG. 268	(meu) amante ☞ NAMORADO, PÁG. 265	o masoquista	

			ČESKY lidé
lesba, lesbička ☞ LESBIČKA, STR. 268	(můj) milenec ☞ PŘÍTEL, STR. 265	masochista	

ENGLISH people	minor, chicken, jailbait, under-age kid	muscleboy	out (of the closet), openly gay ☞ CLOSETED, P. 266 & COME OUT, P. 267
DEUTSCH leute	der Minderjährige	der Muskeltyp, der Bodybuilder	offen schwul ☞ VERSTECKT, S. 266 & COMING-OUT HABEN, S. 267
ESPAÑOL gente	el menor (de edad)	el musculitos, el cachas, el tipo musculoso	abiertamente gay, declarado, blanqueado *(LA)* ☞ NO ABIERTAMENTE GAY, PÁG. 266 & DECLARARSE, PÁG. 267
FRANÇAIS gens	le mineur	le mec musclé, le bodybuilder, le culturiste, le gars musclé *(Qb)*	pas coincé, assumé, ouvert *(Qb)* ☞ COINCÉ, P. 266 & ASSUMER, P. 267
ITALIANO gente	il minorenne	il muscoloso, il mister muscolo, il palestrato, il fusto	apertamente gay, dichiarato ☞ NASCOSTO, P. 266 & DICHIARARSI, P. 267
PORTUGUÊS pessoas	o menor de idade	o garotão, o garoto musculoso	assumido, declarado *(Por)* ☞ INCUBADO, PÁG. 266 & ASSUMIR, PÁG. 267
ČESKY lidé	chlapec pod zákonem	svalovec	neskrývaný (své homosexuality) ☞ SKRÝVANÝ, STR. 266 & OCHALIT, STR. 267

prostitute ☞ HUSTLER, P. 273	queen, mary ☞ FAG, P. 270 & FLAMING QUEEN, P. 278	queeny, faggy, nelly, effeminate, camp *(Br)*	**ENGLISH** people
der Prostituierte ☞ STRICHER, S. 273	die Tunte, die Trine, die Schwuchtel ☞ HOMO, S. 270 & SCHRILLE TUNTE, S. 278	tuntig, weibisch, effeminiert	**DEUTSCH** leute
el prostituto ☞ CHAPERO, PÁG. 273	la loca, la reina ☞ MARICA, PÁG. 270 & LOCA HISTÉRICA, PÁG. 278	mariquita, loca, plumas, afeminado, mariposa	**ESPAÑOL** gente
le prostitué ☞ TAPIN, P. 273	la folle, la pétasse, la tordue ☞ HOMO, P. 270 & FOLLE HURLANTE, P. 278	folle, chouquette, chochotte, effeminé, hystérique, grande *(Qb)*	**FRANÇAIS** gens
il prostituto ☞ MARCHETTA, P. 273	la checca, la pazza, la finocchia, la frocia ☞ FROCIO, P. 270 & CHECCA ISTERICA, P. 278	checca, scheccante, molto donna, effeminato	**ITALIANO** gente
o prostituto ☞ MICHÊ, PÁG. 273	a bicha, a mona, a rainha, a boneca, a perua ☞ BICHA, PÁG. 270 & BICHA LOUCA, PÁG. 278	bichinha, veadinho, mariquinha, efeminado, amaricado *(Por)*	**PORTUGUÊS** pessoas
prostitut ☞ PROSTITUT, STR. 273	teta, buzna ☞ TEPLOUŠ, STR. 270 & VELMI VYKROUCENÁ BUZNA, STR. 278	vykroucený, zženštilý	**ČESKY** lidé

ENGLISH people	flaming queen, screaming queen	to queen it up, to camp it up, to fag out	sadist
DEUTSCH leute	die schrille Tunte	sich tuntig benehmen	der Sadist, der Sado
ESPAÑOL gente	la loca histérica	hacer la loca, hacer mariconadas, mariconear, hacer la reinona, sacar las plumas	el sadista
FRANÇAIS gens	la folle hurlante, la géante (Qb)	faire la folle, faire la chouquette (Qb), faire la chochotte (Qb), chochotter (Qb)	le sadique, le sado
ITALIANO gente	la checca isterica	scheccare, fare la donna	il sadico
PORTUGUÊS pessoas	a bicha louca, a deslumbrada	soltar a franga, embonecar	o sádico
ČESKY lidé	velmi vykroucená buzna	chovat se vykrouceně	sadista

sadomasochist	sexy, hot, hot-looking, hunky	sexy guy, hot guy, cute guy, hunk, babe	**ENGLISH**	people
der Sadomasochist, der Sadomaso	sexy, heiß, geil, aufreizend, heiße Nummer	der Süße, der geile Typ, der gut gebaute Typ, der tierische Typ	**DEUTSCH**	leute
el sadomasoquista, el sadomasoca	sexy, bueno, macizo	el tipo buenísimo, el muñeco, el bonbón	**ESPAÑOL**	gente
le sadomasochiste, le sadomaso, le SM	sexe, sexy, aguichant	le beau mec, le (mec) canon, le beau gars *(Qb)*	**FRANÇAIS**	gens
il sadomasochista	sexy, bono, arrapante, figo, eccitante, sensuale	il bel ragazzo, il ragazzo bono, il figone	**ITALIANO**	gente
o sadomasoquista	sexi, tesão, tesudo, fogoso, quente *(Por)*	o tesão, o gatão, o gostoso, o tesudo, o matulão *(Por)*	**PORTUGUÊS**	pessoas
sadomasochista	sexy, vzrušující	pěkný kluk, hezoun, krasavec, sekáč, hřebec, frajer	**ČESKY**	lidé

ENGLISH people	sleazy	slut, tramp, whore, tart *(Br)*	slutty ☞ EASY, P. 268
DEUTSCH leute	schmutzig, versaut	die Schlampe, die Nutte, das Flittchen, die Hure	nuttig, schlampig ☞ LOCKER, S. 268
ESPAÑOL gente	sucio, vicioso, guarro, gamberro	la puta, el pendón	puta, muy puta, pendón ☞ FÁCIL, PÁG. 268
FRANÇAIS gens	cul, cochon, hard, sale, sexe	la salope, la pute, la putain, la guidoune *(Qb)*, la cochonne *(Qb)*	gros coureur, gros baiseur, salope, pute ☞ FACILE, P. 268
ITALIANO gente	squallido, sporco, sordido	la troia, la puttana, il porco	troia, puttana, porca, troiesco, puttanesco, porco ☞ FACILE, P. 268
PORTUGUÊS pessoas	baixaria	a piranha, a puta, a galinha, a biscate, a rameira, a meretriz	piranha, apiranhado, um tipo de puta, galinha, biscate, rameira ☞ FÁCIL, PÁG. 268
ČESKY lidé	slizký	kurva, štětka, coura, čubka	provařený ☞ KTERÝ JDE S KAŽDÝM, STR. 268

sugar daddy	top, topman	trade	**ENGLISH** people
der Sugardaddy	der Aktive	*(NE)* der Hetero, der manchmal schwulen Sex hat	**DEUTSCH** leute
el espónsor, el protector, el viejo generoso	el activo	*(NE)* el hétero que a veces va con gays; el buga *(LA)*	**ESPAÑOL** gente
le papa gâteau, le motté *(Qb)*, la vache à lait *(Qb)*	l'actif	*(NE)* l'hétéro qui parfois va avec des pédés, le faux straight *(Qb)*	**FRANÇAIS** gens
il papà generoso; uno che mantiene un ragazzo	l'attivo	*(NE)* l'etero che a volte fa sesso gay	**ITALIANO** gente
o coronel, o rico protetor, o "marido" rico	o ativo	o bofe; o careta que ás vezes dorme com gays	**PORTUGUÊS** pessoas
bohatý strýček, sponzor	aktivní kluk, mrdák	*(NE)* normální kluk, který občas spí s kluky	**ČESKY** lidé

ENGLISH people	transsexual, tranny *(Br)*	transvestite, drag queen, female impersonator ☞ IN DRAG, P. 268 & DRAG SHOW, P. 313	trick, pick-up, one-night stand ☞ TO TRICK, P. 310
DEUTSCH leute	der Transexuelle	der Transvestit, die Transe, die Fummeltrine ☞ IM FUMMEL, S. 268 & TRAVESTIESHOW, S. 313	der One-Night-Stand, die Fickbekanntschaft, jemand für eine Nacht ☞ EIN NUMMER MACHEN, S. 310
ESPAÑOL gente	el transexual	el travesti, el travestido, la reinona, la «vestida» *(LA)* ☞ TRAVESTIDO, PÁG. 268 & ESPECTÁCULO..., PÁG. 313	el ligue (de un día), la aventura (de una noche), la conquista ☞ LIGAR, PÁG. 310
FRANÇAIS gens	le transsexuel	le travesti, le trav, le travelo ☞ TRAVESTI, P. 268 & SPECTACLE DE TRAV, P. 313	le coup, la conquête, le sauté *(Qb)* ☞ TIRER UN COUP, P. 310
ITALIANO gente	il transessuale	il travestito, la travestita ☞ TRAVESTITO, P. 268 & SPETTACOLO DI TRAVES- TITI, P. 313	la scopata, il rimorchio, l'avventura (di una notte) ☞ FARSI UNA SCOPATA, P. 310
PORTUGUÊS pessoas	o transsexual	o travesti ☞ EM TRAVESTI, PÁG. 268 & SHOW DE TRAVESTI, PÁG. 313	a cantada, a "aventura de uma noite", um "cari- nha", um "tipinho" ☞ TER UMA NOITADA, PÁG. 310
ČESKY lidé	transexuál	travestie, travestit ☞ OBLEČENÝ DO ŽEN- SKÝCH ŠATŮ, STR. 268 & TRAVESTIE SHOW, STR. 313	sbalení, kluk na jednu noc, kluk na jeden mrd ☞ MÍT NÁHODNÝ SEX, STR. 310

anus	ass, arse *(Br)* ☞ BUTT & BUNS, P. 284	asshole, arsehole *(Br)*	**ENGLISH**	body
der After, der Anus	der Arsch ☞ HINTERN & ARSCH-BACKEN, S. 284	das Arschloch	**DEUTSCH**	körper
el ano	el culo ☞ TRASERO & NALGAS, PÁG. 284	el ojo del culo	**ESPAÑOL**	cuerpo
l'anus	le cul ☞ DERRIÈRE & FESSES, P. 284	le trou du cul	**FRANÇAIS**	corps
l'ano	il culo ☞ SEDERE & CHIAPPE, P. 284	il buco del culo	**ITALIANO**	corpo
o ânus	o rabo, a bunda ☞ TRASEIRO & NÁDEGAS, PÁG. 284	o cu	**PORTUGUÊS**	corpo
konečník, anus, řiť	prdel ☞ ZADEK & PŮLKY, STR. 284	díra do prdele	**ČESKY**	tělo

ENGLISH body	balls, nuts, bollocks *(Br)*; testicles	buns, cheeks, butt-cheeks ☞ BUTTOCKS, P. 285	butt, backside, rear, tush, can, bottom *(Br)*, bum *(Br)* ☞ ASS, P. 283
DEUTSCH körper	die Eier; die Hoden	die Arschbacken ☞ HINTERBACKEN, S. 285	der Hintern, der Po ☞ ARSCH, S. 283
ESPAÑOL cuerpo	los huevos, los cojones, las pelotas, las bolas *(LA)*; los testículos	las nalgas ☞ NALGAS, PÁG. 285	el trasero ☞ CULO, PÁG. 283
FRANÇAIS corps	les couilles, les bonbons, les valseuses, les balles *(Qb)*, les boules *(Qb)*; les testicules	les fesses, les miches, les joues *(Qb)*, les poupounes *(Qb)* ☞ FESSES, P. 285	le derrière, l'arrière-train, le bahut *(Qb)*, le califourchon *(Qb)* ☞ CUL, P. 283
ITALIANO corpo	le palle, i coglioni; i testicoli	le chiappe ☞ NATICHE, P. 285	il sedere, il fondoschiena, il deretano ☞ CULO, P. 283
PORTUGUÊS corpo	as bolas, os colhões *(Por)*; os testículos	as nádegas ☞ NÁDEGAS, PÁG. 285	o traseiro, a bunda ☞ RABO, PÁG. 283
ČESKY tělo	koule; varlata	půlky ☞ PŮLKY, STR. 285	zadek, zadnice ☞ PRDEL, STR. 283

buttocks ☞ BUNS & BUTT, P. 284	circumcised, cut ☞ UNCIRCUMCISED, P. 288	cock, dick, prick, rod, tool, pecker, peter, wiener, schlong, willy *(Br)* ☞ PENIS, P. 287	**ENGLISH** body
die Hinterbacken ☞ ARSCHBACKEN & HINTERN, S. 284	beschnitten ☞ UNBESCHNITTEN, S. 288	der Schwanz, das Glied, der Piller, der Pimmel, das Ding, der Willi ☞ PENIS, S. 287	**DEUTSCH** körper
las nalgas ☞ NALGAS & TRASERO, PÁG. 284	circuncidado ☞ NO CIRCUNDIDADO, PÁG. 288	la polla, el rabo, el pito, la pinga *(LA)*, el bicho *(LA)*, el chile *(LA)*, el churro *(LA)*, la pija *(LA)* ☞ PENE, PÁG. 287	**ESPAÑOL** cuerpo
les fesses ☞ FESSES & DERRIÈRE, P. 284	circoncis, décapité *(Qb)* ☞ NON-CIRCONCIS, P. 288	la bite, la queue, la verge, la pine, l'affaire *(Qb)*, le bâton *(Qb)*, le batte *(Qb)* ☞ PÉNIS, P. 287	**FRANÇAIS** corps
le natiche ☞ CHIAPPE & SEDERE, P. 284	circonciso ☞ NON CIRCONCISO, P. 288	il cazzo, l'uccello, il pisello, la minchia, la verga, la nerchia, il pistolino ☞ PENE, P. 287	**ITALIANO** corpo
as nádegas ☞ NÁDEGAS & TRASEIRO, PÁG. 284	circunciso, circuncisado ☞ NÃO CIRCUNCISO, PÁG. 288	o pau, o perú, o caralho, a rola, a pica, o cacete, a picha *(Por)*, a tranca *(Por)* ☞ PÊNIS, PÁG. 287	**PORTUGUÊS** corpo
půlky ☞ PŮLKY & ZADEK, STR. 284	obřezaný ☞ NEOBŘEZANÝ, STR. 288	čurák, péro, ocas, pták ☞ PENIS, STR. 287	**ČESKY** tělo

ENGLISH body	cockhead	erection; hard-on, boner, woodie, stiffy *(Br)* ☞ TO GET IT UP, P. 300	foreskin
DEUTSCH körper	die Eichel	die Erektion; der Ständer, der Steife ☞ EINEN HOCHKRIEGEN, S. 300	die Vorhaut
ESPAÑOL cuerpo	el capullo	la erección; la polla tiesa, la pija dura *(LA)*, la pinga parada *(LA)* ☞ PONERSE DURA, PÁG. 300	el prepucio
FRANÇAIS corps	le gland, le cass *(Qb)*	l'érection; la trique, le gourdin, le bandage *(Qb)* ☞ BANDER, P. 300	le prépuce, la peau du cass *(Qb)*
ITALIANO corpo	la cappella	l'erezione; il cazzo duro ☞ INDURIRE, P. 300	il prepuzio
PORTUGUÊS corpo	a cabeça do pau	a ereção, a erecção *(Por)*; o pau duro, a tenda armada, o pau ereto ☞ ENDURECER, PÁG. 300	o prepúcio; a pelezinha que envolve a cabeça do pau
ČESKY tělo	žalud	ztopořený penis; tvrdý čurák, tvrdé péro, postavený čurák ☞ POSTAVIT SE, STR. 300	předkožka

nipples ☞ TITS, P. 288	penis ☞ COCK, P. 285	pubic hair, crotch hair	**ENGLISH**	body
die Brustwarzen, die Nippel ☞ TITTEN, S. 288	der Penis ☞ SCHWANZ, S. 285	die Schamhaare	**DEUTSCH**	körper
los pezones ☞ TETAS, PÁG. 288	el pene ☞ POLLA, PÁG. 285	el vello púbico, la pelambre, el pelo de los cojones, los pendejos *(LA)*	**ESPAÑOL**	cuerpo
les tétons, les mamelons ☞ SEINS, P. 288	le pénis ☞ BITE, P. 285	les poils pubiens, les poils du cul *(Qb)*	**FRANÇAIS**	corps
i capezzoli ☞ TETTE, P. 288	il pene ☞ CAZZO, P. 285	i peli pubici	**ITALIANO**	corpo
os bicos do peito ☞ TETAS, PÁG. 288	o pênis ☞ PAU, PÁG. 285	os cabelos púbicos, os pentelhos	**PORTUGUÊS**	corpo
bradavky ☞ PRSA, STR. 288	penis ☞ ČURÁK, STR. 285	chlupy	**ČESKY**	tělo

ENGLISH body	scrotum; ballsac ☞ BALLS, P. 284	tits ☞ NIPPLES, P. 287	uncircumcised, uncut ☞ CIRCUMCISED, P. 285
DEUTSCH körper	der Hodensack; der Sack ☞ EIER, S. 284	die Titten, die Brust ☞ BRUSTWARZEN, S. 287	unbeschnitten ☞ BESCHNITTEN, S. 285
ESPAÑOL cuerpo	el escroto ☞ HUEVOS, PÁG. 284	las tetas ☞ PEZONES, PÁG. 287	no circuncidado ☞ CIRCUNCIDADO, PÁG. 285
FRANÇAIS corps	le scrotum ☞ COUILLES, P. 284	les seins, les tétons ☞ TÉTONS, P. 287	non-circoncis, pas décapité *(Qb)* ☞ CIRCONCIS, P. 285
ITALIANO corpo	lo scroto ☞ PALLE, P. 284	le tette ☞ CAPEZZOLI, P. 287	non circonciso ☞ CIRCONCISO, P. 285
PORTUGUÊS corpo	o escroto; o saco ☞ BOLAS, PÁG. 284	as tetas, os peitos ☞ BICOS DO PEITO, PÁG. 287	não circunciso, não circuncisado ☞ CIRCUNCISO, PÁG. 285
ČESKY tělo	šourek; pytel ☞ KOULE, STR. 284	prsa ☞ BRADAVKY, STR. 287	neobřezaný ☞ OBŘEZANÝ, STR. 285

to come on to, to hit on, to make a pass at	to cruise ☞ PICK UP, P. 290	to go cruising, to be on the make, to go trolling *(Br)* ☞ CRUISING SPOT, P. 313	**ENGLISH**	pickups
anmachen	flirten mit, anmachen ☞ ABSCHLEPPEN, S. 290	auf Anmache gehen, aufreißen gehen, jemanden für's Bett suchen, cruisen ☞ AUFREIßGEBIET, S. 313	**DEUTSCH**	abschleppen
hacer un pase a, piropear a, trabajarse a	ligar con, trabajarse a ☞ LIGAR, PÁG. 290	ir de ligue, hacer la carrera ☞ LUGAR DE LIGUE, PÁG. 313	**ESPAÑOL**	ligues
aborder, draguer, faire une passe à *(Qb)*	draguer, cruiser *(Qb)* ☞ RENCONTRER, P. 290	aller draguer, courir, courailler, cruiser *(Qb)*, être sur la cruise *(Qb)* ☞ LIEU DE DRAGUE, P. 313	**FRANÇAIS**	draguer
provarci con	rimorchiare, battere ☞ RIMORCHIARE, P. 290	andare a rimorchiare, andare a battere ☞ ZONA DI RIMORCHIO, P. 313	**ITALIANO**	rimorchi
dar em cima de, cantar a, engatar *(Por)*	caçar, paquerar, engatar *(Por)* ☞ CANTAR, PÁG. 290	ir caçar, ir ao engate *(Por)* ☞ ÁREA DE CAÇAÇÃO, PÁG. 313	**PORTUGUÊS**	cantadas
sbalit	sledovat, flirtovat s ☞ SBALIT, STR. 290	holandit, lovit chlapy ☞ HOLANDA, STR. 313	**ČESKY**	balení

ENGLISH pickups	flirt *(n)*	to flirt with, to make eyes at	to pick up ☞ TO CRUISE, P. 289
DEUTSCH abschleppen	der Flirter	flirten, anbaggern	abschleppen, aufreißen ☞ FLIRTEN, S. 289
ESPAÑOL ligues	el coqueto	flirtear con	ligar con, levantarse a *(LA)* ☞ LIGAR, PÁG. 289
FRANÇAIS draguer	le flirt, le flirteur	flirter avec	rencontrer, draguer ☞ DRAGUER, P. 289
ITALIANO rimorchi	il filarino, il flirt	flirtare con qualcuno filare con, fare il filo a	rimorchiare, beccare ☞ RIMORCHIARE, P. 289
PORTUGUÊS cantadas	o flerte	flertar com, namoricar	cantar, pegar, caçar ☞ CAÇAR, PÁG. 289
ČESKY balení	*(NE)* kluk, který rád flirtuje, koketa	flirtovat s, koketovat s	sbalit, vybrat si ☞ SLEDOVAT, STR. 289

date *(event)*	to date	to go Dutch, to split the bill, to split the check	**ENGLISH**	dating
die Verabredung, das Date, das Rendezvous	sich treffen, ausgehen, mit einander gehen	getrennte Kasse machen, die Kosten teilen	**DEUTSCH**	verabreden
la cita (para salir)	salir con	pagar a la americana, pagar a escote, dividir la cuenta	**ESPAÑOL**	citas
le rendez-vous, la date *(Qb)*	sortir avec, fréquenter, sortir steady avec *(Qb)*	partager l'addition, partager les frais	**FRANÇAIS**	rendez-vous
l'appuntamento (per uscire)	frequentare, uscire con	dividere il conto, pagare alla romana	**ITALIANO**	uscire
o encontro	namorar	rachar a conta	**PORTUGUÊS**	namoros
schůzka, rande	chodit s	zaplatit napůl, zaplatit každý zvlášť	**ČESKY**	chození

ENGLISH sex	anal sex, anal intercourse ☞ BUTTFUCKING, P. 293	to beat off, to wack off, to jerk off, to jack off, to beat the meat, to wank *(Br)*	to buttfuck, to assfuck, to fuck in the ass, to bugger *(Br)*
DEUTSCH sex	der Analverkehr, der anale Sex ☞ ARSCHFICK, S. 293	wichsen, sich einen runterholen, onanieren	arschficken
ESPAÑOL sexo	el sexo anal, el coito anal ☞ FOLLADA POR EL CULO, PÁG. 293	hacerse una paja, pajeársela, meneársela, machacársela, hacerse una chaqueta *(LA)*	follar por el culo, dar por el culo, encular
FRANÇAIS sexe	le rapport sexuel anal ☞ ENCULAGE, P. 293	se branler, se faire une queue, se palucher, se toucher, se crosser *(Qb)*	enculer
ITALIANO sesso	il sesso anale ☞ INCULATA, P. 293	farsi una sega, farsi una pippa	inculare, mettere in culo, scopare in culo
PORTUGUÊS sexo	o sexo anal, o coito anal ☞ ENRABAÇÃO, PÁG. 293	bater punheta, tocar punheta	foder no cu, enrabar, levar no rabo
ČESKY sex	anální sex, anální styk ☞ MRDÁNÍ DO PRDELE, STR. 293	vyhonit si čuráka	mrdat do prdele, šukat do prdele, dělat do prdele, dělat do zadku

buttfucking, assfucking, bumfucking, *(Br)*, buggery *(Br)* ☞ ANAL SEX, P. 292	buttplug	cockring	**ENGLISH**	sex
der Arschfick ☞ ANALVERKEHR, S. 292	der Buttplug, der Plug	der Schwanzring, der Cockring	**DEUTSCH**	sex
la follada por el culo ☞ SEXO ANAL, PÁG. 292	el tapón para el culo	el cockring, la anilla (para la polla)	**ESPAÑOL**	sexo
l'enculage ☞ RAPPORT SEXUEL ANAL, P. 292	le plug, le buttplug	le cockring	**FRANÇAIS**	sexe
l'inculata ☞ SESSO ANALE, P. 292	il buttplug	il cockring, l'anello per il cazzo	**ITALIANO**	sesso
a enrabação, a foda no cu, a trepada anal ☞ SEXO ANAL, PÁG. 292	o tampão anal	o coqueringue, o anel para o pau	**PORTUGUÊS**	sexo
mrdání do prdele, šukání do prdele ☞ ANÁLNÍ SEX, STR. 292	špunt do prdele, buttplug	kroužek na čurák, kroužek na penis	**ČESKY**	sex

ENGLISH sex	coitus, intercourse ☞ FUCK, P. 299	condom, rubber, durex *(Br)*	to deep throat, to fellate ☞ TO FELLATE, P. 296
DEUTSCH sex	der Koitus, der Sexualverkehr, der Geschlechtsverkehr ☞ FICK, S. 299	das Kondom, der Pariser, der Gummi, der Präservativ	den Schwanz ganz in den Mund nehmen ☞ ORALVERKEHR HABEN, S. 296
ESPAÑOL sexo	el coito ☞ FOLLADA, PÁG. 299	el condón, el preservativo, la goma	tragársela a fondo, tragársela toda, comérsela entera ☞ HACER UNA FELACIÓN, PÁG. 296
FRANÇAIS sexe	le coït, les rapports sexuels ☞ BAISE, P. 299	la capote, le préservatif	avaler la bite, sucer la bite à fond ☞ FAIRE UNE FELLATION, P. 296
ITALIANO sesso	il coito ☞ SCOPATA, P. 299	il preservativo, il guanto, il profilattico	succhiare a fondo ☞ FARE UNA FELLATIO, P. 296
PORTUGUÊS sexo	o coito ☞ TREPADA, PÁG. 299	a camisinha, o preservativo	chupar até o saco ☞ FAZER UMA FELAÇÃO, PÁG. 296
ČESKY sex	pohlavní styk ☞ MRDÁNÍ, STR. 299	kondom, guma, preservativ	kouřit čuráka hodně hluboko v krku ☞ DĚLAT FELACI, STR. 296

dildo	doggy style, dog style, on all fours, from behind	to ejaculate; to come, to cum, to shoot ☞ TO HAVE AN ORGASM, P. 303	**ENGLISH**	sex
der Dildo	von hinten	ejakulieren; kommen, abspritzen ☞ ORGASMUS HABEN, S. 303	**DEUTSCH**	sex
el dildo, el consolador	a cuatro patas, el perrito	eyacular; correrse, irse, acabar *(LA)*, venirse *(LA)* ☞ TENER UN ORGASMO, PÁG. 303	**ESPAÑOL**	sexo
le gode, le godemiché, la bite en rubber *(Qb)*	à quatre pattes, en levrette	éjaculer; jouir, éclater, cracher, juter, décharger, venir *(Qb)* ☞ JOUIR, P. 303	**FRANÇAIS**	sexe
il dildo, il cazzo di plastica	alla pecorina, a quattro zampe	eiaculare; venire, bagnarsi, sborrare ☞ AVERE UN ORGASMO, P. 303	**ITALIANO**	sesso
o consolo	de quatro, por trás	ejacular; gozar, esporrar, vir-se *(Por)* ☞ TER UN ORGASMO, PÁG. 303	**PORTUGUÊS**	sexo
robertek	na kolenou, zezadu, jako psi	ejakulovat; udělat se, vystříknout ☞ MÍT ORGASMUS, STR. 303	**ČESKY**	sex

ENGLISH sex	to feel up, to grope ☞ TO PET, P. 304	to fellate; to blow, to suck off, to give head, to give a blowjob ☞ TO DEEP THROAT, P. 294	fellatio; blowjob ☞ ORAL SEX, P. 303
DEUTSCH sex	berühren, fingern, fummeln, aufgeilen ☞ TÄTSCHELN, S. 304	Oralverkehr haben; blasen, den Schwanz lutschen ☞ DEN SCHWANZ GANZ…, S. 294	die Fellatio; das Blasen, das Schwanzlutschen ☞ ORALE SEX, S. 303
ESPAÑOL sexo	meter mano, toquetear, apretar, manosear, coger jamón *(LA)* ☞ ACARICIARSE, PÁG. 304	hacer una felación; chuparla, comerla, mamarla ☞ TRAGÁRSELA A FONDO, PÁG. 294	la felación; la mamada ☞ SEXO ORAL, PÁG. 303
FRANÇAIS sexe	peloter, taponner *(Qb)* ☞ SE PELOTER, P. 304	faire une fellation; sucer, sucer la bite, tailler une pipe ☞ AVALER LA BITE, P. 294	la fellation; la pipe ☞ RELATION ORO-GÉNITALE, P. 303
ITALIANO sesso	toccare, palpare ☞ TASTARSI, P. 304	fare una fellatio; fare un pompino, succhiare il cazzo ☞ SUCCHIARE A FONDO, P. 294	la fellatio; il pompino, il bocchino, la succhiata ☞ SESSO ORALE, P. 303
PORTUGUÊS sexo	tocar (sexualmente) ☞ ACARICIAR, PÁG. 304	fazer uma felação; chupar, mamar *(Por)* ☞ CHUPAR ATÉ O SACO, PÁG. 294	a felação; a chupada, a chupetinha, a chupeta, o boquete, a mamada *(Por)*, o broche *(Por)* ☞ SEXO ORAL, PÁG. 303
ČESKY sex	hladit ☞ MAZLIT SE, STR. 304	dělat felaci; kouřit čuráka, vykouřit ☞ KOUŘIT ČURÁKA, STR. 294	felace; kouření čuráka ☞ ORÁLNÍ SEX, STR. 303

fetish	fisting, fistfucking	to have a fling	**ENGLISH**	sex
der Fetisch	das Fisten, der Faustfick	es abgesehen haben	**DEUTSCH**	sex
el fetiche	el fistfucking, la follada con el puño	tener una aventura	**ESPAÑOL**	sexo
le fétichisme, le fétiche *(Qb)*	le fist-fucking	avoir une aventure	**FRANÇAIS**	sexe
il feticismo	il fist-fucking	avere una storia di sesso	**ITALIANO**	sesso
o fetiche	a penetração com o punho	ter um caso, ter uma aventura, ter uma paquera	**PORTUGUÊS**	sexo
fetiš	mrdáni pěstí	mít něco, mít aférku, mít někoho	**ČESKY**	sex

ENGLISH sex	foreplay	French kiss, deep kiss, soul kiss *(n)*	to French kiss, to tongue kiss, to french ☞ TO KISS, P. 301
DEUTSCH sex	das Vorspiel	der Zungenkuß	einen Zungenkuß geben ☞ KÜSSEN, S. 301
ESPAÑOL sexo	los juegos preliminares, los previos	el beso a la francesa, el beso húmedo, el beso atornillado, el morreo	besar a la francesa, darse un beso húmedo, darse un beso atornillado, morrearse ☞ BESAR, PÁG. 301
FRANÇAIS sexe	les préliminaires	le baiser profond, la pelle, le patin, le french *(Qb)*	se rouler un patin, rouler une pelle, frencher *(Qb)* ☞ EMBRASSER, P. 301
ITALIANO sesso	i preliminari	il bacio con lingua, il bacio alla francese, il bacio profondo	baciare con la lingua, baciare alla francese ☞ BACIARE, P. 301
PORTUGUÊS sexo	as brincadeiras, os jogos preliminares	o beijo de língua	dar um beijo de língua ☞ BEIJAR, PÁG. 301
ČESKY sex	předehra, milostná předehra	francouzák	dát francouzáka, líbat po francouzsku ☞ LÍBAT, STR. 301

fuck, screw *(n)*	to fuck, to screw, to ball ☞ TO HAVE SEX, P. 307	gay sex	**ENGLISH**	sex
der Fick, das Bumsen, das Vögeln	ficken, bumsen, vögeln, durchficken, stoßen ☞ MIT JEMANDEM SCHLAFEN, S. 307	der schwule Sex	**DEUTSCH**	sex
la follada, el polvo, el revolcón	follar, joder, tirarse, echar un polvo, chingar *(LA)*, singar *(LA)*, coger *(LA)* ☞ FOLLAR, PÁG. 307	el sexo gay, el sexo homosexual, las relaciones homosexuales	**ESPAÑOL**	sexo
la baise, le coup, la botte *(Qb)*	baiser, prendre, mettre, foutre, tirer un coup, bourrer, planter, niquer, botter *(Qb)* ☞ COUCHER, P. 307	les rapports homosexuels, les relations homosexuelles *(Qb)*	**FRANÇAIS**	sexe
la scopata, la chiavata	scopare, prendere, chiavare, sbattere, fottere ☞ FARE SESSO, P. 307	il sesso gay, il sesso omosessuale	**ITALIANO**	sesso
a trepada, a foda	foder, comer, trepar, meter, encher, meter fundo ☞ FODER, PÁG. 307	o sexo gay, o sexo homossexual	**PORTUGUÊS**	sexo
mrdání, šukání, šoustání, píchání, soulož	mrdat, šukat, šoustat, prcat ☞ MÍT SEX, STR. 307	gay sex, homosexuální sex	**ČESKY**	sex

ENGLISH sex	to get it up, to get hard, to get a hard-on, to get an erection, to get a boner, to get erect ☞ ERECTION, P. 286	hickey, lovebite *(Br)*	horny, hot, hot-to-trot, randy *(Br)* ☞ TURNED-ON, P. 310 & SEX-STARVED, P. 308
DEUTSCH sex	einen hochkriegen, einen Steifen kriegen ☞ EREKTION, S. 286	der Knutschfleck	geil, scharf ☞ GEIL, S. 310 & SEX-HUNGRIG, S. 308
ESPAÑOL sexo	ponerse dura, ponerse tiesa, empalmarse, levantarse, pararse ☞ ERECCIÓN, PÁG. 286	el chupetón, el mordisco, la mordida	caliente, cachondo ☞ EXCITADO, PÁG. 310 & HAMBRIENTO, PÁG. 308
FRANÇAIS sexe	bander, triquer, avoir le bâton ☞ ÉRECTION, P. 286	le suçon, la sucette *(Qb)*	en chaleur, en rut, qui a le feu aux fesses, chaud, excité ☞ ALLUMÉ, P. 310 & EN MANQUE, P. 308
ITALIANO sesso	tirare, indurire, farlo diventare duro, eccitarsi, drizzare, rizzarsi ☞ EREZIONE, P. 286	il succhiotto, il morso	arrapato, eccitato ☞ ARRAPATO, P. 310 & AFFAMATO DI SESSO, P. 308
PORTUGUÊS sexo	endurecer, subir, ficar de pau duro ☞ EREÇÃO, PÁG. 286	o chupão	com tesão, cheio de tesão, enteosado *(Por)* ☞ COM TESÃO, PÁG. 310 & FAMINTO POR SEXO, PÁG. 308
ČESKY sex	postavit se ☞ ZTOPOŘENÝ PENIS, STR. 286	cucflek	vzrušený, nadržený ☞ VZRUŠENÝ, STR. 310 & POSEDLÝ, STR. 308

impotent	J.O. party, jackoff party, jerkoff party	to kiss; to neck, to make out, to suck face ☞ TO FRENCH KISS, P. 298	**ENGLISH** sex
impotent	die Wichsparty, die Safer-Sex-Party	küssen; sich anmachen, schmusen ☞ ZUNGENKUSS GEBEN, S. 298	**DEUTSCH** sex
impotente	(NE) la orgía de sexo seguro, la paja en grupo	besar; besuquearse ☞ BESAR A LA FRANCESA, PÁG. 298	**ESPAÑOL** sexo
impuissant	la jack-off party, la party du cul (Qb)	embrasser; se lécher la pomme, se tripoter, se becoter (Qb) ☞ SE ROULER UN PATIN, P. 298	**FRANÇAIS** sexe
impotente	il jack-off party	baciare; limonare ☞ BACIARE CON LA LINGUA, P. 298	**ITALIANO** sesso
impotente	(NE) a "festa da punheta", a "festa da masturbação", a suruba de sexo seguro	beijar; ficar, malhar, se esfregar ☞ DAR UM BEIJO DE LÍNGUA, PÁG. 298	**PORTUGUÊS** sexo
impotentní	sex párty, safe sex párty	líbat; líbat se, cicmat se, cucat se ☞ DÁT FRANCOUZÁKA, STR. 298	**ČESKY** sex

ENGLISH sex	to make love ☞ TO HAVE SEX, P. 307	to masturbate; to masturbate (someone) ☞ TO BEAT OFF, P. 292	masturbation, self-abuse
DEUTSCH sex	Liebe machen, miteinander schlafen ☞ MIT JEMANDEM SCHLAFEN, S. 307	masturbieren; (jemanden) masturbieren ☞ WICHSEN, S. 292	die Masturbation, die Selbstbefriedigung, die Onanie
ESPAÑOL sexo	hacer el amor ☞ FOLLAR, PÁG. 307	masturbarse; masturbar (a alguien) ☞ HACERSE UNA PAJA, PÁG. 292	la masturbación, el onanismo
FRANÇAIS sexe	faire l'amour ☞ COUCHER, P. 307	se masturber; masturber (quelqu'un) ☞ SE BRANLER, P. 292	la masturbation, l'onanisme, la crossette *(Qb)*
ITALIANO sesso	fare l'amore ☞ FARE SESSO, P. 307	masturbarsi; masturbare (qualcuno) ☞ FARSI UNA SEGA, P. 292	la masturbazione, l'onanismo
PORTUGUÊS sexo	fazer amor ☞ FODER, PÁG. 307	masturbar-se; masturbar (alguém) ☞ BATER PUNHETA, PÁG. 292	a masturbação
ČESKY sex	milovat se ☞ MÍT SEX, STR. 307	masturbovat, onanovat; masturbovat (někoho) ☞ VYHONIT SI ČURÁKA, STR. 292	masturbace, onanie

one-night stand, one-nighter ☞ TO TRICK, P. 310	oral sex ☞ FELLATIO, P. 296 & SIXTY-NINE, P. 308	to have an orgasm, to climax ☞ TO EJACULATE, P. 295		**ENGLISH** sex
der One-Night-Stand, das Sex-Abenteuer für eine Nacht ☞ EINE NUMMER MACHEN, S. 310	der orale Sex, der Oralverkehr ☞ FELLATIO, S. 296 & NEUNUNDSECHSIG, S. 308	einen Orgasmus haben ☞ EJAKULIEREN, S. 295		**DEUTSCH** sex
el ligue (de un día), el rollo (de un día), la aventura (de una noche) ☞ LIGAR, PÁG. 310	el sexo oral ☞ FELACIÓN, PÁG. 296 & SESENTA Y NUEVE, PÁG. 308	tener un orgasmo ☞ EYACULAR, PÁG. 295		**ESPAÑOL** sexo
le coup (d'une nuit), l'affaire d'un soir *(Qb)* ☞ TIRER UN COUP, P. 310	la relation oro-génitale ☞ FELLATION, P. 296 & SOIXANTE-NEUF, P. 308	jouir ☞ ÉJACULER, P. 295		**FRANÇAIS** sexe
l'avventura (di una notte), l'avventura occasionale ☞ FARSI UNA SCOPATA, P. 310	il sesso orale ☞ FELLATIO, P. 296 & SESSANTANOVE, P. 308	avere un orgasmo ☞ EIACULARE, P. 295		**ITALIANO** sesso
uma noitada, a trepada de uma noite, a aventura de uma noite ☞ TER UMA NOITADA, PÁG. 310	o sexo oral ☞ FELAÇÃO, PÁG. 296 & SESSENTA E NOVE, PÁG. 308	ter um orgasmo ☞ EJACULAR, PÁG. 295		**PORTUGUÊS** sexo
mrd na jednu noc, sex na jednu noc ☞ MÍT NÁHODNÝ SEX, STR. 310	orální sex, orálně-sexuální styk ☞ FELACE, STR. 296 & ŠEDESÁTDEVÍTKA, STR. 308	mít orgasmus ☞ EJAKULOVAT, STR. 295		**ČESKY** sex

ENGLISH sex	orgy, group sex, group scene ☞ J.O. PARTY, P. 301	to pet ☞ TO FEEL UP, P. 296	phone sex
DEUTSCH sex	die Orgie, der Gruppensex ☞ WICHSPARTY, S. 301	streicheln, Petting machen, Petting haben, tätscheln ☞ BERÜHREN, S. 296	der Telefonsex
ESPAÑOL sexo	la orgía, el sexo en grupo ☞ ORGÍA DE SEXO SEGURO, PÁG. 301	acariciarse, toquete-arse, sobarse ☞ METER MANO, PÁG. 296	el sexo telefónico, el sexo por teléfono
FRANÇAIS sexe	la partouze, l'orgie (Qb) ☞ JACK-OFF PARTY, P. 301	se peloter, se tripoter, se caresser, se poignasser (Qb) ☞ PELOTER, P. 296	le téléphone rose, le rézo, le sexe au télé-phone (Qb)
ITALIANO sesso	l'orgia, il sesso di gruppo ☞ JACK-OFF PARTY, P. 301	tastarsi, pomiciare, palparsi ☞ TOCCARE, P. 296	il sesso telefonico, il sesso al telefono
PORTUGUÊS sexo	a orgia, a suruba, o sexo em grupo, o sexo grupal, a bacanal ☞ "FESTA DA PUNHETA", PÁG. 301	acariciar, afagar ☞ TOCAR, PÁG. 296	o sexo por telefone, o sexfone
ČESKY sex	orgie, grupáč, grupen-sex, skupinový sex ☞ SEX PÁRTY, STR. 301	mazlit se ☞ HLADIT, STR. 296	telefonní sex

porn, porno, pornography, smut	quickie	raunchy	ENGLISH	sex
der Porno, die Pornografie	die schnelle Nummer, der Quickie, der Schnellfick	versaut	DEUTSCH	sex
el porno, la pornografía	el polvo rápido, el polvete	cochino, guarro	ESPAÑOL	sexo
la pornographie	le coup, le coup rapide, le vite fait, la petite vite *(Qb)*	cul, sale, cochon	FRANÇAIS	sexe
il porno, la pornografia	la sveltina	grezzo, sporco, rozzo	ITALIANO	sesso
o pornô, a pornografia	a rapidinha	sujo, obseno	PORTUGUÊS	sexo
pornografie	rychlovka, rychlý sex	špinavej	ČESKY	sex

ENGLISH sex	to rim, to eat ass	rim job	safe sex, safer sex
DEUTSCH sex	den Arsch lecken	das Arschlecken, das Rimming	der Safer-Sex
ESPAÑOL sexo	lamer el culo, chupar el culo	el beso negro	el sexo seguro
FRANÇAIS sexe	lécher le cul, bouffer le cul, manger le cul	le léchage du cul, le mangeage du cul *(Qb)*	le safe sex, le sexe sans risque, le S.S.R., le sexe sécuritaire *(Qb)*
ITALIANO sesso	leccare il culo	la leccata di culo	il sesso sicuro
PORTUGUÊS sexo	fazer cunete, chupar o cu, lamber o cu	a cunete, a língua no cu	o sexo seguro
ČESKY sex	vylízat prdel	olizování prdele, olizování řítě	bezpečný sex, safe sex, „safe"

to score (with some-one), to get (someone) into bed, to do (some-one), to get into (some-one's) pants	semen, come, cum, jism, sperm	to have sex (with someone), to get laid ☞ TO FUCK, P. 299	**ENGLISH**	sex
(jemanden) ins Bett kriegen	der Samen, das Sperma	(mit jemandem) schlafen, gebumst werden, es machen, es treiben ☞ FICKEN, S. 299	**DEUTSCH**	sex
conquistar (a alguien), tirarse (a alguien), hacerse (a alguien)	el semen, la leche, el esperma	follar (con alguien), hacerlo (con alguien), echar un polvo, sin-garse (a alguien) *(LA)* ☞ FOLLAR, PÁG. 299	**ESPAÑOL**	sexo
faire une touche (à quelqu'un)	le sperme, le foutre, le jus, la décharge *(Qb)*	coucher (avec quel-qu'un), baiser, tirer un coup, le faire, niquer, botter *(Qb)* ☞ BAISER, P. 299	**FRANÇAIS**	sexe
fare centro (con qual-cuno), conquistare (qualcuno)	il seme, la sborra, lo sborro, lo sperma	fare sesso (con qual-cuno), farlo, scopare ☞ SCOPARE, P. 299	**ITALIANO**	sesso
pegar (alguém)	o sêmen, o gozo, a porra, o esperma	foder (alguém), comer (alguém), trepar (com alguém) ☞ FODER, PÁG. 299	**PORTUGUÊS**	sexo
mít (někoho), mít číslo (s někým)	semeno, mrdka, sperma	mít sex (s někým), souložit (s někým), mrdat, šukat ☞ MRDAT, STR. 299	**ČESKY**	sex

ENGLISH sex	sex-starved ☞ HORNY, P. 300	sixty-nine ☞ ORAL SEX, P. 303	to sixty-nine
DEUTSCH sex	sexhungrig, geil auf Sex ☞ GEIL, S. 300	der Neunundsechzig, die Neunundsechzig-erstellung ☞ ORALE SEX, S. 303	Neunundsechzig machen
ESPAÑOL sexo	hambriento, salido ☞ CALIENTE, PÁG. 300	el sesenta y nueve ☞ SEXO ORAL, PÁG. 303	hacer un sesenta y nueve
FRANÇAIS sexe	en manque ☞ EN CHALEUR, P. 300	le soixante-neuf ☞ RELATION ORO-GÉNITALE, P. 303	faire un soixante-neuf
ITALIANO sesso	affamato di sesso ☞ ARRAPATO, P. 300	il sessantanove ☞ SESSO ORALE, P. 303	fare un sessantanove
PORTUGUÊS sexo	faminto por sexo, tesudo ☞ COM TESÃO, PÁG. 300	o sessenta e nove, o meia nove ☞ SEXO ORAL, PÁG. 303	fazer um sessenta e nove, fazer um meia nove
ČESKY sex	posedlý ☞ VZRUŠENÝ, STR. 300	šedesátdevítka, vzájemné kouření ☞ ORÁLNÍ SEX, STR. 303	dělat šedesátdevítku, navzájem se kouřit

to sleep (with someone), go to bed (with someone) ☞ TO HAVE SEX, P. 307	threeway, threesome, trio	titclamps, nipple clamps	**ENGLISH** sex
(mit jemandem) schlafen, (mit jemandem) ins Bett gehen ☞ MIT JEMANDEM SCHLAFEN, S. 307	der Dreier	die Tittenklemmen, die Brustwarzenklemmen	**DEUTSCH** sex
acostarse (con alguien), irse a la cama (con alguien) ☞ FOLLAR, PÁG. 307	el trío, el ménage à trois	las pinzas para los pezones	**ESPAÑOL** sexo
coucher (avec quelqu'un) ☞ COUCHER, P. 307	le plan à trois, le ménage à trois	les pinces à sein, les pinces à jos *(Qb)*	**FRANÇAIS** sexe
andare a letto (con qualcuno), dormire (con qualcuno) ☞ FARE SESSO, P. 307	il triangolo, il terzetto, l'amore a tre	le pinzette per tette, le pinzette per capezzoli	**ITALIANO** sesso
ir para cama (com alguém) ☞ FODER, PÁG. 307	o ménage à trois, a trepada a três, o sexo a três	os grampos de teta, os clips que se põem nos bicos do peito	**PORTUGUÊS** sexo
jít spát (s někým) ☞ MÍT SEX, STR. 307	trojka, švédská trojka	kolíčky na bradavku	**ČESKY** sex

ENGLISH sex	to trick ☞ ONE-NIGHT STAND, P. 303	turned on, aroused, hot, excited, hot and bothered ☞ HORNY, P. 300	water sports, golden showers	
DEUTSCH sex	eine Nummer machen, ein Sex-Abenteuer haben ☞ ONE-NIGHT-STAND, S. 303	geil, erregt ☞ GEIL, S. 300	das Anpissen, die Pißspiele, der Natursekt	
ESPAÑOL sexo	ligar (por una noche) ☞ LIGUE, PÁG. 303	excitado, cachondo ☞ CALIENTE, PÁG. 300	la lluvia dorada, la ducha dorada	
FRANÇAIS sexe	tirer un coup, s'envoyer en l'air ☞ COUP, P. 303	allumé, branché, excité ☞ EN CHALEUR, P. 300	le plan uro, le trip de pisse *(Qb)*	
ITALIANO sesso	farsi una scopata (di una notte) ☞ AVVENTURA, P. 303	arrapato, eccitato ☞ ARRAPATO, P. 300	la pioggia dorata, il pissing	
PORTUGUÊS sexo	ter uma noitada, trepar (por uma noite) ☞ NOITADA, PÁG. 303	com tesão, excitado ☞ COM TESÃO, PÁG. 300	*(NE)* o "chuveirinho", os "esportes aquáticos", mijar em alguém (durante o ato sexual)	
ČESKY sex	mít náhodný sex ☞ MRD NA JEDNU NOC, STR. 303	vzrušený ☞ VZRUŠENÝ, STR. 300	*(NE)* chcání při sexu, čurání při sexu	

affair, love affair, romance	to have an affair	love; love at first sight	**ENGLISH**	love
die Affäre, die Liebesaffäre, das Liebesverhältnis	eine Affäre haben	die Liebe; die Liebe auf den ersten Blick	**DEUTSCH**	liebe
la aventura, el lío, el romance	tener un lío, tener una aventura, enredarse, liarse	el amor; el amor a primera vista	**ESPAÑOL**	amor
l'aventure	avoir une aventure	l'amour; le coup de foudre	**FRANÇAIS**	amour
la storia, l'avventura, la relazione (amorosa)	avere una storia	l'amore; l'amore a prima vista, il colpo di fulmine	**ITALIANO**	amore
o caso, o caso de amor, o romance	ter um caso	o amor; o amor à primeira vista	**PORTUGUÊS**	amor
aférka, milostná zápletka, romance	mít aférku	láska; láska na první pohled	**ČESKY**	láska

	to love	to fall in love with, to fall for	to live together, to move in together, to set up housekeeping
ENGLISH love			
DEUTSCH liebe	lieben	sich verlieben	zusammen leben
ESPAÑOL amor	amar, querer	enamorarse	vivir con, vivir liado con
FRANÇAIS amour	aimer	tomber amoureux, tomber en amour *(Qb)*	se mettre à la colle, vivre ensemble, s'accoter *(Qb)*
ITALIANO amore	amare, voler bene	innamorarsi	convivere, vivere insieme
PORTUGUÊS amor	amar	se apaixonar	viver junto com
ČESKY láska	milovat, mít rád	zamilovat se	žít na psí knížku, žít spolu, žít na hromádce

cruising spot, cruising area, pickup area ☞ TO GO CRUISING, P. 289	darkroom, backroom	drag show ☞ TRANSVESTITE, P. 282	**ENGLISH** places
das Aufreißgebiet, die Anmachecke, der Treffpunkt, die Cruising-Zone ☞ AUF ANMACHE GEHEN, S. 289	das Darkroom, der Dunkelraum	die Travestieshow, die Tuntenshow ☞ TRANSVESTIT, S. 282	**DEUTSCH** orte
el lugar de ligue, el lugar de encuentro ☞ IR DE LIGUE, PÁG. 289	el cuarto oscuro	el espectáculo de travestis, el espectáculo de transformismo, el «drag show» ☞ TRAVESTI, PÁG. 282	**ESPAÑOL** lugares
le lieu de drague, le lieu de rencontre, le spot (Qb) ☞ ALLER DRAGUER, P. 289	la backroom, le coin noir (Qb)	le spectacle de trav, le spectacle transformiste, le show de travelos ☞ TRAVESTI, P. 282	**FRANÇAIS** lieux
la zona di rimorchio, la zona di battuage, il luogo di incontro ☞ ANDARE A RIMORCHIARE, P. 289	la darkroom	lo spettacolo di travestiti ☞ TRAVESTITO, P. 282	**ITALIANO** luoghi
a área de caçação, a área de pegação, o ponto de encontro, o ponto de paquera ☞ IR CAÇAR, PÁG. 289	o quarto escuro, o canto escuro	o show de travesti, o show de tranformista, o espetáculo de travesti (Por) ☞ TRAVESTI, PÁG. 282	**PORTUGUÊS** lugares
holanda ☞ HOLANDIT, STR. 289	temná komora, darkroom, díra	travestie show, transvestitní show ☞ TRAVESTIE, STR. 282	**ČESKY** místa

ENGLISH places	gay bar, gay pub *(Br)*; gay disco	gay bath, gay sauna, the baths	gay beach; nude beach, nudist beach
DEUTSCH orte	die Schwulenbar, die Gay-Bar, die Schwulen-kneipe; die schwule Disco, die Gay-Disco, die schwule Diskothek	die schwule Sauna, die Gay-Sauna	der Schwulenstrand; der Nackstrand, der FKK-Strand
ESPAÑOL lugares	el bar gay, el bar de ambiente; la discoteca gay, la discoteca de ambiente	la sauna gay	la playa gay; la playa nudista
FRANÇAIS lieux	le bar pédé, le bar gai *(Qb)*; la discothèque pédé, la boîte pede, le club gai *(Qb)*	le sauna pédé, le sauna gai *(Qb)*	la plage pédé, la plage gai *(Qb)*; la plage naturiste, la plage nudiste
ITALIANO luoghi	il bar gay; la discoteca gay	la sauna gay	la spiaggia gay; la spiaggia per nudisti, la spiaggia nudista
PORTUGUÊS lugares	o bar gay; a discoteca gay	a sauna gay	a praia gay; a praia de nudismo
ČESKY místa	gay bar, gay lokál, bar pro gaye; gay diskotéka	gay sauna, sauna pro gaye, lázně pro gaye	gay pláž; nuda pláž, nudipláž, nudistická pláž

gay bookstore	gay scene	leather bar ☞ LEATHERMAN, P. 274	**ENGLISH**	places
der schwule Buchladen, die Buchhandlung für Schwule	die schwule Szene	die Lederbar ☞ LEDERTYP, S. 274	**DEUTSCH**	orte
la librería gay	el ambiente, el ambiente gay	el bar leather, el bar cuero ☞ HOMBRE LEATHER, PÁG. 274	**ESPAÑOL**	lugares
la librairie pédé, la librairie gai *(Qb)*	le milieu pédé, le milieu gai *(Qb)*	le bar cuir ☞ MEC CUIR, P. 274	**FRANÇAIS**	lieux
la libreria gay	l'ambiente gay, la scena gay	il bar leather ☞ IL LEATHER, P. 274	**ITALIANO**	luoghi
a livraria gay	o ambiente gay	o bar de couro, o bar de ambiente couro ☞ HOMEM QUE SE VESTE EM COURO, PÁG. 274	**PORTUGUÊS**	lugares
gay knihkupectví	gay scéna	leather bar, bar pro gaye v koženém ☞ KOŽEŇÁK, STR. 274	**ČESKY**	místa

ENGLISH places	sex club	sex shop	tearoom, cottage *(Br)*
DEUTSCH orte	der Sex-Club	der Sex-Shop, der Erotik-Shop	die Klappe, das Klo
ESPAÑOL lugares	el sex-club, el club erótico, el antro	el sex-shop, el emporio erótico	los urinarios (donde se liga)
FRANÇAIS lieux	la boîte à cul, le club de sexe *(Qb)*	le sex-shop, la boutique érotique	les tasses, la pissotière, les toilettes, les chiottes, les becosses *(Qb)*
ITALIANO luoghi	il locale per sesso	il sexy shop	il pisciatoio, il cesso pubblico, i vespasiani
PORTUGUÊS lugares	o clube de sexo	o sex shop	o banheirão, o banheiro de pegação, as retretes *(Por)*, a capelinha *(Por)*
ČESKY místa	sex klub	sex-shop	*(NE)* záchodky kde se mrdá, holanda

AIDS; Acquired Immune Deficiency Syndrome	crabs, crab lice, pubic lice	gonorrhea; the clap	**ENGLISH**	health
das AIDS; das Erworbenes Immundefektsyndrom	die Läuse, die Filzläuse	die Gonorrhöe; der Tripper	**DEUTSCH**	gesundheit
el SIDA; el síndrome de inmunodeficiencia adquirida	las ladillas	la gonorrea; las purgaciones	**ESPAÑOL**	salud
le SIDA; le syndrome d'immunodéficience acquise	les morpions	la blenno, la blennorragie	**FRANÇAIS**	santé
l'AIDS; la sindrome da immunodeficienza acquisita	le piattole	la gonorrea; lo scolo	**ITALIANO**	salute
a AIDS; a síndrome de imunodeficiência adquirida	o chato, os piolhos pubianos	a gonorréia	**PORTUGUÊS**	saúde
AIDS; syndrom získaného selhání imunitního systému	filcky	kapavka	**ČESKY**	zdraví

ENGLISH health	herpes	syphilis	venereal disease, VD, sexually transmitted disease, STD
DEUTSCH gesundheit	das Herpes	die Syphilis, der harte Schanker, das Lues	die Geschlechtskrankheit, die sexuell übertragbare Krankheit
ESPAÑOL salud	el herpes	la sífilis	la enfermedad venérea, la ETS, la enfermedad de transmisión sexual
FRANÇAIS santé	l'herpès	la syphilis	la MST, la maladie sexuellement transmissible, la MTS *(Qb)*
ITALIANO salute	l'herpes	la sifilide	la malattia venerea, la malattia trasmessa sessualmente
PORTUGUÊS saúde	o herpes	a sífilis	a doença venérea, a doença sexualmente transmitida
ČESKY zdraví	opar, herpes	syfilis	pohlavní choroba

Contacts

Contacts